Keeping Pet Birds

A Practical Encyclopedia

DON HARPER

Dominant Pied Opaline Budgerigar

Blitz Editions

The white mutation of the Indian Peafowl (*Pavo cristatus*)

Keeping Pet Birds

A Practical Encyclopedia

DON HARPER

First published in 1986 as
"Pet Birds for Home   and Garden"
by Salamander Books Ltd

Reprinted 1995

Copyright © 1986 Salamander
Books Ltd

ISBN 1-85605-279-6

Printed in the Slovak Republic

Credits

Editor: Geoff Rogers
Design: Grub Street Design, London
Colour reproductions:
Rodney Howe Ltd
Typesetting: Witwell Ltd, Liverpool

THE AUTHOR

Don Harper has kept a wide variety of birds for over twenty years, and this book is based on his extensive practical experience in this field. While pointing out that considerable pleasure can result from keeping birds, Don Harper nevertheless emphasises that these creatures can be extremely demanding pets in many instances. He has written this book to serve as a guide to help those seeking a pet bird for the first time, while also including information of considerable value to the more experienced owner. Mr. Harper has travelled extensively in pursuit of his interest in birds, meeting others with similar interests around the world. As a result, this book will have a truly universal appeal to all pet bird owners.

Gouldian Finch
(*Chloebia gouldiae*)

CONTENTS

PART 1

PRACTICAL SECTION

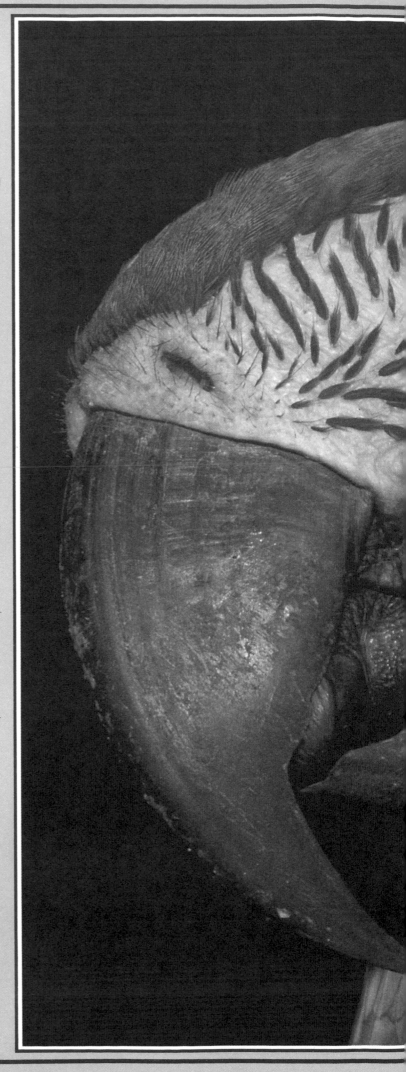

Blue and Gold Macaw
(*Ara ararauna*)

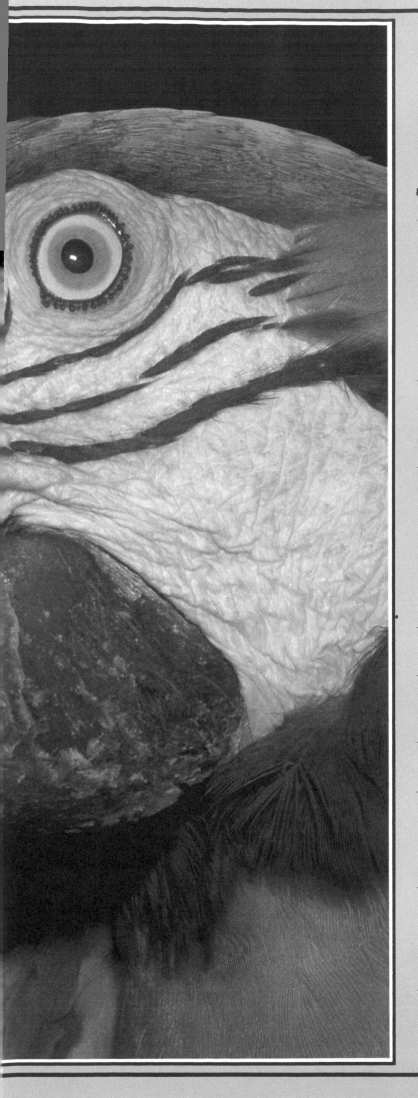

PART 2

SPECIES SECTION

PART 1

PRACTICAL SECTION

A lthough birds have been popular as pets for thousands of years, it is now easier than ever to maintain them successfully. The wide range of prepared foods available enables birdkeepers to offer all types of birds a balanced diet, and modern equipment and accessories have greatly eased the care, feeding and breeding of all species.

The hobby of birdkeeping offers considerable potential, ranging from enjoying a cherished pet budgerigar to keeping tame ducks on a garden pond. Accommodation for birds can be decorative as well as functional; in some cases, it is possible to incorporate plants into their enclosures. If you wish to construct an aviary or a pond, you can now obtain kits from bird farms and other specialist centres to simplify the task considerably. Looking through the columns of pet and birdkeeping magazines it is a useful starting point in tracking down these outlets.

Whether your interest lies in taming and teaching birds to talk, breeding varieties to produce specific colours, exhibiting stock or simply appreciating the natural beauty of these unique creatures, what begins as a pastime is very likely to become a life-long pursuit.

Violet-eared Waxbill
(*Uraeginthus granatina*)

BIRDS AS PETS

THE SCOPE OF THE HOBBY

The keeping of birds as pets is a very old pastime that dates back to the days of ancient Egypt, about three thousand years ago, and may have occurred even earlier in China. Many examples of these early links between birds and humans are still evident. The Egyptian god Horus, for example, portrayed in the form of a falcon, is seen on numerous artifacts of the period. Yet it was not only in the civilized world that birds were seen as being important in cultural terms. Representations of birds feature in the art of many New World tribes, and it is almost certain that parrots have been kept as pets in South America since the early days of human settlement on that continent.

The original reasons that probably first attracted humans to birds are still valid today. It could have been the utilitarian aspect of keeping birds, guaranteeing a source of fresh eggs at the very least, that led to the domestication of the Red Jungle Fowl (*Gallus gallus*) in Asia initially. From here, stock spread to other parts of the world, and today, apart from the commercial poultry, numerous other breeds – including smaller birds described as bantams – have been developed. Apart from their attractive appearance, they can also be relied upon to produce eggs for the table. Similarly, various domesticated breeds of duck are available. These will live contentedly in a typical back-garden environment.

The selective breeding of livestock, known as 'fancying', first came into vogue during Victorian times. The insight into the genetic principles governing inheritance provided by the work of the Austrian monk Gregor Mendel towards the end of the nineteenth century gave the fancy a great impetus for development that would otherwise have been impossible. Selective breeding has been carried out in many groups of birds, but few birds have been developed to such an extent in terms of their physical appearance than pigeons. In some cases, it is hard to believe that two such birds share a common ancestor. Likewise, in terms of colour, a wide array of options now exist for the keen fancier to pursue, particularly in the case of the Budgerigar. The recent surge of interest in the Peach-faced Lovebird, another member of the parrot family, also stems directly from the rapid growth in the number of colour mutations and the resulting colour forms that have been bred.

The main points of a canary

Forehead · Lores · Crown · Upper mandible · Ear coverts (cheek) · Lower mandible · Nape · Chin · Mantle · Throat · Scapulars · Back · Median coverts · Tertials (Top three secondaries) · Breast · Alula · Rump · Greater coverts · Secondaries · Primary coverts · Belly · Primaries · Flank · Upper tail coverts · Tarsus · Vent · Under tail coverts · Tail · Outer tail feather

Observing a bird quietly from a distance will reveal much about its overall state of health. Pay special attention to the eyes, beak and nostrils. Staining of plumage around the vent can indicate a digestive disturbance.

Parrots as pets

Parrots hold a special place in human affection, because of their ability to mimic human speech and other sounds. In some areas of the world, they are regarded as divine for this reason. Furthermore, the tame and devoted nature of a pet parrot towards members of its owner's immediate family provides an unparalleled experience in communication with a fellow creature. Studies are only just beginning to unravel the true extent of the bonds that can be formed in this way. There is now no doubt that, particularly for people living alone, the companionship provided by a tame and talking parrot will actively help the owner's physical and mental health. It is precisely because the large parrots are such demanding pets, in terms of the attention they require, that they are not suitable for people who have to spend much of their time away from home each day.

Sexing adult budgerigars

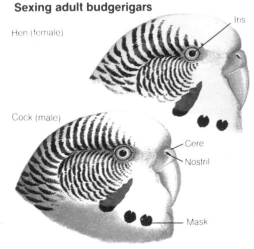

Hen (female) · Cock (male) · Iris · Cere · Nostril · Mask

Above: The cere above the beak provides a useful key to sexing budgerigars. It is brown in a mature hen (Top).

Above: The ceres of cock birds tend to be blue, although they can be purplish in certain instances.

Above: Many people are attracted to the hobby of keeping birds after a visit to a zoo or a bird garden.

Below: The scope is wide. Here at a budgerigar show, the birds are judged to specific standards.

Left: Keeping pet birds can be very rewarding. Parrots especially are likely to become tame and live a long time.

Below: A garden aviary can be an attractive feature, especially if it can be planted or suitably landscaped.

Until recently, it was assumed that parrots did not understand the meaning of phrases that they learnt. Following an American trial conducted at Purdue University, Indiana, using a Grey Parrot, it appears that these birds may well be able to reason in response to their environmental conditions. It has been known for a long time of course that parrots are capable of associating particular events, such as the uncovering of their cage in the morning, with a specific phrase like 'Good morning', which they only utter at that time of day. The actual manner in which parrots speak is unclear at present, however, and is the subject of active medical research, since birds do not possess larynxes and their method of vocalisation may be of help to dumb people. Not all parrots prove talented mimics though, nor will all settle well in the home. Yet the Australian parakeets are highly popular as aviary birds throughout the world and in suitable surroundings their striking colour and graceful flight can be fully appreciated.

A significant factor that has led to an even greater interest in birds as pets during recent years is a better understanding of their reproductive needs. This is reflected in the large numbers of species that are now being bred regularly, and advances in technology have served to improve the situation still further. While the hatching of birds such as ornamental pheasants and waterfowl in incubators has been commonplace for several decades, it has only been during the last ten years or so that parrots have been hatched and reared successfully in the absence of their parents. This in turn has increased the reproductive potential of the birds themselves. If the eggs are removed for incubation, the hen will invariably lay again shortly afterwards, thus doubling the number of offspring that could be bred in a given breeding season.

There are now commercial breeders of parrots, although these businesses are not yet as numerous as those offering game birds and waterfowl. Nevertheless, they provide an unrivalled opportunity to obtain a hand-raised parrot that has always been used to human company, and should therefore develop into a marvellous pet. In order to find the address of such breeders, subscribe to one of the specialist avicultural publications and study the advertisements. You should find a good selection of birds and equipment at your local pet store. If you do not see the species that you are seeking, do not hesitate to ask the proprietor for them, as they can obtain other stock to order. Alternatively, you may decide to try a specialist bird farm, although this will probably mean travelling farther afield. These establishments are often able to display a wide variety of stock, both domestically raised and imported birds.

Birds in the garden

A visit to a zoo or bird park is often the starting point for an interest in a garden aviary. Here again, there is tremendous scope. It is possible to construct an attractive garden aviary, complete with plants, accommodating a mixed collection of birds. The serious breeder, however, will often have to restrict the choice to just one pair of birds in an aviary, or alternatively, provide additional accommodation in the form of a birdroom. This will be essential for the keen exhibitor, who will need extra space to house a number of breeding pairs in individual breeding cages and have facilities for training and preparing stock to look at its best on the show bench.

For those who prefer to keep birds at liberty, and live in a suitable area, then fancy pigeons offer considerable potential; they can provide a great source of pleasure as they return to their lofts. Other types of bird will need to have their powers of flight curtailed if they are to be kept free in the vicinity of the home. For this reason, the operation known as pinioning is carried out on young waterfowl. It is a straightforward and painless procedure that does not inhibit their flight totally but merely serves to restrict them, with just one wing being affected. In adult permanently flighted birds that have not been pinioned early in life, clipping the flight feathers can have a similar

The main points of a fowl

A number of types of bird can only be kept satisfactorily out of doors. Domesticated fowl, like other birds, have been bred selectively to conform to prescribed exhibition standards. The keen exhibitor needs to be aware of the specialist terms that have been evolved to describe areas of the bird's body, as shown here.

Below: The Red Jungle Fowl (*Gallus gallus*) is the original ancestor of all today's breeds of poultry. As in the case of many birds, the male or cock bird is more striking than the hen. These birds are quite hardy, and can be kept outside throughout the year in most areas. Providing adequate winter accommodation is an important consideration with all stock, however, particularly in temperate climes.

Comb
Eye
Ear
Bill
Face
Ear lobe
Wattles
Sickles
Neck hackle
Side hangers
Back
Tail coverts
Main tail
Breast
Wingbow
Wingbar
Keel
Secondary wing feathers
Under-tail coverts
Thigh
Saddle hackle
Primaries
Hock
Shank
Spur

addition to the vocal powers of certain parrots. Feathers and spilt seed in the immediate vicinity of the bird are almost inevitable, for example, and create extra work, especially during the moult when increasing numbers of feathers are being shed. Most birds are not smelly, but some of the larger parrots have a fairly pungent body odour that may be offensive to certain people. Frequent daily cleaning will be essential for birds being kept indoors, especially mynah birds, which have naturally loose droppings.

Also, consider cost quite carefully. A pair of birds may be relatively cheap, yet an aviary to house them satisfactorily is likely to prove relatively expensive. It is possible to buy aviaries in easy-to-assemble kit form, but such structures are not usually reinforced sufficiently to cater for the destructive natures of most parrots. And the cost of constructing an outdoor aviary for parrots is likely to be much higher than an equivalent structure for finches. In addition, one of the larger parrots may be more expensive to buy than most pedigree dogs.

Before setting out to purchase a bird, therefore, try to get some indication of its availability and likely asking price by referring to the various avicultural publications. As a guide, young home-bred stock is likely to be more expensive than an older bird in the short-term. The difference is relative, however, because most birds will live for a decade or longer and obtaining an adult bird of uncertain age and temperament is not always to be recommended.

effect. This needs to be repeated when the birds moult; otherwise they will be free to fly away. In most cases, waterfowl tend not to have the homing instincts of pigeons.

Points to consider

Before deciding to pursue an interest in a particular group of birds, consider honestly whether you can meet their requirements. Most foreign finches and softbills, for example, which are kept for breeding or decorative reasons rather than for their tameness, may look most attractive in a planted flight during the warm summer months, but will you be able to provide satisfactory winter accommodation? In most instances, these birds need warmth and additional light during the winter to enable them to have adequate time to feed. Heating a small garden aviary can prove an expensive undertaking, and is not particularly efficient at the best of times. For this reason, indoor housing, such as a small flight in a spare room, is preferable in many cases, although a well-insulated garden shed can be converted into a temporary birdroom if required. If such a prospect is unappealing, then reconsider your choice of birds.

While most members of the parrot family are sufficiently hardy to winter out of doors satisfactorily without heat, provided they have a dry shelter and a nestbox for roosting purposes, a different problem may arise with these birds. Many are noisy, and some are extremely vocal, with far-carrying calls likely to disturb the neighbours. Similarly, other birds, such as male bantams and peacocks, may also cause complaints, often calling at first light.

Tame birds indoors can also create problems that you should be aware of, in

Above: The Carolina Duck (*Aix sponsa*) can be kept with only a relatively small area of water available. Outside the breeding period, the bright coloration of the male is replaced by duller 'eclipse' plumage.

Below: The magnificent display of an Indian Blue Peacock (*Pavo cristatus*) has ensured the popularity of these birds throughout the world. Unfortunately, their size and loud calls mean that peafowl will not prove suitable for many gardens.

CHOOSING A BIRD

Birds are not characterized by their ability to fly; indeed, some cannot fly, and conversely certain mammals, notably bats, also possess wings. It is the covering of feathers – the plumage – that is unique to birds, and the condition of the plumage plays an important part in revealing a bird's overall state of health.

Plumage and moulting

A fit bird has sleek plumage and will often be seen preening the individual feathers to maintain its appearance. When the bird is moulting, it is possible to see new feathers emerging from quills. These thin waxy sheaths serve to guide the new feathers through the skin, and are removed by the bird's preening action, enabling the individual feathers to uncurl into their normal positions. While this is most apparent for the larger flight and tail feathers, such spikes can also be seen throughout the body feathering, frequently becoming apparent on the head of a budgerigar, for example, while it is moulting.

The frequency of moulting is under hormonal control. Under normal circumstances, most birds will moult shortly after leaving the nest, although they may not drop all their feathers at this stage. (In canaries, for example, the flight and tail feathers are not lost at this moult.) The young birds are then described as 'unflighted' or 'non-flighted' until their first full moult. After the juvenile moult, most birds tend to moult annually, but this

Above: When buying a bird, be sure to look at it carefully beforehand to check that it appears healthy. Pay particular attention to the plumage, beak and head. Be sure to obtain a genuine youngster if you are seeking a pet, whereas older birds can be selected for breeding.

pattern is frequently disturbed in the home, probably as a result of a combination of prolonged light exposure and artificially warm surroundings in which the birds are kept. The condition is often referred to as a 'soft moult', with the bird frequently dropping feathers throughout the year.

A soft moult need not be a cause for concern, bearing in mind that a bird never develops bald patches over its body surface when moulting. If bald patches do develop, especially in tame parrots, it usually indicates that the bird in question is plucking its own feathers. This is a difficult problem to overcome; do not buy such birds. Feather disorders are generally most common in members of the parrot family. Budgerigars, for example, are susceptible to the disease known as French Moult, which shows up in the immediate post-weaning period. (This is discussed on page 29.) The flight feathers may not develop properly, handicapping the bird's flying ability. Although this may not be crucial in a budgerigar to be kept as a pet, such birds should not be used for breeding purposes later in life, as the condition may be transmitted to their offspring.

When you are contemplating buying a particular bird, try to watch it quietly from a distance for a period of time. It should not appear to have ruffled plumage, although the feathering of birds that have been kept inside and not given bathing facilities or a spray tends to look rather brittle and may be rough, noticeably on the breast. Ruffled plumage could indicate the presence of parasites, such as chewing lice. In such cases, it is vital to use a suitable preparation to overcome any infestation, especially if the bird is to be housed in the company of others.

The beak and head

Check the beak; in some cases, there may be a congenital problem that has resulted in

Sexing Zebra Finches

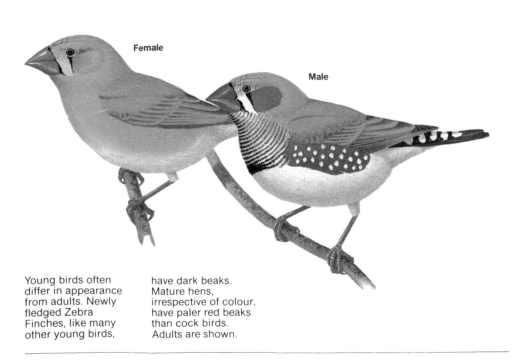

Female

Male

Young birds often differ in appearance from adults. Newly fledged Zebra Finches, like many other young birds, have dark beaks. Mature hens, irrespective of colour, have paler red beaks than cock birds. Adults are shown.

malocclusion, i.e. the upper and lower parts of the beak do not interlock correctly. Such complaints are most common in budgerigars, with the upper mandible growing abnormally over its lower counterpart – giving rise to an overshot beak – or curling into the lower beak and under the tongue – producing an undershot beak. In both instances, the bird is likely to need its beak trimmed at regular intervals throughout its life. Apart from the inconvenience involved, this can also prove costly if you need to call in veterinary help.

Although in many instances it may not be possible to detect parasites that may be affecting a bird, always look closely at the beak of a budgerigar, where the cere joins the beak. Here the early symptoms of scaly face, caused by a mite that actually burrows into the tissue, may be apparent. This parasite can spread rapidly in an aviary – by direct contact and possibly from perches as well – giving rise to coral-like encrustations on and around the beak. The earliest signs may appear to be whitish scratches on the surface of the beak. In severe cases, the mites can weaken the tissue itself, giving rise to abnormal growth of the beak. These mites can also affect the legs. This is the most usual site for these parasites to affect bantams, with the condition then being known as scaly leg.

The head of the bird may well provide the most reliable means of indicating its age. The irises surrounding the pupils of the eyes are invariably dark in the case of young parrots, for example, even if the birds are otherwise similar in appearance to their parents. The eyes should be clear, the nostrils unblocked and of even size. In certain instances, swellings around the eyes can be traced to a nasal infection. You are most likely to see this problem in newly imported parrots. In cases where one of the nostrils appears enlarged, this normally indicates a long-standing minor infection that has caused tissue damage over a period and may flare up when the bird is under stress.

Examination in the hand

You can get a better indication of a bird's state of health by examining it in the hand. (See pages 16–17 for methods of catching and handling birds.) Held in the correct position, it is possible to feel the bird's breastbone or sternum, running down the midline of the body. In a healthy bird, this bone should just be discernible as a bony prominence, but in a bird that is ill and has lost weight there will be a gap either side, reflecting the breakdown of muscle tissue that has taken place. The degree of weight loss depends to some extent upon the underlying cause. A bird affected with the chronic condition described as 'going light' will typically show a very marked loss of weight. If the cause is treated successfully, then the bird should regain weight rapidly.

The remainder of the body, including the

Selecting a healthy bird

A healthy bird, irrespective of its species, should appear alert and lively, especially when approached at close quarters. It is always best to see the bird personally, rather than buying it unseen, even if this entails travelling a fair distance. This is a Crimson Rosella.

Check that nostrils are unblocked and of equal size

Look for clear eyes with no signs of discharge

Plumage should not appear chewed, which could indicate feather-plucking

Check carefully that there is no malformation of the beak

Remember that the bird could be carrying a burden of parasites, which will need treating

Check the breastbone to ensure that the bird is not suffering from weight loss (so-called 'going light')

Ensure that the feet and toes are in good condition, including their undersurfaces

wings, can also be examined easily when the bird is held in the hand. With fancy pigeons, it is well worth inspecting the undersurfaces of the flight feathers for the presence of feather lice. These parasites are apparent as short, dark lines alongside the feather vanes. They can be killed with a suitable preparation in the form of a special aerosol or powder. Be sure to use this as directed.

Choose young stock

As a general rule, try to obtain young stock. There is then less risk of acquiring an adult bird that may be unsuitable for breeding purposes, such as a cock pheasant that persistently savages his mates. In the case of parrots, it may seem preferable to purchase imported adult birds, yet these will probably take several years to settle down sufficiently before they attempt to breed. A young pair of home-bred birds will take an equivalent or slightly longer period of time to mature, but they are likely to be easier to cater for in the short term and have a potentially longer reproductive life.

CATCHING AND HANDLING

The method of catching needs to result in minimum stress and will vary according to the surroundings and the birds involved. Here we look at various methods.

It is relatively easy to catch a small bird in a cage. Simply put your hand in (your right hand if you are right-handed), having first removed unnecessary hindrances such as toys and perches, and take hold of the bird, either on the bars or the cage floor. Try not to grip it tightly. The idea is to restrain it, and providing the wings are confined in the palm of the hand, the bird is unlikely to struggle. Cautiously withdraw your hand and transfer the bird to the other hand, so that you can examine it easily.

You can hold a medium-sized bird, such as a budgerigar, with its head restrained very gently between the first and second fingers. Do not apply pressure with the fingers around the neck; this may in turn narrow the windpipe, which carries air to and from the bird's lungs. Use the other fingers and the thumb to restrain the bird's lower parts, discouraging it from moving.

Using gloves

Clearly, special precautions need to be taken with particular types of birds. Most parrots, for example, have beaks than can inflict a painful bite, and are liable to draw blood if they make contact with the skin. Even budgerigars can give quite a painful nip. It is often better, therefore – particularly if you are not used to handling birds – to wear a pair of gloves for this purpose. A thin pair will be fine for budgerigars, but never use woollen gloves; the bird may get caught up in the strands. Stout gardening gauntlets may be necessary for the larger parrots, al-

Catching birds in the garden
When confronted with the need to catch birds in the garden, try to direct them into their shelter, where they can be caught more easily. Alternatively, use a large net, but try not to create too much disturbance to other birds nearby.

When restraining any bird, particularly large birds such as geese, it is important to keep the wings closed and prevent the head from moving by gripping it gently, as shown here.

though once adequately restrained, parrots do not usually attempt to bite. Their beaks do need to be treated with respect, however, on all occasions; even a tame bird may bite when being closely restrained. And birds may be aggressive at breeding time.

Larger birds

Larger birds, apart from parrots, need to be held in a slightly different manner. Pigeons are easy to handle, since they will not use their beaks, but do not be surprised if you are left with a handful of feathers after holding a pigeon or a dove. This is quite usual – these birds lose their feathers very easily; it may be a defence mechanism against potential predators. Restrain pheasants and

waterfowl with both hands, carrying the bird against your body. Use one hand to hold the neck (especially important for swans) and use the other to support the bird's weight from beneath, ensuring that it is not able to flap its wings. The power of a blow from the wings of a swan, for example, can enable the bird to escape, so that you will have to catch it all over again.

Clearly, catching a large bird is easier in a confined area. Although you can use a large net (see below), it is often preferable simply to catch the bird directly in a corner of its enclosure. Try to get another person to help you by coaxing the bird into the best position so that it can be caught at the first attempt. Stealth is the key to success when

Correct handling

Because some birds, notably parrots, can inflict a painful bite with their beaks, it is important to learn how to handle them correctly and safely. Gloves may be needed in some cases.

Right: It may be easier to catch a bird in an aviary using a net. Ensure that the rim is well padded to minimize the risk of injuring the bird.

INCORRECT

Left: If the budgerigar can twist its head round, it will be able to bite. Keep the head central, but do not press hard on the neck, as this could compress the windpipe.

CORRECT

Right: Holding a budgerigar or small parakeet correctly, with the head positioned between the first two fingers. Do not grip tightly, however.

trying to get hold of a bird at liberty. Move slowly and deliberately so as not to panic the bird unnecessarily, while aiming to drive it towards the chosen spot, such as a corner of the garden. Once the moment approaches to physically catch the bird, do not hesitate, otherwise it will almost certainly get away. This strategy applies to peafowl and other birds at liberty, although an alternative approach is to persuade them to enter a building, with a trail of grain, and simply close the door once they are inside.

The value of darkness

Darkness can be of great value, as it will be much easier to take hold of a roosting bird, providing there are no other birds nearby that may be panicked. (Never disturb aviary birds after dark for this reason.) In some cases, where birds are roosting high up, it will not be possible to catch them in the dark. In the home, however, darkness provides the simplest means of retrieving a bird loose in a room – especially a finch, which is very quick on the wing. Draw the curtains, and the bird will settle down almost at once. It should then be possible to get sufficiently close to catch the bird without any difficulty in the semi-darkness. This will be considerably less stressful than having to follow the bird around the room in the hope of catching it amid furniture and ornaments. Always watch the bird closely; if it starts breathing heavily, panting with its beak open, then let it rest for several minutes before trying again.

Always transfer or transport birds in boxes rather than in cages whenever possible. In dark confines, the birds will not be alarmed, and there is no risk of them injur-

ing themselves. Ventilation holes should be made in the sides of the box before the birds are placed within. Wooden boxes are likely to be more suitable for bigger parrot-like birds, which will be able to chew their way out of cardboard. The larger cardboard boxes used for dogs and cats are also useful for transporting waterfowl. These can be obtained from most larger pet stores, and need to be assembled carefully, so that the bottom will not collapse when the bird is placed within. As an additional precaution, tie the box with string.

Using a net

There will be occasions when a catching net will be useful – in an aviary, for example. Try to contain the birds either in the flight

Above: It is much better to transport birds in boxes rather than in cages; the darkness helps to keep the birds calm. If the birds are destructive, such as large parrots, use a wooden box with adequate ventilation holes. In any event, wood is preferable to cardboard for transporting most birds.

or in the shelter of the aviary, and remove the perches first so that you can move unhindered when catching the birds. Use a net that is well-padded around the rim. Ideally, choose one of the nets specially made for catching birds. Nevertheless, take care when using a net – it is still possible to injure a bird, even if the net has a padded rim. With parakeets, it is often easier to catch them when they rest on the mesh of the aviary. Finches, however, can be driven into the net in flight, by careful movement of the hand.

Once the bird is actually within the net, move rapidly to ensure that it cannot escape and restrain it as soon as possible. Gently remove it, bearing in mind that its claws are likely to be gripping the material inside the net and may have to be prised free. Hold the toes themselves, rather than just attempting to loosen the claws, since the bird will otherwise simply re-insert its claws as soon as they are free. Restraining the toes makes this less likely and will speed removal of the bird.

It can be difficult to catch a bird in an aviary on the first few occasions, especially in a mixed flight housing more than one pair of birds. Try to be aware of where other birds are, so they are not injured inadvertently. Again, watch the bird closely and if it seems to be very distressed, leave it alone to recover for a short period. Take care to create minimum disturbance in the aviary when birds are breeding. Thankfully, young birds are often easier to catch than adults. Take particular care with newly-fledged Australian parakeets, however, since these birds are often extremely nervous, and may even attempt to fly through the mesh when someone enters their aviary, with fatal results. This includes budgerigars.

FEEDING YOUR BIRD

The detailed dietary needs of individual birds are discussed in the second part of the book, but no species covered here will present insuperable demands by virtue of its feeding habits. Indeed, even if you do not live close to a pet store or a bird farm, you can obtain all the foods that your bird may need by mail order from one of the specialist suppliers advertising in avicultural periodicals. If your local pet store does not carry stocks of foods such as pine nuts, they may be prepared to order you a reasonable quantity. Bulk orders may be supplied at a discount, and you can also see the quality of the seed before you buy it.

Canary and budgerigar mixtures

Seed mixtures avoid the need to buy the individual ingredients separately and mix them in the required proportions. Canary mixtures, for example, typically include a mixture of plain canary seed, which is derived from a grass, and red rape, an oil-based seed containing relatively high levels of fat, as well as protein. Other oil seeds present in smaller quantities will be hemp and possibly niger, a thin blackish seed. The major disadvantage of feeding a mixture, especially to canaries, is that certain ingredients will be consumed in preference to others, and it can prove wasteful.

A typical budgerigar mix contains cereal seeds only, which are categorized by their high carbohydrate content and significantly

lower levels of fat and protein. Plain canary seed and millets, including panicum or spray millet, usually feature prominently in the diet of budgerigars and finches. Other cereal seeds, such as groats (oat kernels), are also fed occasionally, while paddy rice, again available from specialist seed merchants, is taken by some finches.

Parrot mixtures

While Australian parrots generally have a mixed diet of cereal and oil seeds, those

Above: Here, a cockatiel feeds on a seed mixture. Although forming the staple diet of these birds, seed alone does not provide a balanced diet. Supply other items, such as greenstuff (including sprouted pulses), particularly for breeding birds.

from other continents are traditionally fed a mixture consisting predominantly of oil seeds. Sunflower seed is the usual basic ingredient, being available in various forms, of which white rather than striped is considered to be the most nutritious. Black sunflower seeds are less popular. Opt, if

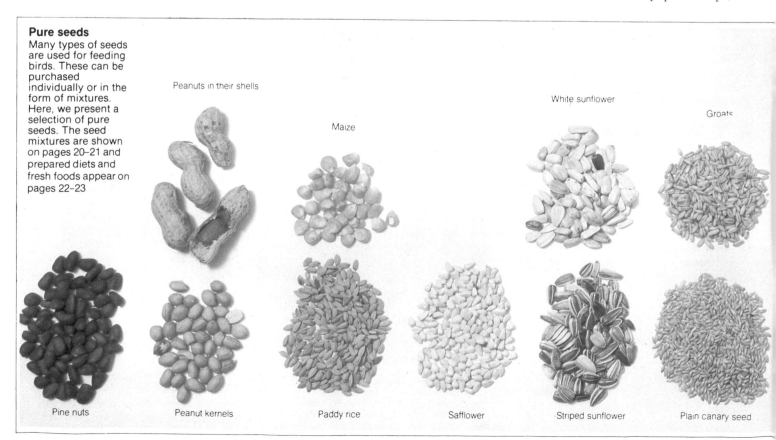

Pure seeds
Many types of seeds are used for feeding birds. These can be purchased individually or in the form of mixtures. Here, we present a selection of pure seeds. The seed mixtures are shown on pages 20–21 and prepared diets and fresh foods appear on pages 22–23

Peanuts in their shells

Maize

White sunflower

Groats

Pine nuts

Peanut kernels

Paddy rice

Safflower

Striped sunflower

Plain canary seed

Nutritional breakdown of commonly used bird foods

The foodstuffs used for feeding birds vary considerably in their nutritional value, as the charts at right reveal. The seeds can be divided into two basic groups: cereals and oil seeds. The cereals, such as canary seed, have a relatively high level of carbohydrate compared with fat. The proportions are reversed in the oil seeds, such as sunflower. The oil seeds also contain only small amounts of water. Green foods are composed largely of water, but provide useful vitamins and minerals. The processed foods shown at far right are intended for specific uses and are likely to offer the best balance of vitamins and minerals.

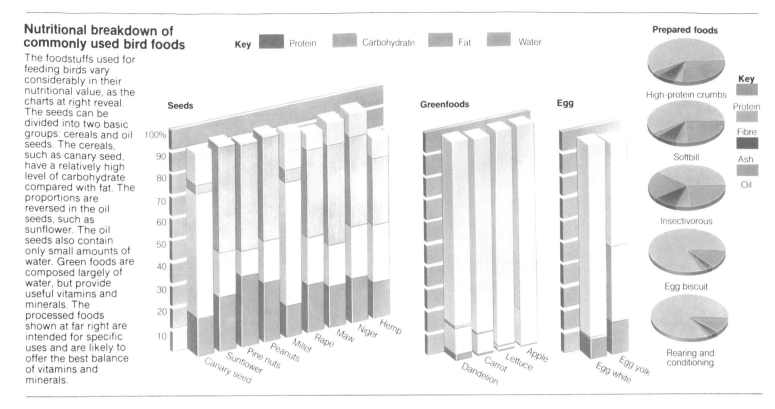

Key ■ Protein ■ Carbohydrate ■ Fat ■ Water

Seeds — Canary seed, Sunflower, Pine nuts, Peanuts, Millet, Rape, Maw, Niger, Hemp

Greenfoods — Dandelion, Carrot, Lettuce, Apple

Egg — Egg white, Egg yolk

Prepared foods — High-protein crumbs, Softbill, Insectivorous, Egg biscuit, Rearing and conditioning

Key Protein, Fibre, Ash, Oil

possible, for small grades of sunflower – the kernel tends to be of fairly constant size and, since the outer husk is discarded, the larger seeds usually prove more wasteful. Peanuts (also known as groundnuts), can be present either loose or in seedpods. Other ingredients in a parrot mixture may include safflower seeds, which are white and fatter in appearance than sunflower seeds, and hemp. Maize may also be included, but is generally too hard for smaller parrots to crack successfully. This cereal seed is valuable, how-

ever, for recently weaned young parrots or birds recovering from illness; boil it until soft and allow it to cool before feeding. In this form, maize is also easily digestible. The only other cereal seed present in most parrot mixtures is oats, but certainly smaller parrots, such as parrotlets, will benefit from the provision of a separate container of a budgerigar mixture, enabling them to feed on the other seeds. Soaked millet sprays are invariably popular with most parrots as well, especially when they have chicks.

Seed can be soaked easily, simply by immersing a quantity in warm water and leaving it for a day. This will start the germination process, and chemical changes occur that raise the protein value of the food. Always rinse soaked seed very thoroughly before offering it to the birds, and never leave any uneaten soaked seed in their quarters for more than twenty-four hours. There is a likelihood that moulds may develop on the seeds and produce toxins that are liable to prove fatal, either in the

Red millet, Panicum millet (Spray form above), Black rape, Teazle, Blue maw, Niger

White millet, Japanese millet, Red rape, Hemp, Pinhead oatmeal, Linseed short or longer term. Millet sprays, plain canary seed and sunflower seeds are often soaked in this way, but a recent trend has been the increasing use of various pulses (such as peas, beans and lentils) as a part of a parrot's diet. Obtain these from health food stores or seed merchants and feed them either soaked or sprouted, taking particular care to wash the sprouted seeds thoroughly before use. Special sprouters can be obtained for this purpose. Prepare only limited amounts at any time, because of their perishable nature, and offer them in a separate container from dry seed.

Game birds and waterfowl

Seeds are also valuable for game birds and waterfowl, but today, greater use is made of poultry rations in their diets. Wheat is the traditional basic diet for pheasants, for example, being augmented with sunflower seed, peanuts and other oil seeds, notably for moulting birds. Now, various suitable types of poultry food are available containing differing levels of protein that correspond to the particular needs of the birds concerned. In a breeder ration the protein level is higher than in the case of a maintenance diet, for example.

The actual presentation of the foodstuffs also varies; an initial chick diet is in the form of small crumbs, with progressively larger pellets being fed as the birds get older. As a general guide, young birds start off on chick crumbs, then progress to growers' pellets and finally to a maintenance ration. When breeding is required, layers' pellets or mash are supplied. A mash is in the form of a powder and is suitable for smaller bantams that may not be able to take layers' pellets.

The digestive tract of a pigeon

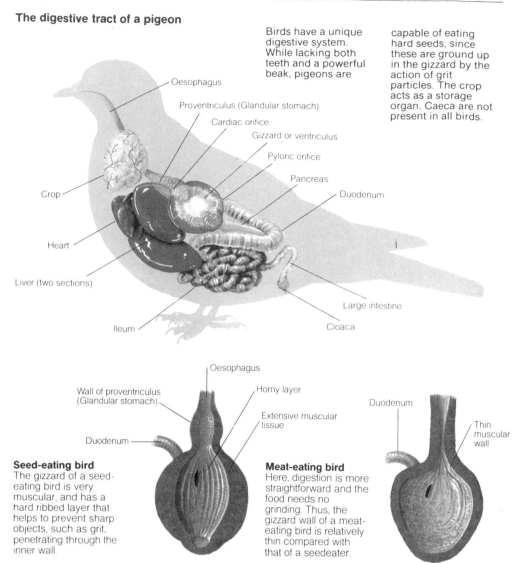

Birds have a unique digestive system. While lacking both teeth and a powerful beak, pigeons are capable of eating hard seeds, since these are ground up in the gizzard by the action of grit particles. The crop acts as a storage organ. Caeca are not present in all birds.

Oesophagus
Proventriculus (Glandular stomach)
Cardiac orifice
Gizzard or ventriculus
Pyloric orifice
Pancreas
Duodenum
Crop
Heart
Liver (two sections)
Large intestine
Cloaca
Ileum

Oesophagus
Wall of proventriculus (Glandular stomach)
Horny layer
Extensive muscular tissue
Duodenum
Duodenum
Thin muscular wall

Seed-eating bird
The gizzard of a seed-eating bird is very muscular, and has a hard ribbed layer that helps to prevent sharp objects, such as grit, penetrating through the inner wall.

Meat-eating bird
Here, digestion is more straightforward and the food needs no grinding. Thus, the gizzard wall of a meat-eating bird is relatively thin compared with that of a seedeater.

Seed mixtures

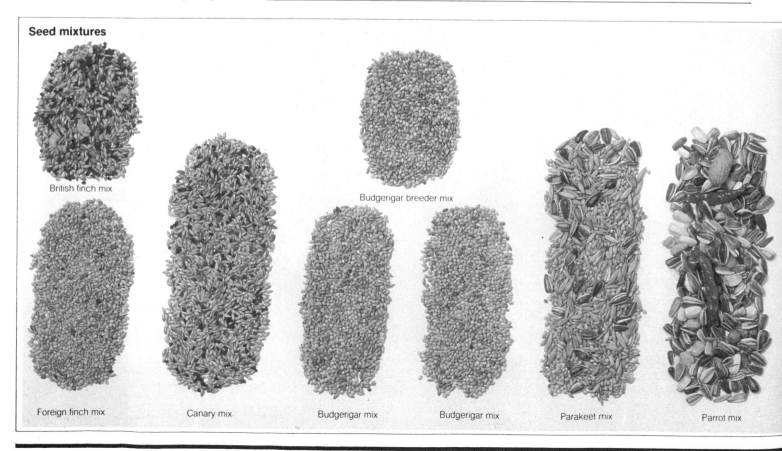

British finch mix

Budgerigar breeder mix

Foreign finch mix

Canary mix

Budgerigar mix

Budgerigar mix

Parakeet mix

Parrot mix

These foods are complete diets, containing all the necessary ingredients, including vitamins and minerals, required to keep the birds in good health. Wheat is still supplied in most instances, however, along with kibbled (crushed) maize and other items, such as greenfood and even insects.

Digestion of foodstuffs

The digestive system of birds differs significantly from that of mammals because, in the first instance, the bird has no teeth with which to chew its food. If seeds are to be digested efficiently, therefore, they must be broken down in the bird's body. This occurs in the organ known as the gizzard. In seed-eating species, the gizzard has thick muscular walls that compress and grind the seed on particles of grit the bird has swallowed. Thus, all seed-eating birds need a supply of grit constantly available to them. Various grades of grit are available; budgerigar grit, for example, is suitable for all finches, including canaries, and most parrot-like birds. Do not be surprised, however, if many parrots do not appear to consume any grit; it is thought that the pieces of wood they gnaw may perform a similar function when swallowed.

Grit falls into two main categories: flint grits which are hard and largely insoluble; and limestone and oystershell grits that dissolve readily in the acid conditions of the bird's gizzard and provide a useful source of minerals. The insoluble grit is necessary throughout the year, whereas oystershell grit is valuable immediately before and during the breeding season, when there is a considerable drain on a laying hen's mineral reserves. Another important source of minerals, especially calcium, is cuttlefish bone, which should be available to all finches and parrots in particular. If necessary, cut slivers from the soft powdery side for the smaller birds.

Feeding softbills

The basic diet for softbills i.e. birds that do not eat seeds, such as mynah birds, will be an insectivorous food, containing a proportion of dry insects and other ingredients, such as fish meal. Some ranges of commercially available softbill foods are more comprehensive than others, so check as to which food is most suited for your particular birds. The oil (fat) level in some diets is lower than

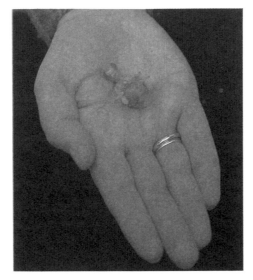

Above: The crop, located at the base of the neck, is clearly visible in this budgerigar chick. This organ acts basically as a food store. In adult pigeons, glands in the crop secrete a protein-rich substance called crop milk used to nourish newly hatched chicks until they can begin feeding for themselves.

others, reflecting the natural food of the species concerned. Those species that feed essentially on fruit, such as fruitsuckers, generally do not require a mixture with a high proportion of fat. Some softbill foods need to be mixed with water before being fed. This applies to mynah bird pellets. A pelleted diet of this type is preferable for birds, such as barbets, that may well experience difficulty in consuming fine loose granules. Unfortunately, pellets are not as readily available as other more traditional types of softbill food.

Let us consider the major types of foods suitable for softbills.

Fruit

Fruit is an important ingredient of the diet of most softbills (as well as parrots) and so always provide a suitable variety. Diced apple can be augmented with other fruits, such as grapes, and softbill food sprinkled over the damp surfaces of the cut fruits. Mix these items together well to minimize wastage of the softbill food. Other items, such as dried fruits, can be given in moderation. Soak dried fruits for a day in water and rinse them thoroughly before feeding them. Even a little grated cheese will be acceptable to the more omnivorous softbills. Both dried fruits and cheese are particularly valuable in terms of their energy value for softbills living in outside aviaries during the colder months of the year.

Livefoods

In the wild, softbills feed on a variety of insects and other invertebrates (as do many finches), especially when they are breeding. Livefood of this nature helps to provide the

Basic pigeon mix   Quail mix   Dove and pheasant mix   Duck and goose mix including flake maize and pellets

essential amino-acids that are deficient in plant foods. Although it is possible to provide alternative and equally nutritious substitutes that in theory should enable chicks to be reared without difficulty, the natural instincts of the birds are such that they must be given livefood for breeding to be successful. A shortage of livefood, particularly in the early days after the chicks have hatched, is likely to result in the offspring being neglected or ejected from the nest. The parent birds' drive to obtain such foods is so strong that they may even mistakenly consume their own chicks for this reason.

It is now possible to buy supplies of livefood in bulk, so there is no need to set up cultures. In the long term, however, this will be preferable, since it should guarantee an uninterrupted supply and will prove considerably cheaper. The following types of livefood can be cultured easily in the home.

Mealworms are the traditional source of livefood for captive birds, and can be easily maintained in a plastic tub with ventilation holes punched in the lid. They are the larval stage in the life cycle of the meal beetle (*Tenebrio molitor*) and extremely easy to cater for. Simply fill the container with bran and place slices of apple on the surface to provide a source of moisture. Meal beetles can be housed in the same surroundings as their larvae. They lay eggs, which hatch out in about six weeks. The major drawback of mealworms is that they are low in calcium. This tends to make them unsatisfactory as a rearing food for young birds, which have a relatively high demand for this vital mineral. Always supplement the bran in which the mealworms are being kept with sterilized bone meal; ingested by the mealworms, this valuable source of calcium will become available to the birds.

Mealworms normally have a relatively hard outer casing that cannot be digested by young birds. As they mature, they undergo a series of moults and at such times they are whitish and relatively soft. Thus, to suit young birds either keep a close watch for moulting mealworms or cut up 'hard-coated' ones before feeding to their parents. The first suggestion is rarely practical, bearing in mind the number of mealworms that may be consumed by a pair of birds with chicks in the nest. The second procedure is unpleasant. For these reasons, other sources of commercially cultured livefood, such as crickets, may be of greater value during the breeding period.

Crickets These insects are available in a variety of sizes, ranging from tiny hatchlings to mature breeding specimens about 15mm (0.6in) in length. They are normally sold in terms of size, so there should be no difficulty in selecting an appropriate grade. Crickets lack the hard, indigestible covering in mealworms, and thus make an ideal rearing food. They are nimble, however. To slow them down, chill them for a short time in a fridge. The birds are then able to take a quantity easily, without the majority of the crickets escaping. If you place the crickets in a fairly deep container, the birds should soon become used to hopping down inside to obtain the insects, particularly if the sides of the vessel are clear. An empty plastic aquarium is ideal for this purpose. Even mealworms will have difficulty in climbing up the smooth sides of such a container.

A simple covered aquarium is also ideal for breeding crickets. Adults can be sexed by the presence of an egglaying tube, or ovipositor, which can be clearly seen at the end of the female's abdomen. Keep the commercially available strains of crickets at a temperature of about 27°C (81°F) and feed them flour and fresh cut grass when available. Moisture is important; provide it in the form of a saturated paper tissue, as the crickets are liable to drown themselves if given a pot of water. A container of sand in the aquarium will attract female crickets about to lay their eggs. If kept warm, these should hatch within about three weeks, thus providing a new supply of small crickets.

Whiteworm culture

Above: Whiteworms are a valuable livefood especially for finches. Culture them in a suitable container of moist peat as here.

Below: Separate the whiteworms from the culture medium simply by dropping a portion of the mixture into a saucer of water.

Fresh and processed foods

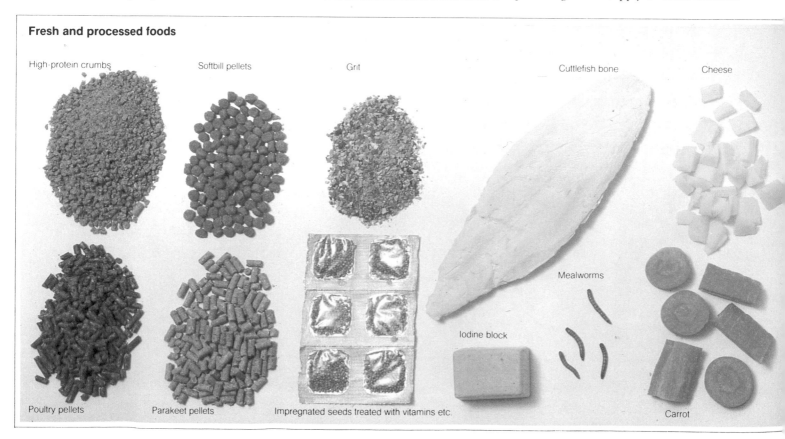

High-protein crumbs   Softbill pellets   Grit   Cuttlefish bone   Cheese

Poultry pellets   Parakeet pellets   Impregnated seeds treated with vitamins etc.   Iodine block   Mealworms   Carrot

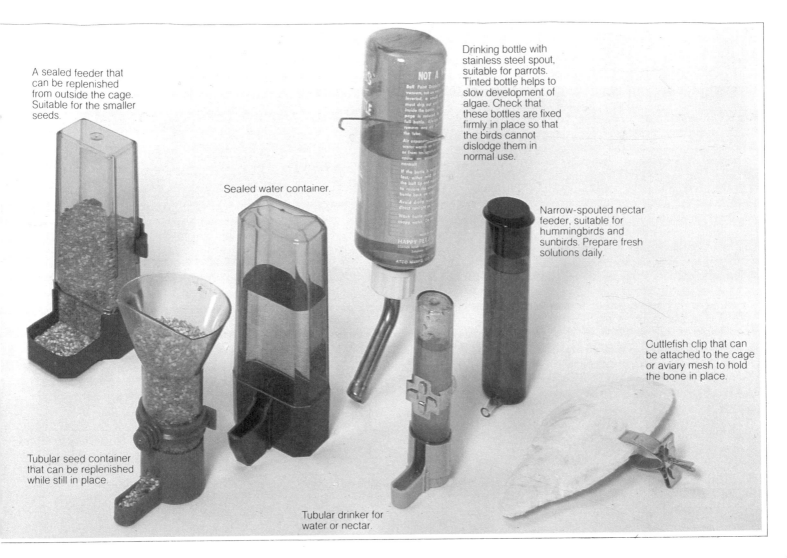

A sealed feeder that can be replenished from outside the cage. Suitable for the smaller seeds.

Sealed water container.

Drinking bottle with stainless steel spout, suitable for parrots. Tinted bottle helps to slow development of algae. Check that these bottles are fixed firmly in place so that the birds cannot dislodge them in normal use.

Narrow-spouted nectar feeder, suitable for hummingbirds and sunbirds. Prepare fresh solutions daily.

Cuttlefish clip that can be attached to the cage or aviary mesh to hold the bone in place.

Tubular seed container that can be replenished while still in place.

Tubular drinker for water or nectar.

Left: Feeders for birds outside must serve to keep the food dry, otherwise arrange for feeding to take place in the shelter. A particular problem with poultry and similar birds ranging free is that wild birds will soon learn to steal their food and may spread diseases in the process, especially if their droppings contaminate the food itself. The feeders shown here are available from specialist suppliers.

bottles are ideal for the more destructive parrots, provided the birds cannot dislodge the container itself. In outside aviaries, never fill drinking bottles to the brim during the winter. If the water freezes, the container will almost certainly crack. In addition, check specifically that the water in the spout has not frozen, thus depriving the bird of fluid, while the main body of water appears unaffected by the low temperature. Conversely, during the summer and especially when there are chicks, you may need to supply an extra water container, as fluid consumption can rise quite dramatically at this time.

Various other utensils have more specific functions. Cuttlefish clips serve to hold the bones firmly in place, enabling the birds to gnaw without hindrance. So-called finger drawers are used by canary breeders to provide softfood easily to breeding pairs, with minimum waste. Small wire racks are provided to act as receptacles for greenfood, but in most instances the birds will simply pull this on to the floor. A bowl is probably just as useful for this purpose.

BASIC HEALTH CARE

Only a veterinarian can give you an accurate diagnosis of avian ailments and offer correct advice on their treatment. Try to find a veterinarian in your area who is used to dealing with birds on a regular basis. This is now likely to be easier, as veterinarians have become more involved with the care of birds as a result of surgical sexing techniques (i.e. using specialized equipment to determine the sex of birds that show no obvious visual differences). Newly acquired birds will be under stress and thus more at risk from illness. As a precaution, keep new arrivals on their own for at least two weeks, partly to let them settle in but also to minimize the risk of spreading disease to other birds. As a general rule, however, birds are very healthy creatures, and rarely fall sick if fed and housed properly.

In this section we look at routine health care, coping with emergencies, early signs of illness, the general care of sick birds, and review a range of conditions and infections that can affect birds in captivity.

Routine health care
One of the basic tasks of routine health care that may be necessary is cutting back your bird's claws or beak at regular intervals. If these become overgrown they will interfere with its eating, preening and perching habits. A bird with abnormally long claws, especially in an aviary, is at much greater risk from becoming entangled and injuring itself as a result. A veterinarian will carry out the

task for you, but many petkeepers and breeders prefer to undertake these simple procedures themselves. If you are unsure as to whether clipping is necessary, compare the bird with others of its kind. Beak shape, for example, can be quite variable, even between members of the same bird family. Macaws have beaks with upper mandibles that are normally quite curved and tapering to a point, whereas a budgerigar's beak is much flatter.

Do not use scissors to clip a bird's claws or beak; they are liable to cause the tissue to

---

Claw clipping

Some birds are likely to need their claws clipped more regularly than others.

Many of the smaller finches tend to have long claws, as do budgerigars in cages.

Above: The first step is to identify the blood supply, visible as a red streak in pale claws.

Below: Cut well clear of this point, using sharp clippers, with the bird restrained (at bottom).

---

splinter, rather than exerting a clean cut. Ideally, use a pair of stout bone clippers. Holding the bird in the usual manner, inspect the length of the upper part of the beak in a good light and establish the extent of the blood supply. This shows up as a dark line down the centre of the beak. Then clip a short distance below this point. If the lower beak is too long, cut the tip off and trim the sides to level it up. If in doubt, check with the shape of a normal beak.

It seems that once the beak has been cut, it tends to grow more rapidly. Since this will necessitate more frequent clipping, try to avoid trimming the beak if at all possible. Providing fresh branches and cuttlefish bone will give the bird an opportunity to wear its beak down naturally. It is normally only budgerigars that are susceptible to overgrown beaks, particularly pet budgerigars kept in cages, which may need their beaks cut back every two or three months. Birds in aviaries rarely need their beaks trimming, unless these were malformed in the nest, which should be fairly easy to ascertain by regular inspection.

Trim claws in a similar way to the beak. First locate the blood supply, visible as a thin streak running down the claw, and then clip the excess growth off cleanly. It is best to hold the bird's foot so that it cannot move during this procedure. The claws of certain birds, notably various finches, grow rapidly and are likely to need regular clipping. When dealing with a bird that has black claws, in which it is almost impossible

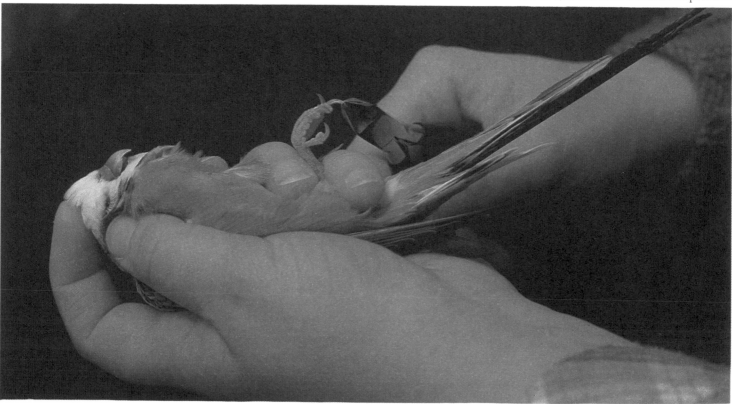

Basic hospital cage
Various designs are available, but the most satisfactory option is to use an infrared lamp as shown here. Unlike fully enclosed hospital cages the bird is able to regulate its own position in relation to the heat source.

Ideally, use a heat source that does not emit any light so that light levels can be regulated separately Maintaining a relatively high temperature is vital for the successful treatment of many bird ailments.

A thermometer will give an indication of the temperature in the cage, but do not position it where destructive birds, such as parrots, can reach it.

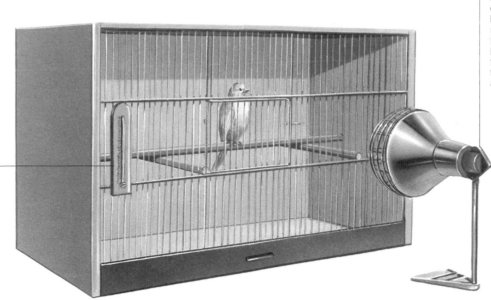

to distinguish the blood supply, err on the side of caution. Remove only a small piece of the dead tissue, so as to minimize the risk of bleeding. See below for advice on first-aid and responding to accidents.

Coping with emergencies
Accidental injuries do occur from time to time and treatment will vary according to the injury. If a bird inadvertently flies into a pane of glass, for example, do not put it into a cage but leave it quietly for an hour or so to recover in a darkened environment, such as a box. There will be nothing you can do in these circumstances, apart from hoping that the injury will not prove fatal.

Bleeding can require immediate first-aid, although in some cases the bird may appear undisturbed, with the only sign being drops of blood on the floor of the cage or flight. A styptic pencil is especially useful for stemming blood loss from a claw that has been torn or inadvertently cut too short. Other, more superficial wounds normally stop bleeding very rapidly, with a clot forming almost immediately. Unlike mammals, birds tend not to develop infected wounds, probably because their higher body temperature does not favour the development of the bacteria that normally contaminate such injuries.

Injuries to the limbs may simply be revealed by the bird's reluctance to use the affected wing or leg, with no trace of blood being apparent. Clearly, under these circumstances, you will need to catch the bird for a closer examination. Handling the bird is the only way to distinguish between a sprain and a fracture. Gently run your fingers up the leg, for example, feeling for a place where the bone appears to move vertically. This is likely to be the site of the

fracture, and in many instances, it is often quite high up in the thigh region. The bird will hold a fractured limb at an abnormal angle and will probably be unable to use it.

Seek veterinary advice, but be prepared to accept that the best course of action may be simply to let healing take place naturally, without even applying a splint to the leg. Indeed, it will probably prove almost impossible to keep a support of any kind on a parrot's leg, for example, and if the site of the fracture is close to the body, splinting

Above: Some problems in later life can be avoided by keeping a close watch on nestlings. This applies in the case of budgerigars, where dirt can readily accumulate inside the beak - particularly in the upper mandible - causing malformation if it is not removed. Use a matchstick or toothpick to remove caked food as part of a daily routine of regular health examination when cleaning out the nestbox.

may not be feasible. Because of the nature of a bird's skeletal system, only external support is usually provided at the site of a fracture, with no attempt being made to fix the broken bones by internal means with screws, plates and other similar devices.

Be sure to keep a bird with a fractured limb quiet, and discourage it from flying. Supply just low perches, so that it will not attempt to fly and land awkwardly, simply complicating the healing process. Under normal circumstances, the ends of a broken bone will re-unite rapidly, within a few weeks. In many cases, especially with limb fractures, there will be no noticeable long-term complications, and such birds can then lead a normal, active life.

Early signs of illness
The early signs of impending illness are likely to be ruffled feathers, a change in the appearance of the bird's droppings and a reduction in its level of activity. It will spend a greater time apparently sleeping, resting for long periods with both feet on the perch; normally, a healthy bird will roost with just one leg supporting its weight. A loss of appetite often occurs early in the course of an infection, and this in turn is responsible, at least in part, for the greenish loose droppings voided by many sick birds. Other factors may however influence the consistency of the droppings, such as the bird's diet. Parrots' droppings are generally greenish in appearance, so other signs need to be taken into account.

General care of sick birds
Warmth can be a very significant factor in the treatment of a sick bird. Maintain a temperature of about 27°C (81°F) to prevent the bird becoming chilled. While many

breeders invest in special hospital cages, with thermostatically controlled heaters, it is possible to devise a suitable emergency unit without too much difficulty. Position an infrared lamp, as used for warming newly hatched chicks, at a suitable distance from the cage, with a thermometer to monitor the temperature inside. Install a thermostat in the circuitry to maintain the temperature at the correct level and gradually reduce the amount of warmth as the bird's condition improves.

Feather ailments

Unfortunately, no straightforward cures exist for the feather ailments described here.

Feather-plucking The plumage disorder of greatest significance to the pet bird owner is undoubtedly feather-plucking, which is most prevalent and serious in parrot-like birds. There is no single cause, and indeed, in many cases, several separate factors may be implicated as possible reasons for feather-plucking. Such behaviour is more commonly seen in mature birds, and it has been suggested that a desire to breed may cause the bird to pull out its feathers totally, leaving not even an underlying layer of downy plumage. Nutritional problems are also clearly a contributory factor in some cases of feather-plucking. Some birds may be affected because they have received a very restricted diet of dry seed, or have refused all other items. Parasitic infestations, involving various mites and lice, are often quoted as leading to feather-plucking because of the irritation that they can cause. In reality,

however, they can be found in very few instances, being particularly uncommon in birds that have been established in a household for a long period of time. Furthermore, where birds, such as bantams, do develop a heavy external parasitic burden, they do not necessarily start pulling their feathers out, although the plumage can often appear frayed and damaged.

It is no coincidence that the parrots commonly regarded as the more intelligent species are the birds most likely to remove their own feathers. In addition, these birds kept in outdoor aviaries very rarely display this vice, although occasionally one bird may pluck another. These factors, when combined, suggest that stress is a particularly significant factor in feather-plucking. It may be that the bird resorts to such behaviour because of boredom. In a small cage, left on its own for much of the day, there will be little stimulus for a parrot, which thus resorts to feather-plucking. It is vital to make immediate improvements in the bird's environment at the first sign of self-inflicted feather damage, if the vice is not to become habitual.

An older parrot living on its own without a mate is even more susceptible to the effects of stress. Most parrots are social birds by nature that form life-long bonds in many instances. Certainly, in some cases, obtaining a mate and providing the birds with a nestbox in a suitable flight will lead to feather-plucking being resolved spontaneously. New feathers are allowed to develop naturally, and the birds may vent their destructive urges on the nestbox instead.

Many parrots naturally enjoy bathing in a shower of rain, yet inside, they are deprived of this opportunity. As a result, their plumage tends to lose its sleek appearance and the bird persists in attempting to preen itself. Thus, some instances of feather-plucking may develop from the bird's intense desire to keep its plumage in order. Again, the remedy is obvious, and regular bathing should be part of the normal management routine. In fact, parrots that are well cared for should rarely resort to feather-plucking. The only exceptions are likely to be an adult bird unused to cage surroundings, or a very tame parrot in a new environment, away from its previous owner. Thoughtful care

Hazards in the aviary

Diseases can be introduced into an aviary by various means. Good hygiene will do much to keep infections at bay, however, and ensure that the aviary occupants remain healthy.

Adding new birds to an established aviary can introduce disease; Always quarantine new stock to be safe.

The woodwork can harbour parasites such as red mite. Some wood preservatives can be toxic to birds.

Wild birds can spread both parasites and disease by way of their droppings or by entering the aviary and mingling with the captive birds. Indeed, the mesh of the aviary should be small enough to exclude birds, such as sparrows, for this reason.

Dirty perches can trigger infections of the feet, known as bumblefoot. Softbills, which wipe their beaks on perches and deposit food particles in the process, are most at risk.

The mesh should not be rusty, otherwise birds that climb around the mesh, such as budgerigars, may ingest particles of rust that may damage the digestive tract.

Never position food and water containers below perches, where they can be contaminated by droppings from above. Keep food dry and change water daily to reduce the risk of harmful micro-organisms developing.

Some birds spend more time on the floor of an aviary than others and are thus more likely to pick up various infections. An earth floor can present particular dangers, favouring the survival of parasitic worm eggs, which may reinfect the birds.

Remember that certain plants and their seeds may be poisonous to birds and exclude these from the aviary.

Rodents may tunnel into the aviary if the foundations are inadequate, or they may even enter directly through the mesh.

Above: The condition known as French Moult is associated especially with budgerigars. The main result of the feather loss is to prevent the bird flying normally. Here, the primary flight feathers are clearly absent. The precise cause remains a mystery.

Left: Feather-plucking is a particular problem associated with parrots and tends to be more prevalent in certain species, such as the macaws.

can again help to overcome the risk of feather-plucking becoming apparent; pay as much attention as possible to a tame bird, and provide an array of suitable playthings to keep it occupied. Keep offering a variety of foodstuffs, even if they are not all accepted, as ultimately the bird's curiosity should lead to it sampling them.

Only a small proportion of cases of feather-plucking will respond to any form of treatment, and relapses are relatively common. Try to establish the cause in the first instance, and take immediate action to overcome the problem. Foul-tasting aerosol preparations are available with which to spray the bird, but these are often useless. Birds only have a restricted sense of taste, and the desire to pluck their feathers usually proves overwhelming.

Feather-plucking may also occur in the nest, with young birds emerging in a partially bald state. The back of the neck is the site most frequently attacked by their parents. This problem is not serious; the plumage rapidly regrows, although the youngsters are more likely to become chilled in the interim. Such behaviour is most apparent in prolific parrots, such as cockatiels, and probably stems from the parents' desire to persuade their early chicks to leave so that they can breed again.

French Moult Budgerigars also may pluck their young to 'oust' their early chicks, but the condition of French Moult is more significant. There have been a large number of potential causes put forward to explain this disease. The possible increase of French Moult caused by overbreeding is discussed on page 100. The symptoms are that young birds lose their flight feathers around the time that they fledge. The effects can range from mild to severe, with some birds appearing to recover spontaneously, while others are handicapped for life. Recent research suggests that a viral infection is responsible for the condition, and at present there is no

effective treatment. The disease does not appear to spread to other birds, such as cockatiels, that may be sharing the budgerigars' accommodation. A good deal of research still remains to be carried out in order to get a full picture of the disease.

Feather cysts Feather cysts in canaries result from an abnormality in the feather structure, so that a swelling occurs at the site where it would normally emerge from the skin. This condition cannot be treated successfully. It may be confused with a tumour, and indeed skin tumours are not unknown in birds (see page 31).

Bacterial diseases

Dirty conditions are likely to give rise to bacterial infections. The disease may start as enteritis affecting the digestive tract and then develop into a generalized infection that is liable to prove rapidly fatal unless treated. Antibiotics are usually effective in combating bacterial disease, although it is vital that treatment begins as soon as possible. The antibiotic may be in the form of a powder preparation to be dissolved in the drinking water, or a veterinarian may decide to inject your bird with a similar drug in the first instance. Dosing by means of tablets is also possible with some species, notably pigeons. Ask your veterinarian for advice.

If a bacterial infection occurs in an aviary, remove any sick birds and clean the environment thoroughly. This will reduce the risk of other birds succumbing to the infection. Wash the food and water pots in particular, since infection can be easily spread by food contaminated by droppings. Dirty perches present a particular threat; they may give rise to a localized bacterial infection leading to swellings on the feet, described as 'bumblefoot'. This is most commonly associated with softbills. Treatment is difficult, often requiring surgery in addition to antibiotic therapy.

Eye infections may also be spread or develop from contact with dirty perches. The affected eye will be kept closed and the surrounding plumage is likely to appear matted. There may also be swelling evident around the eye. Again, antibiotics – in the form of a suitable ophthalmic ointment or

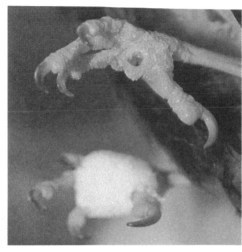

Above: Unclean surroundings are typically responsible for the condition known as bumblefoot. It is most often seen in softbills and poultry and the localized infection can spread up the leg if left untreated. Here, the symptoms are seen on a Mynah.

drops – will rapidly resolve the complaint. To be effective, give this treatment several times a day. Always ensure that you follow the instructions closely; just because a bird appears to have made a spectacular recovery, do not stop treating the infection. Always complete the prescribed course, otherwise complications may develop. This is standard practice for antibiotics.

Viral diseases

Whereas bacterial infections can be overcome by the use of an appropriate antibiotic, there is no effective means of treating viral diseases directly. Mortality can therefore be high in a susceptible population of birds, but thankfully, outbreaks of viral diseases are relatively scarce. The most significant viral infection, essentially because of its economic implications for the poultry industry, is Newcastle Disease, or Fowl Pest. It is for this reason that most countries impose quarantine controls on the importation of birds, especially psittacines (the parrots and parrot-like birds), which may be affected with a particularly severe form of this virus. The symptoms are variable, ranging from sudden death with no prior signs through to neurological and respiratory disorders. In mild infections, a rapid fall-off in the number of eggs being laid is a

Above: Infection of the eye may affect the surrounding skin, as seen here in a Hooded Mountain Toucan (*Andigena cucullata*). If both eyes are affected, this can indicate a more serious condition. Always seek veterinary help.

Above: The result of treatment can be quite rapid. This is the same bird approximately twenty-four hours later, the swelling around the eye having virtually disappeared. Appropriate medication must be applied several times daily, however.

typical effect of the virus in poultry, and one of the possible causes of the so-called 'egg-drop syndrome'.

Other viruses of significance include the pox viruses, which lead to the formation of pustules around the head in most instances, while the bird may also develop breathing difficulties. The discharges are highly infectious to other birds, but if an individual recovers then it will be immune to this particular disease in the future. Pigeons, parrots and canaries are probably most often afflicted with viruses of this type, which may also be spread by biting insects from bird to bird, as well as by more direct means. A virus which appears to be of growing significance in the parrot world belongs to the herpes group, giving rise to the illness known as Pacheco's Disease. It appears that conures may carry the infection with few if any symptoms, yet other parrots coming into contact with them are liable to develop a serious illness, and have little hope of recovery. No treatment is of value, and as yet, no vaccine is available as a preventative measure. By way of contrast, it is possible to vaccinate for the other viral diseases, subject to veterinary recommendation, and government controls in the particular case of Newcastle Disease.

Chlamydiosis (Psittacosis)

None of the diseases mentioned so far can be spread to humans (with the possible exception of Newcastle Disease, which has mild effects), but, as with all animals, there are infections that can be transmitted in this way, and of these, chlamydiosis (also know as psittacosis) is by far the most significant. Yet birds are not the only possible source of human infection; the organism responsible, *Chlamydia psittaci*, can also be acquired from farmstock and even cats. Nor are parrots (psittacines) the only birds that can transmit the infection. With a better understanding of the disease, referring to it as psittacosis is now not strictly correct.

The characteristics of the organism have features in common with both viruses and bacteria. Most significantly, however, the disease will respond to antibiotic therapy. The symptoms in a bird are relatively non-specific, although it is possible to diagnose the infection from the droppings in some instances. A discharge from the eyes and nostrils, coupled with laboured breathing and loose droppings, can be indicative of the disease. If you suspect that a bird may be suffering from chlamydiosis, seek veterinary advice without delay. The disease in humans produces symptoms resembling pneumonia, and clearly, should a member of the family develop a severe respiratory infection of this nature, you should inform the doctor that they could be suffering from chlamydiosis.

On the available data, the actual risk of contracting this disease from birds would appear very slight. In the whole of the United States, for example, a study revealed

Above: Pox viruses can affect many birds, although the symptoms are most often seen in pigeons and canaries.

Below: The signs of illness are relatively non-specific in birds, although clearly this parrot is ailing.

that about forty-six cases of human chlamydiosis occurred annually, and significantly, a number of the people affected had no direct contact whatsoever with birds, with the source of their infection being unknown. Unfortunately, there has been a tendency for birds to be seen as the sole vector for this disease, yet the fact that *Chlamydia psittaci* may be implicated in over ten percent of respiratory infections of cats is rarely mentioned. In some countries, such as the United States, imported birds are treated routinely against psittacosis with appropriate antibiotics. This can create other problems, however, possibly predisposing the birds to fungal disease by lowering the body's natural defences.

Fungal infections

Fungal disease in birds is not very common, but can be seen in particular groups. The organisms responsible may respond to specific antibiotics, as in the case of *Candida* infections. This disease, known as candidiasis, typically affects birds that feed on nectar, such as lories. The whitish colonies produced by the fungus can be seen in the mouth. They can spread lower down the digestive tract, with fatal consequences. A deficiency of Vitamin A, which is normally stored in the liver, may predispose birds to infections of this type.

Hot, humid and poorly ventilated surroundings favour the development of aspergillosis in birds. The fungus usually develops in the respiratory system and can also spread elsewhere in the body. Signs of chronic illness, such as weight loss and laboured breathing, especially after exercise, are typical indicators of this disease. Some remission may be gained with medication,

but, unfortunately, no reliable cure is currently available for this disease.

Parasites

While parasites will be of little concern for anyone keeping a pet bird on its own indoors, they may prove highly significant when a number of birds are being kept together in a confined area. Under these conditions, all the birds can soon become infected. The parasites typically divide into those found on the surface of the bird's body and those occurring within the body.

Although lice are not a great threat to the bird's health, since they only occur on the body and are easily controlled, the same situation does not apply in the case of red mites. These minute parasites may be seen, especially against a white background, as tiny red spots; the reddish colour is most apparent after they have fed on a bird's blood. Red mites live in close proximity to the birds, frequenting nestboxes and other dark localities. They may even cause anaemia in chicks, and are relatively inconspicuous. It pays to take regular precautions, therefore, including spraying the birds' quarters at regular intervals or using a suitable powder. You should be able to obtain preparations of this type that are non-toxic for birds from your pet store. At the end of the breeding period, wash all the cages and boxes thoroughly and apply a suitable treatment against red mites. These parasites can survive for months without feeding, and could still be present at the start of the next breeding season.

Some birds are more susceptible to certain parasites than others, and further details can be found under specific headings in the second part of the book. Budgerigars, for example, are most at risk from the mites that cause scaly face, whereas Gouldian Finches may be afflicted with air-sac mites.

Treating scaly face is fairly straight-forward and simply entails painting the en-

Parasitic worm life cycles

Roundworms

These parasites have a direct life cycle, spreading from one bird to another by infective eggs.

The worms live in the bird's gut, taking in food materials in a digested form.

Tapeworms

These parasites resemble a piece of tape. From a small head they become broader at the tail.

The tapeworm clings to the gut by means of tiny spines and suckers on the head.

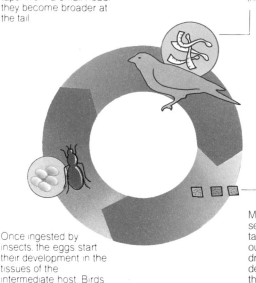

The eggs survive well in damp surroundings and, after a period of time, they become infective for other birds. The eggs can remain viable for several years.

The mature worms produce many thousands of eggs, which pass through the gut and out in the bird's droppings to contaminate the nearby environment.

Once ingested by insects, the eggs start their development in the tissues of the intermediate host. Birds become infected on eating the host.

Mature egg-filled segments of the tapeworms are passed out in the bird's droppings. Control depends on breaking the cycle at a vulnerable point by de-worming.

crustations with a proprietary remedy available from a pet store, or smearing petroleum jelly over the affected area every day. These oily substances inhibit the mites' breathing processes, and they die. Always continue such treatment for a short period after the signs have disappeared, however, to ensure that all the parasites have been eliminated. Be sure to keep affected birds on their own until they are cured, and then thoroughly disinfect their quarters.

Air-sac mites, as their name implies, inhabit the airways. In pheasants especially, another parasite – gapeworms – can cause respiratory distress. Gapeworms have a wide range of hosts, and birds living in the company of pheasants can also be affected if

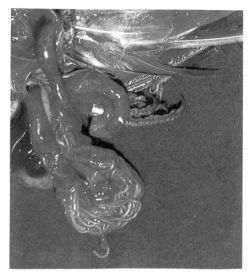

Left: This budgerigar is showing clear signs of scaly face. The mites responsible can cause malformation of the beak in severe cases.

Above: A blockage caused by a build up of parasitic worms in the intestine can prove fatal, as is clearly the case here.

they ingest infective insects. The insects act as intermediate hosts in the parasite's life cycle, having taken the eggs passed out by the bird. After any exertion, an infected bird may be seen with its beak open, gaping, and it may attempt to cough up the parasites, which are anchored in pairs in the lining of the trachea, or windpipe. Young birds are most at risk from this infection, with older stock gaining a degree of immunity.

In addition to treating the birds for the parasites, be sure to clean their environment thoroughly to prevent reinfection as far as possible. This applies especially in the case of Australian parakeets, which are often infected with roundworms. These worms can be spread directly from bird to bird via droppings, with no requirement for an insect to act as an intermediate host. The huge output of eggs from parasites within the bird's gut means that in the relatively close confines of an aviary under poor conditions of hygiene, reinfection will be inevitable. Many breeders routinely deworm their stock, often in the spring before the breeding season and again in the autumn.

Tapeworms tend to be less of a problem than roundworms, since they require an intermediate host in many if not all cases. Yet pigeons often carry a heavy burden of these parasites, and newly imported lories and lorikeets should also be treated with a suitable preparation to remove any tapeworms present in their gut. Seek veterinary advice before embarking on a programme of deworming your stock. Recently, a number of effective new drugs have become available, and in most cases these can only be obtained from a veterinarian.

A bird affected with intestinal worms may show relatively few signs, apart from

appearing off-colour. A more common parasitic cause of diarrhoea is likely to be a protozoal infection. These microscopic creatures are most commonly associated with fowl and game birds, giving rise to the disease often known as coccidosis. Nevertheless, other birds, including finches and budgerigars, can also be at risk. It is possible to obtain medicated foods for susceptible stock. These contain drugs referred to as coccidostats, which are widely used in the poultry industry, where birds are housed under intensive conditions. The protozoa responsible for the disease are spread via the droppings, and clearly, a contaminated food supply presents a serious threat. The groups of drugs known as sulphonamides are traditionally favoured both for control and treatment of coccidosis, but other, newer compounds may be prescribed by your veterinarian. Birds can develop immunity to coccidial infections, and it is for this reason that the most dramatic signs of infection are likely to be apparent in young stock.

Tumours

Budgerigars are at greatest risk from tumours, both of the benign and cancerous types. See your veterinarian if you suspect that your bird is suffering with a tumour. It may be possible to remove a superficial tumour by surgery, but in some cases, with internal tumours, the signs may not even be apparent until the disease is advanced. An internal tumour affecting the kidneys or reproductive organs is frequently the cause of chronic weight loss in middle-aged or older budgerigars. Under these circumstances, the cere may change colour, while the bird generally appears sick, and terminally, it may become unable to perch.

BREEDING YOUR BIRD

In this general overview of breeding, we look at nest boxes, possible problems such as compatibility and egg-binding, the use of incubators, rearing quarters for chicks, and further areas of interest. More detailed breeding information for the different groups of birds accompanies the species descriptions in Part Two.

Nestboxes and nesting materials

Many species of bird that normally nest in tree hollows will use a nestbox for the purpose, either in a cage or an aviary. Indeed, special breeding cages can be bought, or made quite easily, with the metal fronts being produced in various sizes. Most budgerigar nestboxes fix outside the cage, so that the birds have the maximum area available to them within the cage, and it is easy to inspect the contents of the nestbox. In this instance, a wooden or plastic concave (i.e. a depression) provides the area where the hen will lay her eggs. For other parrot-like birds, a more natural set-up may be required. Many species prefer a relatively deep nestbox, and this can be lined with wood chips. The more destructive parrots

Above: The nesting accommodation should reflect the bird's size and destructive power. If supplied with a weak wooden nestbox, parrots may destroy this and cause the loss of both eggs and chicks. This barrel for macaws has been reinforced around the entrance to protect the edge of the wood.

will prefer to gnaw at chunks of softwood to create their own nest lining. For these birds, reinforce the entrance hole to the nestbox with pieces of tin, carefully hammered

around the edges so that the birds will not be able to gnaw the exposed pieces of wood or catch themselves on the sharp edges of the tin sheeting. For Australian species especially, provide a layer of peat in the nestbox. Since the hen may scrape this out, wood chips often prove a more suitable alternative lining.

Although many parrots may nest at a considerable height off the ground in the wild, the nestbox does not have to be placed up against the roof of the aviary. This will make inspection difficult in any event, unless part of a side is hinged. There can be times when it is necessary to check on the progress of chicks, for example, so always allow for looking into the nestbox. If it is fairly deep, provide a ladder of some kind, such as a strip of aviary wire running up to the entrance holder from the interior. Ensure as far as possible that there are no loose sharp edges, and in any event fix the wire in place with netting staples, with battening on top. By this means, even if the birds destroy the wood, the ladder will not fall down, blocking access to the floor of the nestbox where there could be chicks or eggs. Many parrots prefer to roost in a nestbox at night. This is especially recommended in an outside aviary, as the birds will be protected against the elements and marauding animals that may otherwise disturb them at night.

Parrots generally do not require nesting material; the notable exceptions are the lovebirds and hanging parrots, which strip pieces of bark and leaves, as well as making use of other suitable material in the aviary. Yet nesting material is essential for finches. The serins, which include the domestic canary, construct an open nest, and for this reason, may be persuaded to use a plastic nest-pan as a basis on which to build their nest. It is usual to stitch a lining felt into the base of the nest-pan and provide special safe nesting material for the birds. Other items that may be of use include dried moss, available from florists, and even horse or dog hair. While some pairs will accept thick stems of grass, do not offer hay. This is a potential source of fungal spores, which may affect the chicks and even the adult birds. For bantams, use straw to line their nestboxes. Similarly, with pheasants that refuse nestboxes, line their hollow scrapes with a covering of straw. Waterfowl may prefer to construct a nest of twigs, sometimes using a nestbox, depending upon the species concerned. Pigeons, similarly, may prefer to use more bulky material; their nests tend to be sloppy, and it is not unknown for them to collapse. Encourage the birds to use a nesting platform therefore, and place some loose twigs on top to stimulate their interest.

Breeding quarters for large parrots

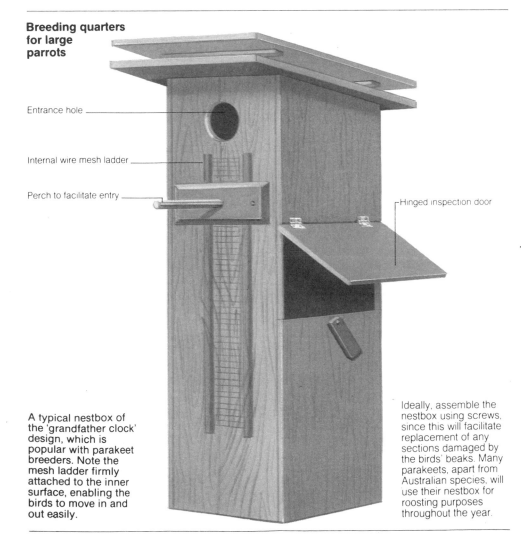

Entrance hole

Internal wire mesh ladder

Perch to facilitate entry

Hinged inspection door

A typical nestbox of the 'grandfather clock' design, which is popular with parakeet breeders. Note the mesh ladder firmly attached to the inner surface, enabling the birds to move in and out easily.

Ideally, assemble the nestbox using screws, since this will facilitate replacement of any sections damaged by the birds' beaks. Many parakeets, apart from Australian species, will use their nestbox for roosting purposes throughout the year.

Breeding quarters for canaries

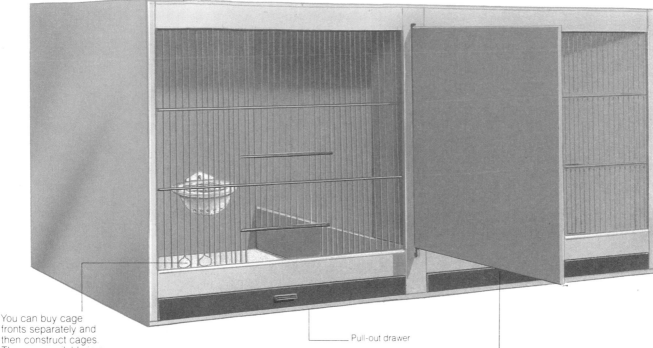

You can buy cage fronts separately and then construct cages. They are available in a variety of sizes, and are held in place by prongs fitting into the wooden struts top and bottom.

This illustration shows a typical cage set-up suitable for breeding canaries, with the nest pan fixed firmly on the back wall of the cage.

Below: The hen canary is responsible for hatching and rearing the chicks. Here, a sitting hen is joined by her attentive mate.

Pull-out drawer

Removable partition

Felt lining

Canary nesting pans are available in various materials, although plastic is the most widely used today. It is lined with a nesting felt.

This is a so-called 'double breeder' with a central removable partition, which offers much greater versatility than using single cages. They can be used as flight cages for young stock after the breeding season is over

Pair compatibility

In most instances, the breeding period will progress without problems. During the early stages, however, watch the birds to ensure that the hen is not being unduly persecuted by the cock bird. This is most likely to occur in Australian parakeets, pheasants and pigeons, and it may be that the hen is not as advanced in terms of breeding condition as the cock bird. Under these circumstances, therefore, remove the cock bird and return it to the hen a week or so later. Never introduce the hen back to the cock, as this will almost certainly lead to further displays of aggression. Further advice on pair compatibility is given in each species description in Part Two.

Egg-binding

During a spell of cold weather, laying birds are more at risk from egg-binding. For this reason, restrict the breeding season in outside accommodation to the warmer months of the year in temperate climates. A hen affected with egg-binding will appear unsteady on her feet, and soon cannot perch. If you suspect egg-binding, take immediate action. As a first step place the bird in a warm environment and, unless the egg is laid within a short period of time, seek expert veterinary help. The bird may be unable to expel the egg from its body if the shell is incorrectly formed; some eggs have a rubbery appearance for this reason, A deficiency of calcium may be responsible,

Breeding quarters for budgerigars

Budgerigars, like other parrots, tend to be hole-nesters, although sometimes they may lay on the floor of the aviary. Nestboxes can be supplied either in the aviary or attached to a breeding cage. Provide as much space as possible, since hens do tend to become rather obese while confined in a breeding cage.

Although plastic nestboxes enjoyed a brief surge in popularity, wooden nestboxes are still the most common. They include a glass inspection panel, which prevents the loss of eggs and chicks when the outer panel is lifted.

The door of cage fronts for budgerigars opens outwards, and the mesh spacing is relatively wide. Again, double-breeding cages with a removable centre partition can be constructed using two cage fronts. Buy these from a pet store or from a mail-order specialist.

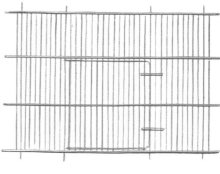

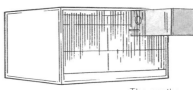

The nestbox can be fitted either at the front of the cage, as shown, which entails cutting a hole in the bars and smoothing off the rough edges, or attached to a wooden side, with a hole cut to correspond to the entrance hole. This takes up more space in a limited area.

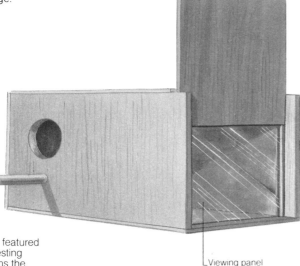

In the design featured below, the nesting concave forms the base of a drawer that slides into the nestbox.

└ Viewing panel

Nesting concave ┐

with certain birds, such as hen Cut-throat Finches, being most at risk.

A complication that may arise after the successful removal of an egg is a prolapse of tissue, which appears as a pink mass hanging out of the bird's vent. While it is possible to manipulate this back successfully, relapses are not uncommon. A veterinarian may have to insert a temporary suture to prevent a repeated recurrence of the prolapse, until the tissue recovers from the trauma. This is most common in birds that have been egg-bound for relatively long periods.

Using incubators

Unfortunately, not all birds will incubate their eggs successfully, and these will have to be fostered or transferred to an incubator for hatching. Early removal of a first clutch of eggs also tends to lead to the hen laying

Budgerigars will breed quite readily, either in cage or aviary surroundings. A pair is shown at the nestbox (left) and the series of photographs shown above traces the development of a group of chicks. A newly hatched youngster along with an older nestmate can be seen at far left. Feathers are clearly visible by three weeks of age, and the young budgerigars will leave the nest when around five weeks old. In the meantime, it is likely that the adult birds will have mated again, and the hen will already have started to lay a second clutch of eggs in the nestbox to begin a new cycle.

Breeding quarters for finches

Finches can be bred successfully using a range of nesting receptacles. Results are likely to be better in flights or aviaries rather than in cages for the non-domesticated species.

Right: The typical finch nesting basket is made of wicker and hooks over the cage bars, or it can be attached to the wooden panels of the cage using netting staples. The birds build their nests inside it

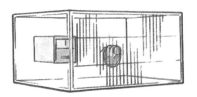

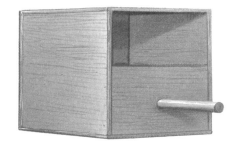

Below left: Wooden nest boxes for finches are typically open-fronted, as shown here.

Below: The bars of foreign finch cage fronts are closely spaced to suit these small birds.

Above: Finches will gather a variety of material with which to build their nests.

Below: A newly hatched Bengalese Finch in its nest, surrounded by eggs yet to hatch.

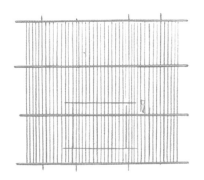

again in a short space of time. Birds divide into two basic groups in terms of the development of their chicks on hatching. While the chicks of the so-called altricial birds, such as parrots and finches, need a subsequent period of parental care before they are able to live independently, this does not apply to the precocial species, such as waterfowl, pheasants, bantams and related species. The latter are more suited to being hatched in an incubator, therefore, simply because the chicks will not require constant hand-feeding every few hours for a period of several weeks after hatching.

There have been rapid developments in incubator technology during recent years, and compact designs, ideal for hatching a small number of eggs reliably, are widely available at low cost. Incubators operating on the moving air principle, recognizable by the presence of a fan close to the roof of the dome, are preferable to the so-called still-air models. Some breeders like to use the latter in the final stage of the incubation period, however, transferring the eggs across.

Apart from maintaining the temperature, an incubator must also be capable of keeping the humidity at the appropriate level. Clearly, having to open the lid regularly to turn the eggs by hand can be a severe handicap in these respects. Ideally, therefore, choose an incubator with an automatic turning device. And choose the location for the incubator with care; never place the machine in a spot where it could be

exposed to direct sunlight, as this could rapidly raise the temperature within to a fatal level for the developing chicks.

Collect the eggs daily, and either store them in a cool locality or transfer them to the incubator immediately. Since the germ within the egg that will develop into the embryo will remain viable for several days at room temperature, wait until you have a number of eggs and put these into the incubator as one batch. This will ultimately facilitate rearing of the chicks, since they should all hatch at the same time.

Check the eggs before you set them in the

incubator. Dirty eggs can introduce disease into the incubator, and often fail to hatch, since bacteria can penetrate the egg via the pores in the shell. Chip off any dirt adhering to the shell very carefully with a finger-nail, or rub the surface with glass paper. Incubate only undamaged eggs, although if there is a minor crack visible, it may be possible to repair this with a coat of nail varnish applied to the damaged area.

Misshapen or small eggs are less likely to hatch, although there is no harm in setting them if space permits. Keep a check on the temperature and humidity throughout the

Hatching eggs in an incubator

A variety of compact incubators, suitable for hatching relatively small numbers of eggs, are now available. An automatic turning device is recommended.

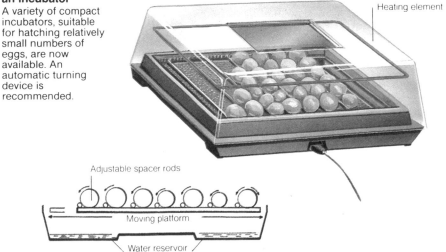

Heating element

Adjustable spacer rods

Moving platform

Water reservoir

incubation period. An instrument known as a hygrometer, commonly available for greenhouses, will provide an accurate reading of the humidity level. Once the chicks start to hatch, leave them in the incubator for a day, depending on the available space, before removing them to a brooder. At first, the young birds will have reserves of food in the yolk sac, which must be used up, so they will not require feeding for the first day or so after emerging.

Rearing the chicks

Rearing quarters for the chicks need not be elaborate; a simple pen with solid walls will do. The most important thing is to keep the birds warm. An infrared lamp, which emits heat and no light, is essential; do not use an ordinary bulb, since excessive levels of artificial light can precipitate feather-plucking, especially in poultry. If you are using the corner of a shed, construct a suitable barrier of hardboard or plywood on the other two sides, with the heat source in the centre of the enclosure. If the chicks get too warm, they are thus able to move slightly away from the heat source to cool off. Suspend the lamp, complete with a reflector, low down but still out of reach of the chicks. Ensure that it is positioned firmly in place and cannot fall on to the chicks beneath. Watching the chicks will give the best indication as to whether they are at the correct temperature. They should not huddle together, which indicates that they are probably too cold, nor lie far apart, suggesting that the temperature is excessively high for them.

Provide food, in the form of a starter diet, close at hand but out of the rays of the lamp. Water is vital, but never provide this in open pots, even to ducklings at this stage. They are liable to get chilled, or even drown, since the natural waterproofing of their feathers is not present at birth. Use sawdust as a floor covering, taking care to avoid treated brands that could prove toxic. Unfortunately, some birds will eat sawdust early in life, and this can lead to impaction, typically of the crop, where food is normally stored. As a precaution, therefore, you may prefer to use coarse shredded paper as an alternative bedding material. Be sure to leave an area clear of bedding where food and water can be supplied.

Always ensure that you have a spare infrared bulb on hand, for the time when a replacement is necessary; this typically occurs at a most incovenient moment, when the shops are closed! Depending on the overall environmental temperature, chilling for any length of time is liable to prove fatal for young chicks. Remember, also, that on a dry diet the birds will be drinking quite considerable volumes of water, and you may need to supply extra as they get older. Reduce the temperature gradually, by raising the infrared lamp further away from the chicks in the enclosure.

Apart from their decorative appeal,

Converting a spare room to a birdroom

An indoor birdroom may be required in areas where the weather precludes keeping birds outside throughout the year. Alternatively, birds that are too noisy for an outdoor aviary, such as many parrots, can be kept indoors in an insulated room, and are likely to rear more chicks in such surroundings. Some birds show a tendency to breed during the winter in northern climates, and thus will benefit from indoor accommodation.

Wire the window over securely but in such a way that it can be opened for ventilation. A blind is ideal for shading the room.

The indoor aviary is constructed on similar lines to an outdoor structure, but the woodwork does not need to be treated.

indoors, dust can become a major problem and the inclusion of an ionizer helps to keep the air fresh and particle free.

Provide plenty of drawer and cupboard space for storing such items as spare perches, feeding pots, drinkers, etc. Store food in a dry place.

Left: Some species make better foster-parents than others. The Muscovy Duck shown here is a popular choice with many waterfowl breeders.

Above: Young budgerigars at five weeks about to leave the nestbox. The hen adult has already started to lay her second clutch of eggs.

bantams are widely used as foster-parents for the eggs of species that would be normally hatched in an incubator. Using bantams in this way is discussed in the chapter relating to their care on page 157. While this system can work very well, it is dependent upon the breeding cycles of the birds concerned being coordinated. As a result, you may need more than one or two hen bantams for the purpose.

Indoor breeding of birds

In some parts of the world, such as Scandinavia, it may not be possible to house birds in outside flights throughout the year because of extreme weather conditions. In urban areas, the limited space available in a garden and the vocal powers of parrots when combined may spur you to provide alternative accommodation inside the house. A spare room can be ideal, and can house a number of cages plus larger flights as well. In the first instance, however, check that there will be no problems in converting a room for the purpose. Replace any carpeting with linoleum or a similar flooring and fix suitable screening over the windows to prevent the birds flying at the glass if they escape, or being exposed to direct sunlight. Some degree of sound insulation may be required for parrot-like birds, because their calls could disturb neighbours. Cockatoos are particularly noisy birds to keep.

When provided with suitable nesting facilities, birds will breed quite contentedly under these conditions. Indeed, in some cases, they can prove more prolific than if housed in outdoor flights. This applies especially to species that tend to nest during the winter months in northern climates. An interesting fact that has emerged from keeping breeding stock indoors is that birds from tropical areas, where there is normally little variation in day length throughout the year, will respond to increasing periods of light, which act as a breeding trigger. Further investigations into other contributory factors that can lead to reproductive success are underway. In the nutritional field, for example, a completely balanced pelleted diet suitable for parrots is currently being marketed in the United States, although not all species will readily accept the dried pellets.

Further developments

Breeding birds, whether a pair of finches indoors or ducks living in the garden, is a fascinating pastime of interest to people of all ages. It is not uncommon for someone who enters the hobby in a small way to want to expand their collection. Try, therefore, to plan with this in mind as far as possible. A single aviary may look very attractive on its own, but you may want to expand the design at a later stage, by building additional flights on to the existing structure. These can then be linked by a service corridor running down the back of the aviaries, obviating the need for individual safety porches. (See also pages 44–47.)

Apart from keeping more birds, there are other avenues that you may wish to pursue. Hand-rearing of baby parrots is a unique and immensely pleasurable task, albeit very demanding in terms of time. Shared between members of the family, however, the problem of repeated feeds at short intervals over a two-month period in many cases can be overcome. Colour-breeding, which will require some knowledge of genetics, is another area that offers considerable scope for the specialist. Alternatively, the exhibition side of the hobby may hold greater appeal for you. Virtually any species can be shown, although it is typically the so-called fancy breeds, ranging from bantams to budgerigars, that are most commonly exhibited and judged according to prescribed standards. (See the sections in Part Two.)

In most areas, there are bird clubs, where people keeping a variety of birds meet and discuss their interests with a full social programme often being arranged, including visits to major shows. Local contacts can be very valuable at holiday time; you may be able to come to a reciprocal arrangement with a fellow fancier living nearby. There are few leisure activities that will prove as relaxing and enjoyable as birdkeeping, whichever aspect appeals to you.

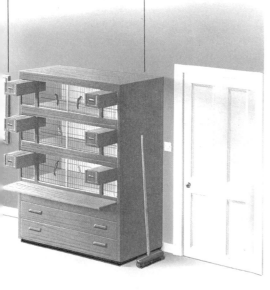

A pinboard is useful for displaying such details as eggs laid and hatched and a calender of important exhibition dates, etc.

Avoid positioning breeding cages directly in front of a window, to avoid direct sunlight during the day and flashing lights after dark.

For good hygiene in the birdroom, choose a floor covering that is easy to keep clean. Vinyl flooring is ideal.

Keeping a record
Accurate record keeping is essential to avoid repeated pairings of closely related stock. With colour mutations, accurate knowledge of the parentage of the breeding stock is vital, in order to maximize the production of chicks of a certain colour.

Above: Pins in a softwood block serve as a breeding record: eggs on the left, chicks on the right of the line. Face pins indicate eggs laid in this nestbox; top pins, eggs or chicks introduced from other nestboxes; bottom pins record eggs or chicks relocated, indicated by top pins elsewhere.

BIRDS IN THE HOME

CAGES AND INDOOR FLIGHTS

In this section we consider the quest for a cage or other suitable indoor accommodation for your bird, the best location for a cage indoors, taming and teaching birds to talk, toys and bathing.

Cages and indoor flights

Looking round at the array of cages stocked by larger pet stores and similar outlets can be an unsettling experience for many people who have kept birds over a period of time. A significant number of the cages currently marketed are either inadequate or plainly unsuitable for their purpose. Tiny bamboo cages, for example, may appear decorative, but may harbour dirt and parasites and will be rapidly destroyed by a budgerigar requiring a more spacious if less scenic environment. Most parrot cages are far too small to house these active and intelligent birds, and economies in their manufacture can render the bird liable to injury from the thin metal

sheeting with sharp edges often present at the base of the cage.

Plastic, although easy to clean, will rapidly be destroyed by a parrot if it can gain access to this material with its beak. Thus, although plastic now appears to predominate, be sure to choose a more suitable material, such as glazed earthenware, for food pots in a parrot's cage. The most recent trend towards using plastic instead of wooden perches in many parrot cages reflects a distinct lack of concern for the bird's welfare. Parrots are destructive birds by nature and should be provided with wood to gnaw; replacement dowel perches are easy to obtain from most timber merchants if natural branches are unavailable. The other serious drawback of plastic is that it appears to be uncomfortable for the bird itself; after a few weeks, some parrots will refuse to sit on plastic perches, preferring to cling to the sides of the cage.

Yet another point of weakness in many parrot cages now available is the door fastening. A door that just clips closed is simply inadequate; the parrot will rapidly learn to open the door and escape into the room. Even a screw-type fastening may not be safe, so invest in a stout padlock.

The shape of the cage is an important consideration. Although for the home an attractive cage is desirable, do not be way-laid by exotic designs. For finches, never purchase one of the upright barrel-shaped cages that are frequently seen. These are totally unnatural, permitting the birds very little flying space. Indeed, all birds being kept indoors will benefit from a rectangular structure that affords them generous flying space. The ideal solution is an indoor flight cage. Since these offer a larger internal area than conventional cages, it will not be so necessary to allow birds to fly free in a room for exercise, which can prove safer in the long term. Indoor flight cages of attractive and functional design are available.

Among other points to consider when assessing a cage is the ease with which it can be cleaned; most designs incorporate sliding trays. Easy access to the interior is also important for such tasks as replacing perches and fixing up a nestbox. Screening may also be significant, with a messy bird such as a mynah, or to give more seclusion if a pair of birds start nesting. Panels can be fitted to the sides of some designs.

In many cases, it is easy to overlook the fact that you may have to spend more on adequate housing than you paid for the bird itself. Kept in more spacious surroundings, birds are likely to remain healthier, and will not succumb to the neuroses, such as feather-plucking and head-weaving, exhibited by many pet birds housed in very confined quarters. In addition, you should be able to house a pair of birds together. As is becoming increasingly evident, many parrots will breed more readily in indoor quarters than in an outside aviary, where probably only one round of chicks will be reared during the course of a year, before the onset of winter.

If you decide to keep finches, you may prefer to construct your own flight for these birds. Since they will not destroy woodwork, a basic wooden box design is ideal and easy to build to any suitable dimensions. Fit a separate frame covered with suitable mesh to the front of the structure, and remember to allow for a sliding tray beneath this part

Cage design

Take particular care over choosing a cage, as many designs available have serious shortcomings. Also examine equipment for the cage closely to ensure that it is suitable for the birds.

If a stand for the cage is required, check that the attachment point on the cage is strong.

Position perches so that the bird's tail does not rub on the cage bars. And perches should not overhang the food pots.

Ornate cage designs may please the human eye but are not always ideal for pet birds. Here, for example, these narrow roof spaces give the cage a spacious look but they are inaccessible to the birds themselves.

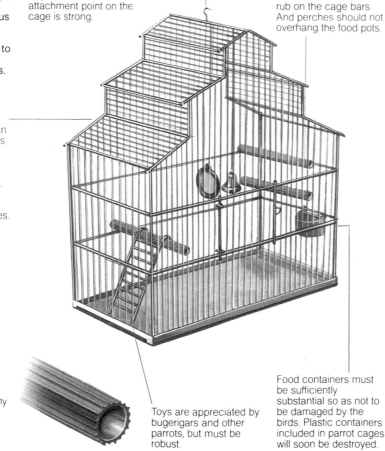

Plastic perches are unsuitable for birds, although now incorporated into many cages. Replace them with a selection of dowelling and natural branches.

Toys are appreciated by bugerigars and other parrots, but must be robust.

Food containers must be sufficiently substantial so as not to be damaged by the birds. Plastic containers included in parrot cages will soon be destroyed.

Positioning a cage
There are a number of factors to consider when positioning a bird cage in a room. If a stand is used, it should be reasonably substantial and not easily tipped over.

Windows should be screened with net curtains, to indicate to the bird that there is an obstruction present

Otherwise, birds may attempt to fly directly through the glass, with fatal consequences. Nets also filter sun

Open-topped fish tanks are a potential danger to free-flying birds. Cover them.

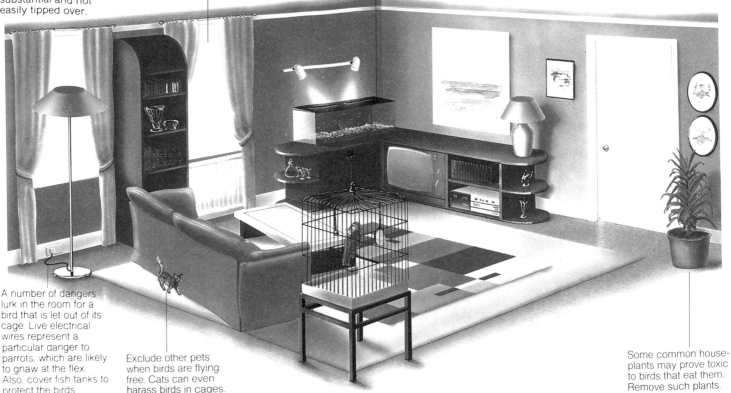

A number of dangers lurk in the room for a bird that is let out of its cage. Live electrical wires represent a particular danger to parrots, which are likely to gnaw at the flex. Also, cover fish tanks to protect the birds

Exclude other pets when birds are flying free. Cats can even harass birds in cages.

Some common house-plants may prove toxic to birds that eat them. Remove such plants.

Left: Only allow birds to fly free in a room when there is someone on hand to supervise them. In many cases, after an initial flight, the bird will settle happily on top of its cage, like this cockatiel. The larger parrots are capable of destroying valuable furniture with their powerful beaks. Ornaments are always at risk with a bird loose in a room and should be removed well beforehand to avoid any accidental breakages occurring

of the unit. This enables the cages to be cleaned with minimum disturbance to the birds, which is particularly important when they are breeding. Newspaper makes an ideal floor lining. The entry to the flight cage should give easy access to the interior, enabling you to catch the bird without difficulty, for example. In a large flight, it may be preferable to include two service doors, one at each end. The whole structure can be painted if required, using a light-coloured emulsion, to improve the overall appearance of the unit. And consider mounting it on castors for convenience.

For messy birds, such as mynahs, it may be preferable to use a melamine-coated wood or chipboard that can be wiped off easily when the sides of the unit become soiled with the bird's droppings and food. Breeding cages, to house individual pairs of finches, canaries and budgerigars can be constructed on identical lines, although if you opt for one of the custom-built cage-fronts, the rest of the design will have to be based on these dimensions.

Locating the cage
The location of the cage is important for the bird's well-being. Avoid the kitchen, where fumes can lead to the development of possibly fatal respiratory problems in birds, notably from non-stick cooking utensils that may become overheated. A conservatory attached to the house might seem an ideal location, especially during sunny weather, but the temperature within can rapidly rise to fatal levels and fall off equally dramatically at night. If you use a conservatory to house a bird, ensure that the cage is adequately screened from direct sunlight and that there is good ventilation to minimize a build-up of heat. Also ensure that the cage fastenings are secure and that neighbourhood cats cannot enter the conservatory to harass the bird. Their presence over a period of time can cause disturbance and stress that may prove fatal, even if the bird is not touched directly.

Similar consequences apply to the use of other rooms in the house, including the avoidance of direct sunlight. Ideally, position the cage in the corner of a room. This will give the bird a sense of security, as it will come to appreciate that it cannot be approached on all sides. Position the cage at about eye-level, and, if a stand is to be used, ensure that it is sufficiently secure for the purpose. If the cage is accidentally dislodged, it could prove fatal to the bird.

Prepare the cage, including food and water, before you release the bird into its new quarters. Ensure that the food can be clearly seen. In some budgerigar cages, the seed pots are covered by hoods that obscure the food when viewed from above. In order to attract the bird's attention, therefore, sprinkle a little food on to the floor of the cage, close to the feeder. Leave the bird alone quietly to recover from its journey, and allow it to settle in its new quarters.

TAMING YOUR BIRD

The taming process will depend to some extent on the individual bird. A parrot that is already tame and talking will probably settle more readily than a youngster reared under aviary conditions. Yet ultimately, the young parrot is more likely to develop into a true personal pet. Simply watch your bird in the first instance to ensure that it has settled properly in its new surroundings, and has been eating on its own. Any abnormalities are also likely to be reflected in the droppings. When offering fruit, always try to encourage the bird to take it by hand in the first instance. Hold the piece relatively close to the bird, so that it is within easy reach. It may be safest to wear a glove throughout the early training procedure, just in case the parrot decides to bite; obviously, this is more significant with those species with powerful beaks. Yet the claws are also sharp and you may feel these being dug into your skin on occasions, especially when the bird first starts to perch on your hand.

The key to successfully training a parrot is first to win the bird's confidence. This bond can only be built up over a period of time; do not rush. Obviously, however, a domestically raised parrot will be much more ready to accept human company. It may already be tame, and so should take food from you without hesitation. Encourage the bird to perch on your hand in the first instance, which may be easier with the bird out of its cage. Parrots will often sit contentedly on the top of their cage, and this can make a convenient training area. Never scare the bird by rapid movements. Start by placing your hand flat on the cage, close to the bird's feet, and slowly move it towards the parrot. It may withdraw slightly, but soon sensing that no harm will result, the bird is likely to step on to the glove, especially when offered a titbit, such as a piece of fruit. Do not attempt to move your hand at first, but then gradually raise it slightly, with the bird still remaining perched on the glove. Then offer a piece of fruit with your other hand, and the parrot should take this and eat it while perched.

Some birds respond faster than others. For the best results, ensure that you are alone in the room, so that the parrot will not be distracted by the movements of other people close by. In any event, before you open the cage door, ensure that pets, such as cats and dogs, are excluded from the room and that the windows and doors are closed.

Use net curtains to cover large windows, since, if the bird decides to fly around the room, it may attempt to fly through the glass. Such collisions can prove fatal, and the bird is likely to stun itself, at the very least.

Many owners prefer to clip the wing of a newly acquired bird that will be allowed out into the room so that it is less likely to injure itself by flying wildly around. This can be carried out in various ways. The least drastic way is to carefully cut the primary flight feathers, while leaving the two outermost primaries in place. Carried out properly, this will not hurt the bird, nor will it be a permanent handicap; the feathers will be moulted normally and replaced at the next moult. Do not clip both wings though, because this will serve to handicap the bird totally. Try to arrange some assistance when cutting the feathers. One person should hold the bird, allowing the other to use both hands to open the wing and cut across the primaries with a sharp pair of scissors. Cut away most of the feather, almost down to the top of the quill. Do not cut any lower, however, in case there is a trace of blood still present at the base of the feather. Carried out carefully and quickly, the procedure will cause little distress to the bird, but it may be withdrawn for a short period afterwards. This is quite normal.

In order to prevent a parrot flying around the room, it is possible to attach the bird to a stand using a leg-chain. While this may not be harmful with a tame bird, there is a considerable risk that a parrot not used to being confined by this means will injure itself. It may attempt to fly and end up dangling from the end of the chain. In some cases, the ring that fits around the bird's leg can actually cut into the leg. If the bird is willing to perch on a stand when out of its cage, this is fine, but do not restrict its movement with a chain.

Birds out of the cage

You must be prepared to supervise a bird that is free in a room. The beaks of some species can inflict considerable damage, and there are many dangers that can harm an unsuspecting parrot, for example. Live electrical wires, poisonous plants and paintwork, and the hazard of an uncovered fish tank can prove fatal for parrots. With a large flight cage, however, there will be less need to allow a parrot out into the room for long periods each day. And some birds, such as finches, are not really suitable to be allowed to fly freely around the room, partly because they will often not make any attempt to return to their cage.

Nevertheless, a parrot will not become

Right: A pet bird can become a unique companion for many years. In the first instance, however, try to obtain a young bird. For many people, a cockatiel, as shown here, is an ideal choice. They are widely available, inexpensive to keep and soon become tame. Young birds have a pinkish cere.

very tame unless it is allowed out of its cage on a regular basis. Generally, parrots are only likely to bite when handled, or when a finger is placed through the mesh of the cage. In the latter instance, the bird may be used to receiving food in this way and responding accordingly. Out in the room, unless directly handled, parrots are not aggressive birds, although their character may change somewhat when they are in breeding condition. Once a parrot has accepted you, however, you should be able to gently stroke the plumage around the sides of the head, close to the back of the head. This is the spot usually preened by the other member of a pair. Such behaviour may even be solicited by the bird sitting with its head rather to one side.

If a tame bird attempts to bite, give it a sharp tap on the beak with your finger. While it used to be thought that this could prove counter-productive, even setting back the training process, it is now clear that birds may fence with their bills in a similar manner in a quest for dominance. A distinct hierarchy exists within a flock of parrots, and clearly, in the domestic situation, it is preferable for the owner to assume the dominant role. Some circumstances are potentially more tricky than others; for example, once a bird is hand-tame, it may start to walk up your arm, resting on your shoulder. Here, it will be attracted by your hair, and may start to preen you. This is fine, provided that the bird does not transfer its attention to your ear. Always supervise contact between a parrot and your

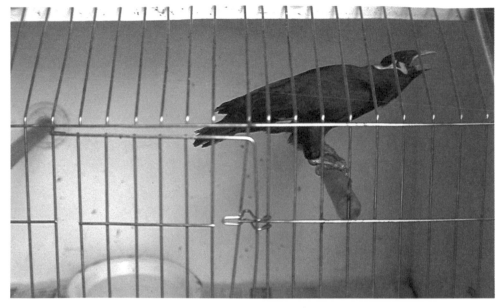

Above: Mynah birds are unsurpassed as mimics and have bold, brash personalities. They make lively, easily tamed pets. Unfortunately, they can also prove extremely messy in the home and really need to be kept in a small flight.

children, to ensure that they are not bitten. And never set a bad example, such as feeding your parrot on a mouth-to-mouth basis. Apart from hygienic considerations, there is always a risk that your lips may be badly bitten inadvertently by the parrot seeking its titbit.

Encouraging birds to talk

It may appear difficult to teach a bird to talk successfully, but in reality, this can be quite straightforward, and training can begin almost as soon as you get the bird home. It is sometimes said that birds find it easier to learn from a child or a woman, but this is not necessarily true. The tone of voice is certainly very important, however. Parrots in particular are sensitive birds and will not respond well to loud or harsh instructions.

Repeat the word that you want the bird to mimic as regularly as possible. For example, when you uncover the cage in the morning, say 'Good morning' to the bird, and then 'Good night' in the evening. Do not confuse the bird by attempting to teach too many phrases all at once; a gradual progression and development of the bird's vocabulary will be much more satisfactory in the long term. It is important to capture the bird's attention during teaching periods, so carry out the process in a quiet room and make the sessions relatively short, lasting for perhaps five minutes or so.

In order to reinforce the patterns of speech you are teaching, it may be worth recording your voice on a cassette tape and playing this to the bird. Pre-recorded records and tapes are available that may assist in encouraging your bird to start talking, but with no-one visible, and an unfamiliar voice audible, such methods may only have limited success. The most effective way is to repeat the words yourself to the bird.

Use a similar strategy to teach a bird a simple tune. Some birds, particularly mynahs, will pick up other sounds from their environment, such as the sound of a door bell. Once a bird has mastered an unwanted phrase or sound, it can be very difficult to persuade it to drop the item from its repertoire. Try to ignore it, or, as with persistent screeching, simply cover the cage for a short time immediately after the bird has transgressed, and this may encourage it to desist in the future.

A number of myths exist about talking birds. The horrendous idea that cutting a parrot's tongue will encourage its powers of mimicry is still prevalent in some parts of

Wing clipping

Waterfowl kept at liberty will need to have their flight feathers on one wing clipped if they were not pinioned shortly after hatching. Clipping a parrot's flight feathers may prevent injury.

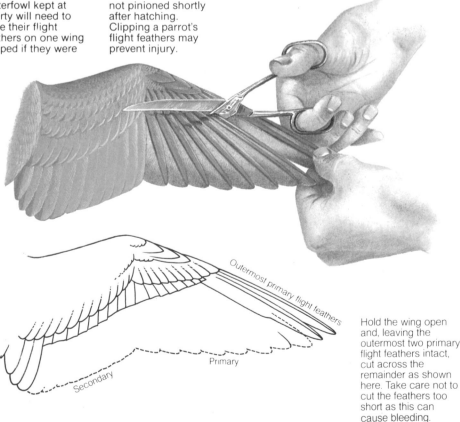

Outermost primary flight feathers

Primary

Secondary

Hold the wing open and, leaving the outermost two primary flight feathers intact, cut across the remainder as shown here. Take care not to cut the feathers too short as this can cause bleeding.

South America in particular. This has no factual basis whatsoever, and is more likely to lead to the bird dying as a result of an acute loss of blood or a subsequent infection. The belief that only cock birds talk well is also untrue. Most owners will not even know the sex of their parrot, since in the majority of larger psittacines, including Grey Parrots and macaws, it is impossible to sex these birds by sight. There is also the idea that a mirror in a cage will prevent a bird from talking successfully, on the grounds that it will communicate naturally with its reflection. Again, there is no real evidence for this view; two birds of the same species can be housed together, and they will continue speaking in a human voice.

Although mirrors do not prevent a bird from talking, they may encourage a cock budgerigar in particular to feed its reflection. Over a period of time, this may develop into a pathological urge, to the extent that the bird actually starts to lose weight. Under these circumstances, it is best to remove the mirror. The regurgitation of food does on occasions signify a more serious medical complaint, however, described as 'sour crop'. The crop under these circumstances becomes full of gas and mucus, causing the bird to vomit. The head feathers becoming stained as a result and the bird looks sick. Recent scientific investigation tends to suggest that a protozoal infection may be responsible for this, so seek immediate veterinary treatment.

Toys

Although budgerigars are quite playful by nature they do not need to have their cages crammed with toys, as you might be persuaded to think by the large selection available. Opt for simple designs in which the bird cannot get caught up or otherwise injure itself. Ladders can prove dangerous; some budgerigars manage to get caught between the rungs if these are widely spaced. Apart from a mirror, therefore, one of the best toys that you can provide for your budgerigar is a ping-pong ball. This is light enough for the bird to push around and yet sufficiently robust to ensure that it cannot be damaged. A further advantage is that it can be kept clean simply by wiping the surface with a damp cloth. Toys for larger parrots need to be correspondingly robust; a block of wood that slides up and down a piece of wire attached in the cage can provide them with considerable enjoyment, and is easy to replace if the wood is destroyed.

Bathing

Some birds are much keener to bathe than others, softbills tend to be among the most ready bathers, entering an open container full of fluid without hesitation. For this reason always provide nectar for such birds in tubular drinkers, and a separate bowl of clean water to enable the bird to bathe if it wishes. Many budgerigars will bathe in a

Spraying a bird
Although some birds, such as mynahs, will bathe in a container of water when kept indoors, others, notably parrots, will need to be sprayed.

A regular spray will help to keep the bird's plumage in good condition. A clean plant sprayer is ideal for this purpose. At first, the bird is likely to be nervous. Therefore, angle the sprayer so that the water droplets fall from above, as this will be less disturbing.

Below: Once used to being sprayed, parrots look forward to a daily shower. Many refuse to bathe in a pot of water

Before starting to spray, place a generous layer of newspaper in the bottom of the cage to absorb excess water.

shower of rain, yet ignore a dish of water provided for this purpose. This has led to the development of a special budgerigar shower, which is activated by the bird entering the bathing chamber. The unit resembles the traditional plastic baths that fix on to the door of a conventional cage.

The importance of bathing is not simply confined to improving the appearance of the bird itself. The water also helps to remove particles of feather debris from the air, which otherwise can give rise to an allergic condition in humans, often resulting in tight-chested breathing. The situation is likely to be worse during a moult, and certain species produce more feather dust than others; cockatoos are notorious in this respect. A similar situation can arise with pigeons. Ionizers are now available for both the home and birdrooms and can prove useful by reducing the level of dust in the atmosphere. (Ionizers cause dust to precipitate out from the air by putting a minute electric charge on the particles.)

Indoors, if a bird refuses to bathe then you will need to give it a regular spray. At first, the bird may be scared of the procedure, but will rapidly grow to accept it as part of the daily routine. Use a fine nozzle sprayer, such as those sold for spraying houseplants, filled with tepid water. Plumage conditioners added to the contents of the sprayer may have a limited effect. The best time to give the bird a light spray is immediately before cleaning out the cage.

The value of ionizers

Ionizers help to purify the air in an enclosed space by removing dust and other airborne particles, including viruses. They are particularly valuable in rooms containing several cages, where levels of feather dust in the air can be high.

Left: This is a typical ionizer suitable for use in a room housing several bird cages. Ideally, fix it high up and in an unobstructed position. It connects to the mains electricity supply and is safe and silent in use.

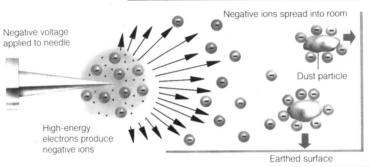

Negative voltage applied to needle

High-energy electrons produce negative ions

Negative ions spread into room

Dust particle

Earthed surface

How ionizers work
High-energy electrons produced at the needle tip collide with molecules in the air and change them into negative ions that shoot out into the room. Dust particles bombarded with these ions become negative and precipitate out on earthed surfaces.

Remove food pots beforehand and point the nozzle towards the bird from outside the cage. Aim the sprayer at a slightly vertical angle so that the water droplets fall from above, rather than spraying directly at the bird. It will probably find this less disturbing, especially at first. Only half a dozen sprays may be required to get an adequate covering of water droplets. Do not saturate the bird, particularly if it has not bathed for a long time, since there is an increased risk of it developing a chill as a direct result.

A regular spray two or three times a week will keep the bird in excellent condition. An added advantage of spraying birds that will be transferred later to an outside flight is that the natural waterproofing in their feathers will not be lost. Rain-bathing species can otherwise become so enthusiastic at the sight of rain that they become absolutely saturated when first housed in an outdoor flight, after being kept indoors.

A typical budgerigar cage with toys and accessories

When selecting toys for budgerigars, choose only those that can be cleaned easily. Elaborate toys soiled with droppings will prove difficult to keep clean. Never clutter the cage unnecessarily with toys.

The selection of toys shown here includes bells, a ladder, mirrors (including an unbreakable stainless steel type), plus some general playthings. The coloured ping pong balls are ideal, being safe and easy to clean.

Male budgerigars kept on their own are likely to attempt to feed their reflections in a mirror. They may act in a similar way towards other toys.

For most parrots, natural perches are greatly appreciated as a means of exercising their beaks. Few manufactured toys are suitable for them.

Some budgerigars will use a bath that attaches to the front of their cage as shown here, although most prefer a spray. For this reason, a shower unit has been devised that turns on when the bird enters the chamber.

Use the sprayer as directed in the text. The simple bath with a mirror base may suit some birds. The curved brush with metal bristles is for cleaning the perches.

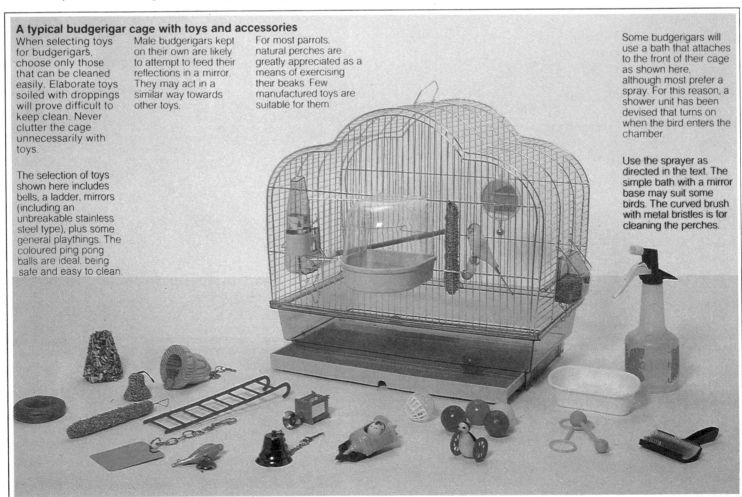

BIRDS IN THE GARDEN

AVIARIES AND FLIGHTS

A garden aviary is ideal for many species, although the dimensions will vary according to the birds concerned. It is possible to construct a similar structure to accommodate waterfowl in the garden and to protect them from potential predators, such as foxes.

Building a basic aviary

A basic aviary consists of an outside flight area connected to a shelter, where the birds are able to roost and feed. A more elaborate set-up entails the construction of a birdroom where birds can be fed indoors and flight cages included. Outside flights are also usually connected to a birdroom.

Using electric heating and lighting during the winter months makes it possible to overwinter all the smaller and more delicate species that otherwise would need to be brought inside for this period. With just a single aviary of mixed finches, however, it is usually more economical to bring them into the home for the winter rather than pay an additional heating bill. All the family can appreciate the birds and no-one has the unenviable task of venturing outside on cold wet winter days. A small flight is easy to make and decorate to your taste.

The techniques used in constructing an indoor or outside flight are basically similar, although in the home you can use unjointed frames simply by nailing or screwing the pieces of wood together. For garden flights, use a more rigorous method of building, entailing proper jointing. Even simple joints will lend overall stability to the finished structure and prevent the wood twisting.

Aviaries need a solid base. Ideally, position the flight on top of brickwork that extends for about 30cm (1ft) below ground level. Apart from ensuring stability, this also serves to exclude rodents and foxes. Bolt the flight to this base. Set the bolts upright in the mortar before it dries and, using corresponding pre-drilled holes, position the structure in place and tighten the nuts firmly. Bolt or screw adjoining panels together.

Small aviary

A wide range of aviary designs can be seen, built around the basic module of a flight unit linked to a shelter. The materials used in their construction will depend on the birds to be housed within.

Wooden battening can be used to cover sharp ends of wire mesh that could otherwise injure the birds once the aviary is assembled. A different technique is required for destructive birds, notably parrots.

This is 19G wire mesh with a mesh size of 2.5×1.25cm (1×½in) Suitable for most finches and softbills, as well as budgerigars.

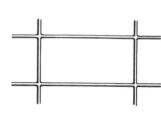

Some protection over the roof area of the flight is recommended. This may extend over the whole area, but will then deny the birds an opportunity to bathe in the rain.

A safety porch will ensure that birds cannot escape from the aviary even if they fly out of the door. It is especially useful with finches, which are very fast on the wing.

Attaching the flight frames to the brickwork base can be achieved using bolts. A damp-proof course of roofing felt will help to prevent premature rotting of the wood in this situation.

A low entrance door facilitates access to the flight for quail and similar birds.

Perches can be set in the floor or hung across the aviary.

Additional protection may be necessary during periods of bad weather. Use a simple framework supporting ultraviolet-resistant plastic sheeting.

One of the more unusual aviary designs is the octagonal structure. Careful siting is required, however, to ensure that the birds have additional protection from the elements, as it is exposed on all sides. The inner core of the structure provides the shelter for the birds, with a covered roof. In exposed localities, the back of the structure will also need to be covered with plastic. Like other aviaries, octagonal designs are available in kit form for home assembly. Be sure to provide a firm foundation for these.

Birdrooms are also produced commercially. They are made in sections like the traditional garden shed. Be sure to anchor them to a solid base, ideally concrete. A course of brickwork and a damp-proof layer will prevent the structure rotting prematurely. Where it is not likely to be destroyed by birds, treat the wood at regular intervals with a recommended preservative.

The majority of finches and softbills can be housed quite adequately using aviary mesh made from 19 gauge (19G) wire with a mesh size of 2.5cm × 1.25cm (1 × ½in), which will keep mice and other rodents out of the aviaries. Finches and most softbills will not damage the woodwork but for parrot-like birds, excluding the smallest species such as the hanging parrots and parrotlets, you will need to take extra precautions to protect the aviary against their beaks. Some aviary manufacturers offer a standard design flight, plus a reinforced version suitable for parrots, at extra cost. If you are building the flight yourself, choose heavier 16G mesh, while for the most destructive species, 12G may be a better choice. Ensure that the whole of the wooden surface is covered with

Ready built aviaries and flights

There is no need to worry about building an aviary or indoor flight, since a number of specialist firms manufacture such structures. Some designs are highly flexible and can be added to as required at a later date. Individual components, such as doors and panels, are produced in standard sizes, enabling you to build up an aviary of a specific size. More ornate structures, such as octagonal designs, are also available. These shapes, although attractive, are rather exposed and some sides will need covering to give the birds protection, particularly against the wind. Mount these aviaries on a solid base as previously described.

Medium-sized aviary

The size and shape of the aviary will depend on the site available. Even in a limited area, it is still possible to build an outside flight, as shown here. An aviary of this type would be useful for lovebirds or other small parrots.

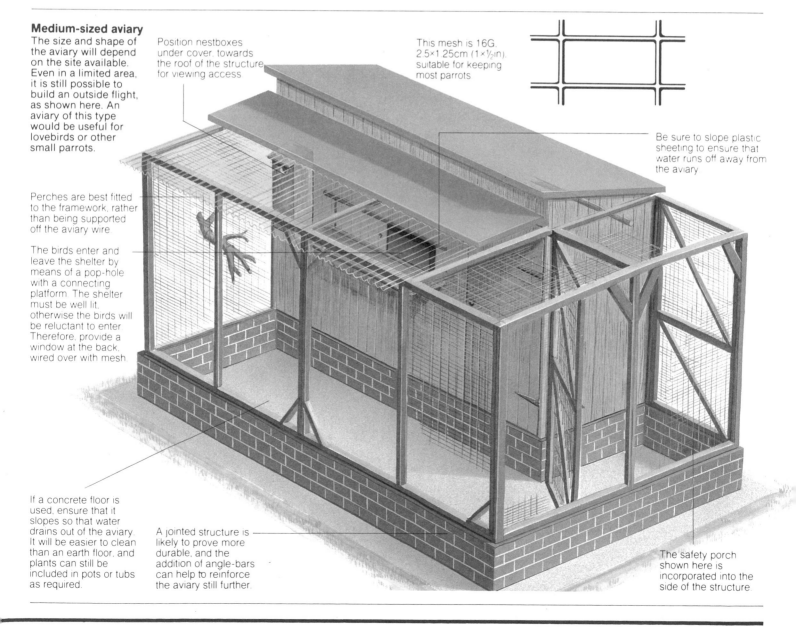

Position nestboxes under cover, towards the roof of the structure, for viewing access

This mesh is 16G, 2.5×1.25cm (1×½in), suitable for keeping most parrots

Be sure to slope plastic sheeting to ensure that water runs off away from the aviary

Perches are best fitted to the framework, rather than being supported off the aviary wire.

The birds enter and leave the shelter by means of a pop-hole with a connecting platform. The shelter must be well lit, otherwise the birds will be reluctant to enter. Therefore, provide a window at the back, wired over with mesh.

If a concrete floor is used, ensure that it slopes so that water drains out of the aviary. It will be easier to clean than an earth floor, and plants can still be included in pots or tubs as required.

A jointed structure is likely to prove more durable, and the addition of angle-bars can help to reinforce the aviary still further.

The safety porch shown here is incorporated into the side of the structure.

Large aviary

The same basic construction guidelines apply to all aviaries, irrespective of their size. Large aviaries can be arranged in blocks, with a central service corridor behind. Adjoining faces where the birds could come into contact with each other must be double-wired, however, to prevent fighting.

It is possible to use larger mesh on parrot aviaries. Although this will reduce the cost somewhat, it is almost certain that rodents will be able to enter the aviary and disturb the birds. They may also introduce disease.

An adequate supply of wooden perches will serve to divert the birds' attention from the aviary structure. They will need to be replaced as they are whittled away

Reinforce vulnerable areas in the aviary with thin metal sheeting, as shown here around the entrance hole.

Over a period of time, both the brickwork and floor of the flight may become encrusted with algal growth. This can be scrubbed off as necessary.

Choose a level site for the aviary to facilitate the building process. Sound foundations are important, especially in areas of high winds. Special standards may be required in parts of the world where hurricanes occur.

A bed of tightly compacted hardcore, surrounded by concrete provides a sound base.

Exterior woodwork should be treated with a non-toxic wood preservative.

As an alternative to a water-butt, a soakaway can be included. Under these circumstances, try to ensure that drainage of water from the floor of the flight can be connected into this system as well.

mesh, and that there are no cut edges exposed to the birds. To do this simply run the mesh on to the adjoining faces of each panel. When the flight is erected, all edges will be out of the birds' reach.

With more nervous birds, such as quails, include a false roof of fine plastic mesh. Fixed taut, this will prevent the birds injuring their heads, and possibly killing themselves, if they fly up vertically, as they might do when frightened. Attach a separate panel below the mesh of the aviary roof for this purpose. A proper rigid outer layer is required, however, to prevent potential predators gaining access to the flight by simply tearing the netting. During the winter, any

accumulation of snow is also likely to split thin netting.

You can cover the entire roof of a flight with plastic sheeting, although this will mean that the birds cannot bathe in a shower of rain, so it is best to leave at least 90cm (3ft) open to the elements. Slope the sheeting to facilitate run-off of water, and, with a concrete base, ensure that this is adequately built up so that water drains away rapidly, rather than settling in puddles on the floor of the flight. Although it may seem attractive to include a pond in an aviary housing a mixed collection of birds, this can prove rather dangerous. Small birds can drown very easily, especially if it is dif-

Above: Plan the site of the aviary to allow for easy expansion at a later stage. Building work is best carried out after the breeding period to avoid disturbing the birds more than necessary. They may have to be moved to temporary quarters during the building work.

The roof of the shelter should slope away from the flight. Guttering can be used to collect the run-off, and in turn can be linked to a water butt. Ideally, use several layers of heavy duty roofing felt

Left: A well-planted aviary offers plenty of cover for the birds during the breeding period and will also attract livefood

Below: Some birds may tend to monopolize a single container, so ensure there is a choice available in a communal aviary

There are various ways of protecting the woodwork of the flight frames from the birds' beaks. Here, the mesh is continued over the full face of the frame and tacked in place on the opposing faces, so that when the frames are assembled, all the woodwork is covered.

Above: The aviary shown at left after extension. Increasing the flight area has enabled more birds to be kept without overcrowding, allowing them to exercise to maintain their normal weight and condition. The roosting facilities were also enlarged. Using pre-fabricated panels saves time.

ficult for them to get out of the water. Newly-fledged youngsters are most at risk from drowning. As a general rule, therefore, only include ponds in duck enclosures. See pages 50–51 for advice on keeping waterfowl.

Planted aviaries

A well-planted aviary can look particularly attractive during the summer months. Remember though that this will be harder to clean than a flight with a concrete floor. The main perches, running from one side of the aviary to the other, can be positioned either above paving stones or over an area of concrete. This will not detract significantly from the overall appearance of the flight, but should ensure that the majority of the droppings can be cleaned up easily. The choice of plants will depend on the climate and on the species of birds to be kept in the flight. Certain finches prove more destructive to growing plants than others, with bullfinches, for example, being capable of inflicting considerable damage. Aim to provide security in the first instance; dense shrubs or conifers provide seclusion, and this should encourage birds to build nests. Then consider plants that will be of value in providing livefood; those, such as nasturtiums (*Tropaeolum majus*), that attract aphids and grow readily in poor soil are ideal.

Bear in mind the growth potential of the plants. Over a period of time, many climbing plants will damage the aviary mesh, unless their growth is curtailed by regular pruning. You may prefer to fix posts and trellis work within the flight and train climbing plants accordingly, rather than using the aviary mesh as a support. The trellis will, in any event, provide additional perching areas for small birds. Russian Vine (*Polygonum baldschuanicum*), Virginia Creeper (*Parthenocissus* sp.), Clematis and even Pyracantha, which will produce berries for the birds in the autumn, can all be considered for inclusion in the flight.

Use grass as the basic floor covering. If you grow this from seed, ensure that it has not been treated with any toxic dressing, in case the birds consume any spilt seed that fails to germinate. Provide good drainage to prevent the grass being spoiled by an invasion of moss. Incorporate a suitable path, lined with gravel, as a means of walking through the flight; in a smaller aviary, set paving slabs into the turf. Ornamental grasses may also be useful in the flight, especially for providing cover for birds that prefer to nest on or close to the ground. In a tall or open enclosure, Pampas Grass (*Cortaderia* sp.) is ideal for the purpose, and also looks attractive when in flower. Perennials of this type are preferable to annual grasses, although annuals will be appreciated by seedeaters as an additional source of food after the flowering period. Indeed, a handful of canary seed can be planted in the flight, and should germinate quite rapidly under favourable conditions.

Flowering plants of various types can also be included, but take care to avoid any that are known to be poisonous, such as lupins (*Lupinus* sp.). Since some birds may damage flowers, select plants that bloom freely and need little attention over a long period of time, such as dahlias. Before planting the aviary, draw up a plan that shows the dimensions, means of access and the perches. This in turn will show how much space is available for planting and help you to work out the most decorative way of arranging the plants. Leave the vegetation undisturbed as far as possible during the summer months, except for making arrangements for watering the covered part of the flight. Try to encourage the birds to nest here, so that nestlings will not be soaked, possibly with fatal consequences, during wet weather, as can happen in the exposed section. A light spray from a hose, avoiding known nesting sites, should be sufficient to water the plants, and avoids the need to enter the aviary at sensitive times.

HENHOUSES AND DOVECOTES

V arious commercially made pens and sheds are available to accommodate fowl. These vary in size depending on the number of birds to be kept, ranging from basic ark designs, which are essentially triangular, to more elaborate fold units that are moved around a grassy area at regular intervals. A typical size of a fold unit would be 3 × 1.2m (10 × 4ft), with the fold incorporating suitable nestboxes and a roosting area. While you can keep birds at liberty in the garden, it will undoubtedly be safer to keep them penned up, especially at night. It is important to wire the undersurface of a run, so that foxes cannot simply tunnel beneath or even tilt the structure to gain access to the birds. In addition, runs and pens should be portable so that the poultry can have access to fresh grass, and existing areas of lawn are not permanently damaged by the presence of the structure, leading to bare patches developing beneath.

For breeds with plumage extending down to their legs, it may be preferable to house them permanently in a suitable shed, opting for a deep-litter system of management. The dimensions of the structure will be influenced by the breed of poultry concerned. As a guide, a shed with floor dimensions 90cm (3ft) square will suit for four smaller bantams. The height of the structure is less critical, although, if you opt for a larger area,

it will be useful to have sufficient headroom to enable you to enter and service the interior easily.

As a general rule, do not buy secondhand poultry houses or aviaries. Although sectional designs can be dismantled quite easily, they can be a source of disease and parasites, such as Red Mite. If you do opt for an older building, however, disinfect it thoroughly before placing new birds inside

Above: Accommodation suitable for bantams, with nestbox and run. With birds kept in a state of semi-liberty, ensuring their protection against potential predators assumes greater importance. In many urban areas, foxes are well established.

it. The exterior of the structure will need to be thoroughly treated with a nontoxic wood preservative, in any event, and it may be several weeks before this has dried thoroughly. Check also for signs of any rotting

Accommodation for poultry
Accommodate poultry in a special house where the birds can roost and lay their eggs, or alternatively convert a garden shed for this purpose, with nestboxes inside.

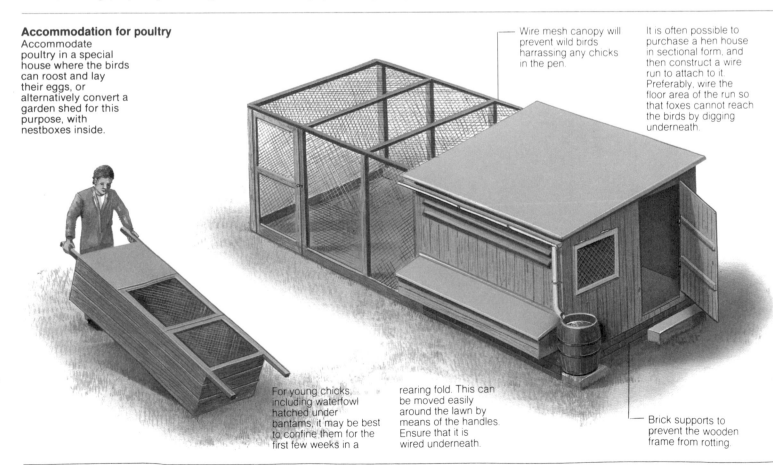

Wire mesh canopy will prevent wild birds harrassing any chicks in the pen.

It is often possible to purchase a hen house in sectional form, and then construct a wire run to attach to it. Preferably, wire the floor area of the run so that foxes cannot reach the birds by digging underneath.

For young chicks, including waterfowl hatched under bantams, it may be best to confine them for the first few weeks in a rearing fold. This can be moved easily around the lawn by means of the handles. Ensure that it is wired underneath.

Brick supports to prevent the wooden frame from rotting.

wood, especially around the base of the house if it has been standing on grass. Preferably, mount sheds (like aviaries) on a course of bricks or blocks to increase their lifespan. This will not be possible with arks, however, since the birds are to have access to the grass.

Treat nestboxes for poultry with a safe insecticidal powder to minimize the risk of a serious outbreak of Red Mite, and then line them with straw. A number of different designs are available and they are usually positioned in the darkest area of the shed. To give the birds easy access to the nestboxes, fix perches about 60cm (2ft) above the ground. Since most of the droppings will be beneath the perches, locate them so that there is plenty of access for cleaning purposes. Square-section perches are the norm for poultry houses, most breeds requiring perches approximately 5cm (2in) square. Be sure to smooth the edges of the perches and check that there are no splinters which could penetrate the birds' feet and lead to infection developing. Rubbing the timber with glasspaper will be sufficient.

Dovecotes

While ornamental pigeons can be kept in flights or allowed to fly free, the dovecote remains a popular means of housing such birds. Dovecotes can range from simple wooden boxes to highly decorative designs. To build one, base the design on a square floor area measuring 90cm (3ft) on a side. This will allow sufficient space for an open yet protected area at the front, serving as a landing platform to give access to the

Above: Dovecotes can be made from a variety of materials, such as this beer cask. Food can be provided within, where it will keep clean and dry. A white dovecote has high 'visibility'.

interior. Use either stout plywood or, preferably, tongue-and-grooved timber for the sides and roof to create a snug interior. Ideally, partition the structure into two units, which should accommodate two pairs of birds satisfactorily, and make suitable

entrance holes at the front. Fit an apex roof and cover it with plain roofing felt. Paint the roof and rest of the structure white; this makes the dovecote clearly visible to the birds, enabling them to find their way back with greater ease.

A variety of permutations are possible on such a basic design. Consider making tiered structures, for example, but always ensure that each unit is easily accessible, incorporating service doors where necessary to facilitate cleaning. A door at the front can be useful to close the birds in when necessary; if they are shut in at night, they are easy to catch in the morning.

Many aviary manufacturers include dovecotes in their range. Thus, you should be able to buy everything from a large-scale loft to house a number of birds to a simple dovecote for one or two pairs. Dovecotes are also made in various ornate designs, but be sure to select a type that enables the interior to be cleaned easily.

As with aviaries, it is vital that dovecotes are mounted securely. If you position a dovecote on a wooden stake, be sure to set the stake some distance into the ground. Take care to ensure that the wood is not in direct contact with the soil, since over a period of time it will rot away. During windy weather, an unstable dovecote may be blown over, with fatal consequences. Stake supports, produced for use with fencing poles, are ideal for fixing dovecotes into the ground.

Locate the dovecote in a relatively open position where there will be no risk of cats jumping on to the structure and seizing one of the birds. Unfortunately, birds such as young Fan-tailed Pigeons have relatively trusting natures and are especially vulnerable in this respect when kept in a dovecote.

Deep litter system
An internal view of a deep litter hen house. Bacterial action in the litter breaks down waste products.

The deep litter system is essentially self sustaining, needing a substantial cleaning about every six months.

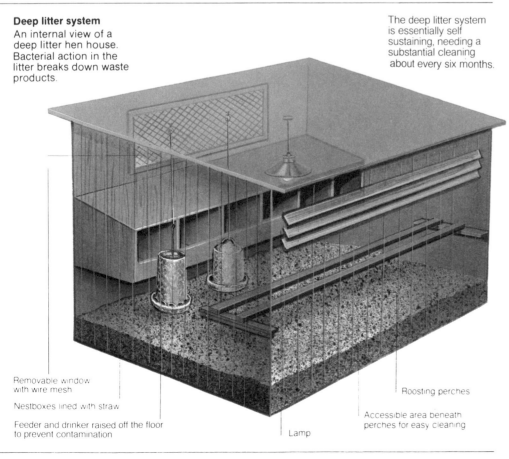

Removable window with wire mesh

Nestboxes lined with straw

Feeder and drinker raised off the floor to prevent contamination

Lamp

Roosting perches

Accessible area beneath perches for easy cleaning

ENCLOSURES FOR WATERFOWL

Even if you allow your birds to roam at liberty around the garden, you will still need effective fencing to stop them escaping on to neighbouring land. It is essential that the birds are wing-clipped, even if not actually pinioned, so they will not fly off. Remember that clipping needs to be carried out at each moult, otherwise the birds are likely to fly away if they are not confined within an aviary-type structure.

The ideal height for any barrier depends on whether there are foxes in the area, which could attack the birds. It is surprising how far these animals have penetrated success-fully into urban areas, often escaping detection because of their nocturnal habits. A fence to exclude foxes will need to be at least 2.1m (7ft) in height, and must be bent horizontally at the top for about 30cm (12in) so that they cannot climb over into the enclosure. At the base, set the wire into the ground to a depth of about 45cm (18in) so that there is no risk of foxes tunnelling in from beneath the fence. Although wooden stakes can be used to support the fence, metal poles will prove more durable, with the mesh being attached by twisting strands of wire around the poles to hold it in place. A thin 19G mesh is quite satisfac-tory, so such fencing need not be an ex-cessively expensive item. It can appear unattractive, however, unless adequately screened.

Although broad-mesh wire is often recommended, since it is relatively cheap, do not opt for anything larger than 2.5cm (1in) square. This is because rats and similarly aggressive creatures, such as stoats, may otherwise be able to gain easy access to the enclosure via the mesh. It will be virtually impossible to contain such creatures if they are running in and out of the pen, and serious problems may result, particularly during the breeding season, with a loss of eggs and chicks. Perhaps surprisingly, some dogs will also persecute waterfowl if allowed to do so; make sure that they are not allowed access to the birds' enclosure. Some of the more predatory birds, such as crows, may also persecute sitting ducks during the breeding season. For these reasons, it may be best to house the smaller species of water-fowl in an enclosed aviary.

Constructing a pond
If you are fortunate enough to have a stream on your land, you should be able to con-struct a series of individual pens for water-fowl that extend across the water. Careful planting of shrubs and fast-growing conifers will help to hide the external perimeter fencing in any event, but do not position these so close to the fence that cats or foxes can simply climb over by this route.

In the absence of a stream or natural pond, you will need to construct an artificial pond. Yet now there is no need to spend hours shovelling concrete for this purpose; simply obtain a pond liner, available from many garden centres and aquarist shops. The most satisfactory type, with an almost indefinite lifespan, is made of butyl rubber and should be 0.75mm (0.03in) in thickness. There are other options available, such as PVC pond liners, but these tend to deteriorate much more rapidly.

Once you have decided upon the size of the pond, it is straightforward to work out the area of liner required for the job. Simply take the maximum length and width, and add double the depth of water at the deepest point to both these dimensions. Because of the flexible nature of butyl rubber, it will stretch naturally as it fills with the weight of water, and no extra allowance is needed for

perimeter measurements. In all cases, the depth need not be greater than 90cm (3ft). The actual area of water will vary according to the species concerned, with swans needing a considerable area of water. If pos-sible, plan to construct a reasonably large pond, simply because, in most instances, the full appeal of waterfowl cannot be appre-ciated over a small area. For this reason, the vast majority of prefabricated pools on the market are unsuitable for waterfowl. There is also the problem of keeping the water relatively clean; clearly, a small pond will become soiled more quickly than a larger volume of water. Before excavating the hollow, mark out the perimeter of the pond on the ground using stakes. To take much of the effort out of the construction phase, consider hiring a small excavator from a local plant hire company. Be sure to decide in advance what to do with the excavated

Building a pond
A duck pond can form an interesting garden feature. Many species of waterfowl will be content with a fairly modest area of water in the garden.

Predators are always a threat to waterfowl. Use fox-proof fencing to protect stock. Solid foundations will prevent foxes and other vermin tunnelling underneath.

soil. Only the surface soil will be directly valuable for horticultural purposes; the sub-soil could be used to form the basis of a rock garden or perhaps a waterfall.

Once the hollow has been dug out, check the surface where the liner will be fitted and remove any protruding stones or other sharp objects that might puncture the liner. Ideally, line the hollow with a layer of sand to smooth out any irregularities in the contouring and provide an even surface for the liner. Next, fit the liner roughly in position, with the edges evenly spread around the perimeter of the site and anchored securely with paving slabs. As you fill the pond by means of a hose, the increasing weight of water forces the liner firmly into place on the bed of sand. Keep a close watch on the liner, however, and manipulate the rubber sheeting as necessary to prevent creasing, while keeping the weights in place to stretch it. Once the pond is full, set paving slabs around the perimeter to conceal the excess liner beneath. An edging of this type will also help to prevent the pond becoming excessively muddy, as the waterfowl move into and out of the water.

Consider fitting a filter to remove organic matter from the water and generally enhance the appearance of the pond. Effective pond filter units are widely available, operating off a suitable electrical supply. Safety is obviously of paramount importance under these conditions, and if in doubt about fixing an external supply, contact a professional electrician. Alternatively, use a pond pump to build a basic external filter, with the water being passed over gravel after being withdrawn from the pond. Once the pond is established, top up the water level when necessary and provide a soak-away in case the pond overflows.

Using plants

While it might seem idyllic to include plants in a pond with waterfowl, this is very rarely successful, unless the area is very large. Apart from being eaten in some cases, plants will not be able to withstand the wash created by the birds in a small area. Water lilies, for example, will not thrive under such conditions, preferring static water.

By way of contrast, however, the enclosure itself should definitely contain plants.

These will offer the birds a sanctuary from the weather and may encourage successful breeding. In a fairly large area, as distinct from the confines of an aviary, you will be able to feature shrubs such as Buddleia, as well as Pampas Grass and small stands of bamboo. Arrange the other plants to provide maximum cover for the bamboo, because it can be slow to grow. Typical plants associated with water, such as weeping willows and irises, can be included near the pond, but try to ensure that the invasive roots of weeping willows do not come into contact with the pool liner from beneath.

Give over a substantial part of the area to grass, but avoid overcrowding the enclosure with birds to prevent the grass rapidly being replaced by unattractive areas of mud. If necessary, cut the grass during the summer, but preferably by hand in a small area so as not to disturb sitting birds. Certain waterfowl, notably Widgeon of various species, as well as geese, will graze quite effectively so that cutting may then be unnecessary. Another option is to include some tame rabbits or guinea pigs, provided that they are penned away from the pond.

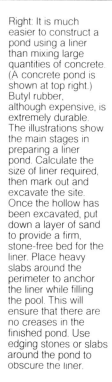

Provide a simple small shed for roosting, suitable for the species. In any event, the birds' food can be kept dry if placed within the entrance to the shelter.

Include some shrubs in the surrounding enclosure. The lawn area will be kept largely in trim by the birds themselves. Most plants in a duck pond will be destroyed by the birds. Duckweed on the surface grows rapidly and will be eaten greedily by waterfowl. Rushes in containers may survive, and be used as a breeding site.

Right: It is much easier to construct a pond using a liner than mixing large quantities of concrete. (A concrete pond is shown at top right.) Butyl rubber, although expensive, is extremely durable. The illustrations show the main stages in preparing a liner pond. Calculate the size of liner required, then mark out and excavate the site. Once the hollow has been excavated, put down a layer of sand to provide a firm, stone-free bed for the liner. Place heavy slabs around the perimeter to anchor the liner while filling the pool. This will ensure that there are no creases in the finished pond. Use edging stones or slabs around the pond to obscure the liner.

Below: Encourage waterfowl to leave and enter the water at one spot by providing a gentle incline. Arrange for a bed of shingle to extend on to the bank of the pond, as shown.

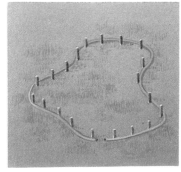

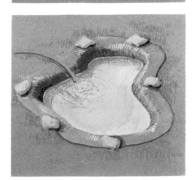

PART 2

SPECIES SECTION

This part of the book features a wide selection of the most popular and widely kept species of birds. As a general rule, closely related species are listed together in natural sequence. Significant groups are prefaced with a brief introduction; in other cases, representative examples are simply included.

Throughout the section, emphasis has been placed on those birds that are relatively undemanding in their requirements and that can be housed together in a mixed collection, although this does not apply in every case. Indeed, the compatibility of individual birds does vary. This is especially the case at breeding time, when displays of aggression are likely to become more obvious. Keeping an eye on the birds during these periods should help to prevent serious problems developing.

Think carefully about the accommodation required for the birds featured in this section. While the cost of the bird may not seem excessive, the expense of providing suitable housing can prove considerable. The more destructive birds, such as parrots, are correspondingly more expensive to accommodate. Also bear in mind that the far-carrying calls of certain birds render them unsuitable for an outdoor aviary in urban areas.

A colourful collection of lively finches, including Zebra Finch, Orange-cheeked Waxbill, Blue-headed Waxbill, Red-headed Parrot-finch and Bengalese Finch.

FINCHES

The birds of this particular group are categorized by their dependence on seed as a major item in their diet. Thus, they are sometimes described as 'hardbills', possessing beaks able to crack seeds, dehusking them before swallowing the inner kernel. The power of their beaks is variable, however, and many of the smaller birds can only cope with certain millets, being unable to break the casing on sunflower seeds or other similar ingredients present in some 'aviary' seed mixtures.

The appeal of finches as pet birds stems from their lively, active nature and colourful appearance. These birds do not become tame or learn to talk like parrots and certain softbills. Many species will nest, however, either indoors or in garden aviaries, and can be accommodated together successfully in mixed groups. A number have been effectively domesticated, and are now bred in a range of colour forms. The majority do not sing, although certain breeds of the Domestic Canary, bred from wild finches found on some islands off the western coast of Africa, have been evolved specifically as songsters.

While various finches are bred exclusively in captivity, others are imported in large numbers, particularly from parts of Africa and Asia. In the wild, huge flocks of these birds can descend on agricultural areas, causing enormous damage locally. Controlled trapping provides some compensation. Senegal, in West Africa, is one country that exports finches under government control. The quotas established for this trade take account of fluctuations in the natural populations that may arise in the face of drought, for example. Although criticized in some quarters, trade prevents mass destruction of birds – often carried out by means of napalm bombs dropped on to roosting sites and the use of flame-throwers and poison – thus conserving the environment generally. The mortality of these small birds in the wild is very high; studies involving a species of African Fire-finch (*Lagonosticta* sp.) have revealed that there is an annual turnover in the population of approximately 80 percent.

Finches rank among the least expensive and most freely available birds, being often seen in pet stores alongside budgerigars. Yet they are extremely active by nature and need to have adequate flying space, ideally being kept, for example, in a 'double-breeding' cage with the central partition removed. Although not as aesthetically appealing as some of the ornate cages available, designs of this type provide much more satisfactory accommodation. It is quite possible to build a similar box-type cage using melamine-faced chipboard and fitting on the appropriate foreign finch or canary cage front. This will create a more attractive result than using a breeding cage made of plywood or hardboard. It will also be much easier to keep such a cage clean by wiping the melamine at regular intervals with a damp cloth. Remember to allow for a partition to be fitted in the cage, should one pair of birds start to breed.

Standard equipment for keeping finches includes a tubular water container, a pot for grit and a seed hopper of some kind. This can be simply a jam jar containing a mixture of canary and millet seeds inverted on a special plastic base, or an earthenware pot on the floor of the cage, positioned away from perches so the contents cannot be soiled. Also include a cuttlefish holder.

This section first looks at a selection of African finches, plus some interesting species that extend from Europe into northern Asia, and then concentrates on the commonly kept finches that originate in the varied environments of Australasia.

Right: **Orange-cheeked Waxbill**
This is one of many African finches that, once acclimatized, will flourish and breed in captivity.

AFRICAN FINCHES

The best-known members of this group are frequently described as waxbills, because of their dull reddish beaks, said to resemble sealing wax in appearance. Imported birds require particular care. Keep them warm, especially when first obtained, and subsequently during the winter months. The cocks of other species, notably weavers and whydahs, develop nuptial plumage at the onset of the breeding season. They need considerable amounts of livefood if the chicks are to be reared successfully and, partly for this reason, breeding success is more likely in a planted aviary, where the birds will be able to forage for insects themselves. The following is a representative selection of the species often available.

Cordon Bleu
Uraeginthus angolensis

- **Distribution:** Across a wide band of southern Africa
- **Size:** 12.5 cm (5 in)
- **Diet:** Small seeds, with a relatively high level of insects
- **Sexing:** Hens are usually paler and duller, depending on the race concerned
- **Compatibility:** Can be difficult at breeding time
- **Pet appeal:** Colour and overall beauty

The Cordon Bleu is a typical representative of the group sometimes described collectively as the Blue Waxbills. These attractive finches usually feed on the ground, seeking out small grass and weed seeds, although they will also take winged insects in flight. Their diet must include regular supplies of invertebrates, such as moulting mealworms, spiders and small crickets. Livefood of this type will become increasingly important during the breeding period, providing the essential animal protein to ensure that the chicks develop well.

Indeed, in the absence of livefood, it is highly unlikely that the parents will rear their offspring satisfactorily.

Once established in their surroundings, Cordon Bleus may live for a decade or more, although they can prove difficult to establish in the first instance. While being allowed into an outside aviary in temperate climates during the summer months, Cordon Bleus should not be regarded as being able to survive without artificial heat and light in the cold winter months. It is nevertheless cheaper, and preferable, to bring them indoors during this period.

Related species, such as the Red-cheeked Cordon Bleu (*U. bengalus*) and the Blue-headed Waxbill (*U. cyanocephala*) are similar in their requirements. The latter is often regarded as being more prolific under aviary conditions, but breeding results with all species are not uncommon, providing care is taken with their diet.

Below: **Red-cheeked Cordon Bleu**
A pair, with the male showing the characteristic bright red cheek patches. Protect them from harsh winter weather in temperate areas.

Purple Grenadier
Uraeginthus ianthinogaster

- **Distribution:** East Africa, from Somalia to Uganda
- **Size:** 12.5 cm (5 in)
- **Diet:** Small seeds, small livefood and softfood
- **Sexing:** Hens tend to be whiter around the eyes, with speckling on their breasts
- **Compatibility:** Aggressive
- **Pet appeal:** Stunning appearance and lively nature, but not really for the novice

Ranking among the most striking of the African finches, the Purple Grenadier is also equally costly, and only irregularly available. It is closely related to the Violet-eared Waxbills (*U. granatina*), and acclimatization for both species can prove a tricky period. These waxbills are highly insectivorous throughout the year, and do not take kindly to damp, cold conditions. They need to be housed alone in individual pairs, since they will fight between themselves and with related species such as the Cordon Bleus. These birds are really for the specialist, in view of their

Above: **Purple Grenadier**
A male of this handsome species. This is an excellent subject for the enthusiast but not suitable for beginners to birdkeeping. Supply insects and other livefood.

more demanding requirements.

Like other *Uraeginthus* species, the cock bird often displays by holding a piece of grass in his beak and bowing up and down in front of the female. If she reciprocates then mating takes place. Their nests are constructed in a suitable bush, with the interior being lined with feathers by the male. Having built its nest in the wild, this waxbill may play unwitting host to the eggs and then the chicks of Fischer's Whydah (see page 68-69). In common with other waxbills, the clutch may consist of up to five eggs, which take just under two weeks to hatch. Both sexes are involved in incubating the eggs, with the cock sitting in the daytime. The chicks fledge when about three weeks old, and possess the characteristic blue swellings either side of their beaks for slightly longer. These stimulate the parent birds to feed their offspring.

Golden-breasted Waxbill

Amandava subflava

- **Distribution:** Ranges over most of Africa, southwards from the Sahara Desert
- **Size:** 9 cm (3.5 in)
- **Diet:** Small seeds, small livefood and softfood
- **Sexing:** Hens can be recognized by the absence of the red stripes above the eyes, and are duller in overall coloration than cock birds
- **Compatibility:** Quite social
- **Pet appeal:** Lively disposition and attractive coloration

This is one of the smallest waxbills, occurring in the more arid areas throughout its extensive range. There is a southern subspecies, which is larger and sometimes described under the alternative name of Clarke's Waxbill. Certain individuals may be darker than others, which is a reflection of the relative level of the dark pigment melanin in their plumage; it does not appear to be an inherited characteristic.

As with many of the African finches, Golden-breasted Waxbills cannot be considered hardy in temperature climes; if they are housed outside in the summer, they should be brought back indoors before the onset of frosts. In view of their diminutive size, ensure that the mesh used in accommodating them is no bigger than 1.25 cm (0.5 in) square; otherwise they may escape, with fatal consequences.

These waxbills are kept more for their colour than their song, which, coupled with their lively social natures, makes them most attractive. It is unlikely that they will breed in a cage, although it is a possibility if they are given a finch nesting basket, suitable material and adequate seclusion. Golden-breasted Waxbills sometimes occupy the disused nests of other birds in the wild, and this behaviour may also be apparent under aviary conditions. They tend not to be aggressive, and may therefore be housed in the company of related species and small doves if desired.

Below: **Golden-breasted Waxbill**
A male perching on the nest, with the female just visible inside.

Orange-cheeked Waxbill

Estrilda melpoda

- **Distribution:** West Africa
- **Size:** 10 cm (4 in)
- **Diet:** Small seeds, livefood and softfood
- **Sexing:** In some instances, orange areas may be reduced in size in hens, but this is not entirely reliable as a guide in every case
- **Compatibility:** Can be difficult, particularly when breeding
- **Pet appeal:** Attractive, but tends to prove shy

These unmistakable waxbills, with their characteristic cheek patches, are often available but, unfortunately, they tend to prove nervous, particularly in a cage where no cover is available. This behaviour relates to their natural environment, since they occur in areas of tall grass that affords seclusion.

In the wild, bushes are favoured for nesting purposes, and the resulting structure may be located

Above: **Orange-cheeked Waxbill**
Distinctive in coloration, these African waxbills will feel more at home in a planted aviary that offers suitable cover to reduce their natural nervousness. Provide a good varied diet and avoid undue disturbance when they are breeding.

very close to the ground. In a planted aviary, Orange-cheeks will often start nesting enthusiastically, but show a tendency to abandon their attempts, even with chicks in the nest. Always try to provide adequate seclusion, therefore, and then leave the birds alone as much as possible at breeding time. It has proved feasible, with care, to rear these waxbills successfully in cages. For those with only limited space available, it might be possible to breed this species successfully indoors. When breeding, the adults can turn decidedly aggressive, even towards larger occupants or a community flight, and pairs of Orange-cheeked Waxbills should never be overcrowded for this reason.

Black-cheeked Waxbill

Estrilda charmosyna

- **Distribution:** Arid regions in Somalia to Kenya and Uganda
- **Size:** 12.5 cm (5 in)
- **Diet:** Small seeds, such as panicum millet, suitable livefood and greenfood
- **Sexing:** The abdomen is greyer in the hen than in the cock bird
- **Compatibility:** Generally safe to house in the company of related species
- **Pet appeal:** Lively and social

There is often some confusion over the common name of this species, which it shares with the closely related waxbill also described as the Black-faced Waxbill (*Estrilda erythronotos*). In fact, they are similar in appearance, but the East African species listed here tends to be pinker in overall coloration, and this has given rise to another alternative description of Pink-bellied Black-cheeked Waxbill. The young of these species are harder to distinguish,

however, although the offspring of the Pink-bellied may be paler overall.

Outside the breeding season, these birds congregate in flocks, but pairs nest on their own. Their aviary needs to be well planted and with adequate cover available. Unlike some species, the Pink-bellied Black-cheeked Waxbill normally builds at least four metres (13 ft) from the ground, constructing a fairly elaborate nest. This may be the reason why they are generally loathe to breed in cages, although aviary successes are quite common. A clutch normally consists of between four and six eggs, with an incubation period of twelve days.

You will need to supply plenty of livefood if the chicks are to be reared successfully, and other items, such as an insectivorous mixture, should also be available, in the hope that the birds will sample such foods. Greenfly are said to be favoured by breeding pairs, as their soft bodies present no problems for newly hatched chicks. Breeding failures may often be traced to an

inadequate supply of livefood during the crucial early stages.

It seems that these waxbills will naturally take a significant proportion of insects as part of their normal diet. In addition, they have been seen feeding on the flowers of fruiting trees, presumably taking nectar as well as pollen. The relevance of such items in their daily food intake is unclear, but both species of Black-cheeked Waxbills have gained a reputation for being relatively difficult to establish in captivity. Apart from a regular supply of livefood, therefore, also offer a nectar solution on a daily basis as suggested for lories and lorikeets (see page 130 for further details). Also, sprinkle pollen granules in among their seed or on softfood. See also pages 18-25 for a wider coverage of foods and feeding.

Right: **Black-cheeked Waxbill**
Keep these active birds in a spacious planted aviary with a warm, dry shelter. Livefood is very important for successful breeding.

St. Helena Waxbill

Estrilda astrild

- **Distribution:** Most of southern Africa
- **Size:** 11.5cm (4.5 in)
- **Diet:** Small seeds, greenstuff and livefood of the appropriate type
- **Sexing:** The abdomen is a significantly paler pink in the hen
- **Compatibility:** Can be less social than related species
- **Pet appeal:** Probably one of the easier waxbills to cater for

This waxbill ranges over such a wide area that it is sometimes known simply as the Common Waxbill. Not surprisingly, therefore, they are adaptable birds in captivity, and will breed either in indoor cages or outside aviaries. Their nests are often found close to ground level, and in aviaries a low bush is a favoured nesting site. The pair construct a false nesting chamber on top of the real nest to confuse potential predators. This chamber remains empty, and is described as the cock's nest. Similar structures may also be included in the woven nests of related species. If alarmed, the birds may appear to show great interest in the cock's nest, although the eggs are laid beneath. Access to the nesting site proper is by means of a tunnel-shaped entrance.

Both sexes share the task of incubation, with the eggs hatching after a period of twelve days. The chicks grow rapidly, and may well fledge before they are three weeks old. At this stage, the youngsters are duller than adults in overall coloration, their beaks being black rather than red. They attain adult plumage when about two months of age and are mature shortly afterwards, although young birds are not usually encouraged to breed until they are at least nine months old to help ensure success.

This species is slightly hardier than its relatives and can survive on a diet of little more than panicum millet. Nevertheless, keep the birds warm during the winter months and offer a suitable variety of seeds, insects and greenfood, especially if chicks are to be reared successfully. Some pairs develop a liking for hard-boiled egg, and can even be persuaded to take egg-food when there are chicks in the nest.

The way these waxbills take food in the wild can cause problems in captivity. The claws, which serve to anchor the bird on the rough stalks of seeding grasses, tend to be naturally long and spindly and can lead to the bird becoming caught up within the aviary. Therefore, trim the claws regularly, taking care not to cut them too short, as this will result in bleeding. A good time to check is when the waxbills are being transferred to an outside aviary during the late spring. This provides an opportunity for close inspection, and avoids the need to catch the birds unnecessarily.

Below: **St. Helena Waxbill**
This is one of the more robust waxbills for keeping in captivity and should breed successfully in suitable surroundings, indoors or outdoors.

Red-billed Fire-finch
Lagonosticta senegala

- **Distribution:** Occurs over much of Africa south of the Sahara.
- **Size:** 11.5 cm (4.5 in)
- **Diet:** Small seeds, suitable insects and greenstuff
- **Sexing:** Hens have brownish grey backs; cocks red-brown backs
- **Compatibility:** Pairs can usually be housed safely with waxbills
- **Pet appeal:** Attractive, often ready nesters

The fire-finches as a group are not the easiest of birds to establish and need very careful acclimatization if they are to be kept outdoors for part of the year. Bring them inside into heated accommodation for the duration of the winter in temperate climates. This particular species can often be found close to the ground, seeking spilt seeds and insects. They may even nest in a suitable tussock of grass, building a typical domed structure associated with the members of the Family Estrildidae. The clutch is likely to consist of three or four eggs, with both birds being responsible for the incubation duties and rearing of the chicks. They should hatch after twelve days and fledge within three weeks, becoming fully independent in about a further week. The young fire-finches are predominantly brown in colour at this stage, although cock birds may show a reddish tinge overall. Young birds, lacking the white spots on the breast, start to moult into adult plumage as young as six weeks old.

To ensure breeding success, be sure to provide an adequate supply of insects and rearing foods for the adult fire-finches. If a pair are reluctant to breed, you may be able to persuade them to do so by providing an artificial nesting site lined with dried grass. Once a pair start breeding, however, it can be difficult to persuade them to stop; they are capable of rearing three rounds of chicks through the summer months. Ensure that the aviary is roofed over as far as possible, so that the nest and young chicks will not be saturated in a rainstorm, with fatal consequences. Water any plants in the aviary individually, taking care not to disturb the sitting birds in the process.

In total, there are eight species of fire-finch, and all have similar requirements to those of the Red-billed. Some are rarely available, however, although the Black-bellied Fire-finch (*L. rara*) is quite often seen. Hybrids with several *Estrilda* waxbills and with other fire-finches have been reported. In fact, an unpaired fire-finch in a mixed collection may well pair up with a bird of a related species. Unfortunately, it appears that fire-finches have a naturally short lifespan, compared with other related waxbills, although this to some extent is compensated for by their high reproductive rate, especially under aviary conditions.

Left: **Red-billed Fire-finch**
A handsome pair, with the male bird showing the typical bright colour.

Cut-throat
Amadina fasciata

- **Distribution:** Across northern Africa, occurring in arid country to the north of the tropical forests from Senegal eastwards into the Sudan and southwards into the Transvaal, northern Orange Free State and Mozambique
- **Size:** 12.5 cm (5 in)
- **Diet:** Small seeds, livefood and greenstuff
- **Sexing:** Hens are paler, and characteristically lack the red throat band
- **Compatibility:** Can turn aggressive, especially when breeding, and thus should not be housed with waxbills. May live in harmony with munias
- **Pet appeal:** Unusual coloration, and often keen to nest

The common name of these birds is derived from the prominent band of red plumage across the cock bird's throat, resembling blood in appearance. They were first bred in Europe as long ago as 1770, when a pair nested in France. Since then, countless Cut-throats have been reared successfully both in aviaries and in cages. Cock birds sing quite freely when in breeding condition, although their vocal prowess is limited. A small nestbox will suffice for Cut-throats, although suitable nesting material must also be supplied. This is normally collected by the cock and passed to his mate, who is responsible for building the nest on her own. Incubation of the resulting four or five eggs is shared, with the chick hatching after twelve days, and then fledging about three weeks later. Livefood is not vital during the rearing phase; a softfood, augmented with soaked seed, for example, will often suffice. The main drawback in attempting to breed Cut-throats successfully is the apparent susceptibility of hen birds to egg-binding, which can prove fatal

unless rectified speedily. An affected hen is likely to appear in considerable discomfort, and will be unsteady on her legs. Catch egg-bound hens with particular care, ensuring that the egg causing the blockage is not accidentally broken by rough handling, as this in itself can prove fatal.

In order to minimize the risk of egg-binding, administer a calcium supplement in the drinking water to susceptible birds for a short period before the breeding season. Ensure also that cuttlefish bone is freely-accessible, cutting off slivers from the soft side with a knife in case the finches have difficulty pecking at the bone. The use of a so-called 'natural' light over birds housed indoors may assist in the synthesis of Vitamin D_3, which also has a crucial role to play in the process of shell formation by mobilizing and controlling the body stores of calcium, which is the major ingredient of the eggshell. Finally, do

Above: **Cut-throat**
The male of this pair clearly shows the blood-red markings at the throat. A hardy and unusual bird.

not allow hens to have more than two clutches of chicks in a season. Breeding can prove a taxing time on the body's reserves, and the incidence of soft-shelled eggs, which in turn are liable to lead to egg-binding, will increase if the hen is allowed to lay repeatedly throughout most of the year.

Always allow hen Cut-throats to mature before they are encouraged to breed; they should be about a year old. The sexes of the youngsters can be determined by the time they leave the nest, since cock birds already show their red throat band. It is possible to breed these birds on a colony system, and may be preferable to housing them in a mixed collection. Cut-throats kept together gradually synchronize their breeding behaviour and are not

Above: **Aurora Finch**
An attractive, lively finch that will thrive in warm, dry conditions. Be sure to acclimatize it carefully.

normally aggressive towards each other, providing there is an adequate choice of nesting sites available.

An unusual feature of the Cut-throat's behaviour, more commonly associated with sparrows, is its fondness for dust-bathing. The bird excavates a small hollow in a suitable area of dry soil, immersing itself in the dirt just as if it were water. Cut-throats naturally hail from arid areas, and it seems likely that this activity may help to keep the plumage in good condition and free from parasites, acting rather like a dry shampoo, and possibly removing excessive natural oil from the plumage. Once acclimatized properly, the Cut-throat is quite a hardy bird, and has much to offer as an aviary occupant.

Aurora Finch
Pytilia phoenicoptera

- **Distribution:** Semi-arid regions of northern Africa, in a band from The Gambia eastwards to Sudan and Uganda
- **Size:** 11.5 cm (4.5 in)
- **Diet:** Small seeds, including spray millet, suitable invertebrates and greenfood chopped into pieces
- **Sexing:** Hens tend to be duller, with a brownish tinge overall
- **Compatibility:** Pairs can be kept with other waxbills, but some cock birds may become aggressive when breeding
- **Pet appeal:** Colourful, and keen to nest

Like other small finches, the Aurora Finch (also known as the Red-winged Pytilia) needs careful acclimatization. Never place these birds in an outside aviary until the weather is relatively warm and there is no risk of frost. Furthermore, keep

newly-acquired individuals destined for a garden aviary inside for a short period to check that all is well with them beforehand. If their plumage appears ruffled and fluffed up, the temperature may be too low for them. This is a reliable indicator for all foreign finches, although it may also be a symptom of illness.

Pairs may choose to build their own nests in the aviary or adopt a nestbox for the purpose. Wicker nesting baskets are favoured by some pairs, with both partners sharing the task of gathering material. The clutch may number up to five eggs, which start to hatch about thirteen days after laying. Again, livefood or a substitute source of protein, such as a canary rearing food, must be available if the chicks are to be reared successfully. Although probably of equal nutritive value, most inert foodstuffs do not hold the same appeal as live insects for breeding birds, which have been conditioned over generations to seek

such foods when chicks are present.

Young Aurora Finches fledge within three weeks of hatching and should be independent about two weeks later. Ideally, remove them at this stage if possible because the adult birds will probably be seeking to nest again, and will not want the distraction of their earlier youngsters. In a mixed collection, however, where there may well be other birds sitting on eggs or with chicks, the disturbance caused by catching the immature finches may outweigh the potential advantage. Having been first bred during 1872 in Germany, Aurora Finches have nested quite freely in many countries, with some pairs producing over ten young in the course of a breeding season.

Related species include the Melba Finch (*Pytilia melba*) and the Yellow-winged Pytilia (*P. hypogrammica*), which is also known as the Red-faced Aurora Waxbill. Although these birds tend to inhabit more arid areas of scrubland, they need similar care.

Golden Song Sparrow
Passer luteus

- **Distribution:** A wide area of northern Africa, from Nigeria eastwards to Sudan, Somalia, Ethiopia and Arabia
- **Size:** 12.5 cm (5 in)
- **Diet:** A mixture of small seeds, including spray millet; some livefood and greenfood
- **Sexing:** Hens are brownish overall; cocks are predominantly bright yellow
- **Compatibility:** Probably best kept in groups on their own, rather than in the company of waxbills, as they can prove aggressive
- **Pet appeal:** Colourful and lively

Although frequently seen, these small sparrows are not always easy to acquire in pairs, as there is often a preponderance of cocks available. Their common name is rather misleading, in that these birds do not sing, but have a rather dull chirping call. While hens show the typical lively curious natures associated with sparrows, cocks tend to be extremely flighty. Pairs, therefore, need to be accommodated in fairly spacious surroundings, such as an

indoor flight. The best way of keeping this species is to purchase several pairs simultaneously and set up a small colony. Breeding results tend to be rather sporadic compared with some other African finches, however, and this is almost certainly because Song Sparrows need the stimulus of others of their kind if they are to be persuaded to nest. An interesting and unusual feature of cock birds of this species is that their beaks darken considerably at the onset of the breeding season, turning completely black, and then fade again later in the year.

Golden Song Sparrows naturally nest in thorn bushes, which afford a degree of protection against potential predators. In aviary surroundings, they may adopt clumps of gorse bush for this purpose. Alternatively, they may be persuaded to use a nestbox, which they line with suitable material in a rather sloppy manner. The greenish-white eggs are laid on a bed of feathers. The incubation period is about eleven days, and the youngsters fledge when they are about two weeks old. It appears that livefood is not vital for rearing purposes, especially if the birds will take a softfood plus greenfood, such

Above: **Golden Song Sparrow**
A pair of these delightful birds, the cock showing the typical yellow coloration. Breed these lively birds on a colony basis in a spacious flight planted with suitable shrubs.

as chickweed, cut into fine pieces. Nevertheless, a supply of suitable invertebrates should be maintained if possible.

Although Song Sparrows can be kept safely out of doors throughout the year if the winter is mild, be prepared to bring them into moderately heated quarters. Do not keep newly imported birds in an outside aviary during their first winter: they require a longer period of acclimatization. Apart from the cold, the lack of daylight during the winter reduces the feeding time available, so that there is a long gap overnight between feeds at a time when the birds are expending a considerable amount of energy (derived from their food) in maintaining their body temperature. You should provide additional lighting in the depths of winter, even for established or home-bred stock, to give them an adequate opportunity to feed and thus keep warm.

Pearl Silverbill
Lonchura griseicapilla

- **Distribution:** East Africa, from Southern Ethiopia to Kenya and Tanzania
- **Size:** 11.5 cm (4.5 in)
- **Diet:** Smaller seeds, with some livefood and greenstuff
- **Sexing:** Cannot be sexed visually
- **Compatibility:** Social; best kept in groups
- **Pet appeal:** An undemanding and cheerful bird

A member of the Munia group, which extends into Asia, this species shows the typically subdued coloration of its type. No bright red, yellow or orange plumage, but an attractive combination of grey, black, white and brown, which has given rise to its alternative name of Grey-headed Silverbill. Like the related African Silverbill (*L. cantans*), it is impossible to sex these birds by sight, and so a group should be housed together in the hope of obtaining at least one breeding pair. Patience may be required before the birds show any clear sign of breeding behaviour, possibly taking a year or so to settle in new quarters.

Subsequently, they can prove quite prolific in captivity.

Pearl Silverbills construct relatively bulky nests, which are usually lined inside with feathers and soft material. Strands of grass, small twigs and even old millet sprays will be used to form the exterior, with the birds entering via a hole in the side of the nesting chamber. They may also use a nesting box with an open front positioned under cover in the aviary. Cock birds display to intended mates by singing and bobbing up and

down, holding a piece of nesting material in their beaks. The hen should then respond, and ultimately, the cock bird drops the item from its beak as a prelude to mating. Close observation of the birds once they are established in their surroundings can make it easier to sex individuals even if they are not breeding. The use of celluloid split rings of different colours is advocated by some breeders in such cases, so that the birds then carry a permanent marking, serving to distinguish their

sex. Split rings are easy to fit on the leg at any stage of growth.

The incubation period for this species is about eleven days, with up to six eggs forming the clutch. Munias generally are less dependent on livefood for the rearing of their chicks than waxbills, and this certainly applies to the Silverbills. Nevertheless, providing suitable items of this nature, as well as soaked seed and greenfood such as chickweed, should help to ensure that the maximum number of

Above: **Pearl Silverbill**
Handsome rather than colourful, this is an excellent bird that will reward patience with a readiness to breed once it has settled in.

offspring are reared successfully. Fledging is likely to take place from about three weeks onwards. At this stage, the young Pearl Silverbills are paler in coloration than their parents, with a buff tinge to their plumage. They lack the white spots present on the heads of adult birds.

Speckle-fronted Weaver
Sporopipes frontalis

- **Distribution:** Senegal to the Sudan, and south to Tanzania
- **Size:** 11.5 cm (4.5 in)
- **Diet:** Canary seed and millets, with some livefood and greenstuff
- **Sexing:** No visual differences between the sexes
- **Compatibility:** Can be kept in groups, but not in the company of waxbills, as these weavers may prove quite aggressive
- **Pet appeal:** Interesting and present a challenge for the serious breeder

The two members in this genus (the other one is the Scaly-crowned Weaver - *S. squamifrons*) are unusual, since they show affiliations with both waxbills and members of the Family Ploceidae, which includes the weavers. Their relatively dull coloration has led to them being christened 'sparrow weavers'. They are quite often available, but tend to be overlooked in favour of their more gaudy relatives. The Speckle-fronted Weaver naturally occurs in arid regions, including urban areas throughout its range. Outside the breeding season, these weavers form relatively large flocks and construct their nests in quite close

proximity to each other, almost on a colony basis.

When first acquired, Speckle-fronted Weavers can be difficult to establish. It is essential to keep them in heated surroundings for the duration of the winter in temperate climates. They are adaptable birds, however, and will soon settle within the confines of a cage and may even become quite tame. Since they will normally roost within a nest at night, provide a suitable box for this purpose. If a pair do go to nest, the cock bird in particular may become aggressive towards other occupants of an aviary. The usual clutch consists of between three and five

Above: **Speckle-fronted Weaver**
These energetic birds will adapt well to living in an aviary. Keep them warm during the winter months and provide a nestbox for roosting.

eggs, with the hen being largely responsible for incubating them. They should hatch after two weeks. Be sure to provide an adequate supply of suitable livefood to ensure that the chicks are reared successfully. Indeed, it is thought that these weavers may feed their offspring totally on insects for the first part of the rearing period. Also provide soaked seed and greenfood throughout this crucial phase.

Red-headed Quelea
Quelea erythrops

- **Distribution:** Northern Africa, from Senegal to Ethiopia, extending south to Angola
- **Size:** 11.5 cm (4.5 in)
- **Diet:** Typical finch diet of mixed millets and canary seed, greenstuff and livefood
- **Sexing:** Males in breeding colour have red heads.
- **Compatibility:** Can be housed with related species, but preferably not with waxbills
- **Pet appeal:** Lively birds with interesting breeding habits

The Red-headed Quelea is a member of the group of birds known as Weavers, so called because of their desire to build ornate pendulous nests. They are colony birds, and breeding success is more likely when a number are housed together in a colony aviary. Although occurring in large flocks, it appears that there is a strong bond between individual members of a pair. Unfortunately, these weavers cannot be sexed outside the breeding period; for the remainder of the year both are basically brownish in overall coloration. There may be slight traces of red apparent on the crown of cock birds, however, and the beaks of hens also tend to be lighter in colour. The Red-headed Quelea is said to be less aggressive than related species, such as the Red-billed Quelea (*Quelea quelea*), which may be more readily available.

Reed beds in the wild are popular breeding sites for *Quelea* species, providing a ready supply of material for the cocks birds to weave their pendulous nests. Once a pair start nesting, they take it in turns during the day to incubate the eggs, which number up to four in a clutch. The eggs hatch after fourteen days, with the chicks fledging about three weeks later. Insects and other invertebrates are important during the rearing period.

Once acclimatized, Queleas are reasonably hardy in captivity, but be sure to provide them with a suitable shelter where they can retreat during periods of bad weather. The Red-headed species is probably more suitable than the Red-billed for keeping indoors in a flight cage, as these birds tend to prove less nervous. The only other species, the Cardinal Quelea (*Quelea cardinalis*), which is also sometimes described as the Red-headed Quelea, can be distinguished by the lack of black markings on the throat of cock birds in breeding plumage. For the remainder of the year, it has brown streaks on the head. The Cardinal Quelea is the smallest member of the genus and has identical requirements to the other Queleas described here. Its nest has an entrance hole at the top, which may be constructed so that it is obscured by leaves above.

Below: **Red-headed Quelea**
A fine male in typical breeding colour. Skilled nest builders.

Fischer's Whydah
Vidua fischeri

- **Distribution:** East Africa, from Somalia to Uganda and parts of northern Tanzania
- **Size:** Overall length about 30 cm (12 in), for a male in nuptial plumage. Body size 10 cm (4 in)
- **Diet:** A mixture of small cereal seeds, with livefood and greenstuff
- **Sexing:** Cock birds develop magnificent tail plumes at the onset of the breeding season, but resemble the brownish hen for the remainder of the year
- **Compatibility:** A cock with several hens should be kept alongside specific waxbills for breeding purposes
- **Pet appeal:** Magnificent appearance of cock birds, coupled with fascinating breeding habits

Whydahs are closely related to weavers. The males of all species undergo a dramatic seasonal moult at the approach of the breeding season. They then develop the long, sometimes ornate tail plumes characteristic of the group. Females, by comparison, are very dull and drab. Outside the breeding season, these birds may be advertised as being O.O.C. (out of colour), when it is difficult to distinguish between the sexes. A male whydah usually has a harem consisting of several hens.

Whydahs can be divided into two groups on the basis of their breeding behaviour. This division is made on the basis of whether or not the hens incubate their own eggs or lay them in the nests of other passerines, notably waxbills, which in turn incubate the eggs and rear the resulting chicks. There is a close relationship between the host species and the whydah that parasitizes it; the usual host for Fischer's Whydah is the Purple Grenadier Waxbill (*Uraeginthus ianthinogaster*). The male whydah is capable of mimicking the calls of these birds perfectly to attract a female whydah to a suitable nesting site. Very few species of parasitic whydah appear able to make use of a range of waxbills as foster parents; the Pin-tailed Whydah (*U. macroura*) is almost exceptional in this respect.

As you might expect, whydahs are not cage birds in the traditional sense, although they can be kept quite satisfactorily in a spacious indoor flight. Take particular care with the arrangement of perches in aviaries housing whydahs, so that cock birds cannot damage their magnificent tail plumes. They tend to prefer feeding on the ground, and may be seen digging for seeds on an earth floor. Once acclimatized and afforded adequate shelter, these birds can generally be overwintered in an aviary, but if they appear uncomfortable, bring them inside for the duration of the winter and place them outside again during the spring in the company of waxbills. Provide a fairly large aviary, if only to appreciate the graceful flight of the cock whydah with the tail plumes streaming in a horizontal position behind it. They are surprisingly fast on the wing.

The key to successful breeding appears to revolve around the host species. When the waxbills start nesting, this acts as a trigger for the whydahs. The latter are polygamous, so house two or three hens with a single cock bird. They lay their eggs in the waxbill's nest and these are incubated and hatch at the same time as the host's chicks. There is no direct competition between the chicks, as with the cuckoo, where the natural offspring are ejected from the nest. The hatchling whydahs mimic the waxbills, even to the extend of possessing the characteristic markings within the mouth that serve to identify each particular species to the adult birds.

It is remarkable how these close relationships have developed. A possible transition stage in the evolutionary links between these different avian families can be seen in the behaviour of the Senegal Combassou or Indigo Bird (*Vidua chalybeata*). In most instances, these particular whydahs parasitize fire-finches (*Lagonosticta* sp.), but in the absence of such birds they have been known to rear their own chicks successfully. Various forms of this relatively dull whydah are known.

The *Vidua* whydahs as a group present a considerable breeding challenge. Not surprisingly, relatively few are bred in aviaries at present, although viable breeding populations have been maintained in Australia for a number of years, without the introduction of new stock because of importation restrictions. Repeated success has also been reported from southern Africa, where a pair of Paradise Whydahs (*Vidua paradisaea*) nested successfully in an aviary containing Melba Finches (*Pytilia melba*) over a four year period. In spite of difficulties over breeding *Vidua* whydahs, however, they are extremely easy birds to cater for and may live for twenty years or so.

Left: **Fischer's Whydah**
The superb tail plumes of the male clearly distinguish it from the females of this species. Provide a spacious aviary for these birds.

Above: **Orange Bishop**
A splendid male in nuptial plumage. Colour food will help to maintain this.

Orange Bishop
Euplectes orix

- **Distribution:** Across northern Africa, from Senegal to Ethiopia and Tanzania, ranging south into Angola and South Africa
- **Size:** 12.5 cm (5 in)
- **Diet:** A mixture of smaller cereal seeds, such as canary seed, with livefood and greenfood
- **Sexing:** In breeding condition, cocks can be easily recognized by the orange neck ruff. For the remainder of the year they closely resemble hens, but may have scattered black feathers through their otherwise brown plumage
- **Compatibility:** Can be kept with other birds of similar size but likely to do best in groups of the same species
- **Pet appeal:** Unusual coloration

There is some confusion over the actual status of this species. A number of distinctive subspecies are recognized, with some being accorded full specific status by various authorities. Nevertheless, the striking appearance of the male Orange Bishop in nuptial plumage is unmistakable. They are easy birds to cater for. Once established, they can be relatively hardy, but be sure to provide adequate shelter during the winter months. Successful breeding, however, tends to be uncommon, although there is no reason why this should be so. Many people simply prefer to house these weavers as part of a mixed collection, which is not conducive to breeding success.

In order to breed Orange Bishops, the most important first move is to keep one cock bird in the company of several hens. These weavers are naturally polygamous, and do not maintain a strong pair bond. The cock bird will often adopt a bush as the site for constructing a nest, and you can supply raffia or even dried grass for this purpose. Having constructed the framework of the breeding site, the cock persuades a hen to complete the task, before laying her bluish eggs within. The clutch size can be quite variable, ranging from two to seven eggs, and the incubation period is about two weeks. The hen incubates the eggs alone throughout and is also responsible for rearing the chicks. The cock bird in the meantime will normally have mated with another hen, repeating the process. It is important that several hens - as many as six - are housed with a single cock bird. On a one-to-one basis, a cock will persecute an individual female with chicks and this can lead to fatalities.

Provide a selection of rearing foods, including a regular supply of invertebrates, when a hen is rearing offspring. The youngsters fledge after about two weeks in the nest, and become independent about a fortnight later. Remove the young weavers as soon as possible, as they too may be persecuted by the cock. Unfortunately, it can be difficult to distinguish between immature birds and adult hens, although newly-fledged chicks display a yellow striping close to the eyes and are paler overall. The orange coloration of cock birds tends to fade over successive moults, unless a colour food is supplied to reverse this change.

In common with certain other species of perching birds that live in reedbeds, the claws of these weavers tend to become overgrown quite rapidly in aviary surroundings. Regular clipping is recommended.

A related species, known as the Golden Bishop or Napoleon Weaver (*E. afer*) has identical requirements, but does not need to be colour fed. Again, house only one cock bird in the company of several hens.

Grey Singing Finch
Serinus leucopygius

- **Distribution:** Across much of northern Africa, from Senegal eastwards to Ethiopia and Sudan
- **Size:** 10 cm (4 in)
- **Diet:** Predominantly a canary seed mixture, to which plain canary seed can be added to increase the overall content. The smaller oil-based seeds, such as maw and rape, will also be taken
- **Sexing:** Impossible to sex by plumage differences
- **Compatibility:** Can cause a disturbance in a mixed aviary
- **Pet appeal:** Excellent songsters, if rather dull in colour

Sometimes also known as the White-rumped Seedeater, these serins are often available, and cocks are admirable songsters. The main drawback is that these birds cannot be sexed easily; four birds may have to be obtained in the hope of acquiring a breeding pair. Cocks may compete with each other, but serious conflicts are uncommon; if a fight seems inevitable, however, separate the potential combatants and transfer one to alternative accommodation.

When first acquired, imported birds can prove delicate and need to be kept warm. Providing livefood and greenstuff can help them through this difficult phase. A pair can be housed in a suitably spacious cage, and may attempt to nest, although successful breeding is more likely with birds kept in a planted aviary. Canary nesting material can be supplied, and will be used to build the typical cup-shaped nest. This may be located in a canary nesting pan or even a partially open-fronted nestbox. The male will sing repeatedly throughout this phase and proves attentive to his mate. She lays a clutch of three or four eggs and incubates them on her own, being fed by the cock throughout this time, although she will also come off the nest for brief periods. The chicks should hatch after two weeks, but this period can be prolonged slightly, depending on when the hen actually started to sit in earnest.

Hen Grey Singing Finches usually prove highly attentive to their newly hatched offspring and tend not to leave the nest for the first few days after hatching. Livefood is essential at this stage, although these birds will also often take a canary rearing food mixed as directed. The female is solely responsible for the care of the chicks until they fledge, from about two weeks onwards, when the cock bird will start feeding the youngsters. Immature Grey Singing Finches can be recognized by an increase in the dark streaking on the chest region, compared with that of the adult birds.

Once they start breeding, pairs are likely to prove prolific, and a second clutch of eggs will probably soon follow. At this stage, remove the earlier youngsters to prevent them being persecuted by the cock. It is quite usual for Grey Singing Finches to construct a new nest for each clutch of eggs, so ensure that

suitable sites and additional nesting material are freely available. They may choose to nest in the winter if the opportunity arises, but prevent this if possible; the chances of success in an outdoor aviary are minimal at this time of year in temperate climes. Indeed, do not keep adult Singing Finches outside

without heat unless the weather is extremely mild. Under good conditions, individual birds may live for eighteen years or so.

Other related species often available include the Green Singing Finch (*Serinus mozambicus*) and the Giant Green Singing Finch or St. Helena Seedeater (*S. flaviventris*),

Above: **Grey Singing Finch**
Aptly named for its melodious song, this small African finch will fare well in captivity once it has become acclimatized to new conditions.

both of which need similar care and conditions to that recommended for the Grey Singing Finch.

colour, but if you do opt for a colour food, ensure that you feed it in the correct quantities. Although unlikely to be toxic, excessive usage of these preparations is likely to spoil the canary's appearance until the next moult, as well as turning the droppings reddish in the short term.

The coloration of Red Factor Canaries is also influenced by their feather structure. In some individuals, the feathers have whitish borders, which has led to them being described as frosted; these birds also have slightly softer plumage compared with the non-frosted canaries. This difference is also seen in all other breeds of canary, but may not be so clearly apparent. The respective terms for feather texture in other breeds are buff and yellow, although the feather type itself is not influenced by the colour of the bird. As a general rule, breeding pairs should consist of one bird of each feather type. Repeatedly pairing buff canaries together can

give rise to feather cysts, where the plumage is so soft that it cannot emerge in the normal manner, but curls under the skin, leading to the formation of swellings, typically on the back of the bird.

The Gloster Fancy
The above problem is definitely associated with certain of the so-called 'type' breeds. These are bred essentially to conform as closely as possible to official standards, being judged accordingly when they are exhibited. One of the most popular canaries in this group is the Gloster Fancy, which has suffered during recent years with an increasing incidence of feather cysts. The Gloster is a relatively new breed, which only became popular after the Second World War, although it was first developed during the 1920s. Both crested and non-crested birds of this breed are available, being described as Coronas and Consorts respectively. Coronas are not paired

together, however, but always to non-crested individuals, because a so-called lethal factor will prevent the survival of a percentage of the chicks likely to result from a crest-to-crest pairing.

Apart from their exhibition following, Gloster Canaries are attractive birds for keeping as pets or in garden aviaries. They have lively, active natures, and are capable songsters, which is probably a reflection of the Roller Canary blood in their ancestry (see the text and photo on pages 74-75). A further advantage of this breed is that hens usually prove reliable parents, a trait not associated with all breeds; indeed, some breeders use Gloster Fancy birds for fostering the eggs of other varieties.

Below: **Border Canary**
A Clear Yellow cock, one of several appealing colours that are available. These canaries are particularly popular as lively pet birds.

The Border Fancy
Probably the most popular of the type breeds at present is the Border Fancy. These canaries were developed during the nineteenth century in the Border region between England and Scotland, and have since gained an international following. They have been bred in a wide range of colours and hold a considerable appeal for the pet-seeker. Pure yellow Border Fancies, as well as white, blue and cinnamon birds, are available. There are various terms that have been evolved to describe canaries and their markings. White or yellow birds, with no dark areas of plumage are known as 'Clears', whereas in green and blue canaries, lacking any variegation, the term 'Self' is applied. Variegated individuals may be either lightly or heavily marked, depending on whether light or dark areas predominate in their plumage. (The breeding of canaries is an absorbing subject in its own right.)

The Lizard

The Lizard is one of the oldest surviving type breeds of canary and also the most distinctive. The unique pattern of markings on its body, said to resemble a reptile's scales in appearance, are a vital consideration for judges of the breed. Lighter coloured (buff) Lizard Canaries are known as Silvers, whereas the yellow form is called the Gold. Apart from the characteristic body markings, the Lizard may also have a clear unbroken area of plumage on the top of its head. This is known as the cap. It can be divided into two parts, in which case the description of broken-capped is applied to the canary in question. Non-capped birds are also known, and there are futher subdivisions in these groups. The Lizard Canary, unlike both the Border and Gloster Fancies, is usually colour-fed, but again, this is not essential from the bird's viewpoint in terms of health.

While many pet stores stock canaries, these are likely to be the most popular breeds already mentioned, apart from the Lizard. Many such birds may not bear a close relationship to the show standards prescribed for the variety in question, and may even result from the crossing of Border Fancies with Glosters, for example. Such pairings are frowned upon by serious breeders, who are devoted to the development of their particular breed. Indeed, the Canary Fancy in the UK and Europe and also, to a lesser extent, in the United States has tended to remain rather localized. As a result, specific breeds with historical links with particular areas may not be seen in any numbers elsewhere, unless they undergo a surge of popularity.

The Fife Fancy

This situation has happened in the UK with the rise of the Fife Fancy.

Above: **Clear-capped Lizard Canary**
This highly distinctive and long-established variety offers a breeding challenge to enthusiasts.

The breed is almost identical to the Border Canary, except notably in terms of size. The original Border Fancy was a relatively small bird, but had become progressively bigger over the course of recent decades. The Fife Fancy, originally developed as a breed in Scotland during the 1950s, reflected a desire among breeders in the area to rekindle the former appearance of the Border Fancy. They persevered in the face of some opposition, and today the Fife Fancy has undergone a remarkable growth in popularity, being seen at shows throughout the United Kingdom.

The Yorkshire Canary

During the course of time, the appearance of some breeds has changed dramatically, not just in terms of size. The Yorkshire Canary, long associated with the coalmines of its native area, served to act as a sentinel for the presence of deadly methane gas down the pits, being taken underground by the miners in special cages that were sometimes even equipped with a small oxygen supply in case of an emergency. During the latter part of the nineteenth century, the Yorkshire Canary was popularly regarded as being slim enough to slide through a wedding ring. Today, the breed is considerable broader, while remaining one of the tallest canaries, with an overall length approaching 18 cm (7 in). The Fife Fancy, by comparison, is only 11.25 cm (4.4 in) long - a considerable difference.

Some canary breeds have been lost, while others have declined dramatically in numbers during recent years. Indeed, the Lizard at one stage was considered imperilled

after the Second World War but has now undergone a substantial revival in numbers. Practical problems have led to the demise of some breeds, linked particularly to breeding difficulties. A poor reproductive rate and a preponderance of feather cysts were responsible for the decline of the Norwich Fancy, which has never fully recovered from these setbacks, although retaining a loyal following, especially in East Anglia, which is the native region of this large breed in the UK..

The Roller Canary

While most of the popular 'type' breeds have been evolved in the UK, it is in mainland Europe where interest has been keenest in developing the song of the canary to maximum effect. The best known of the breeds in this category is the Roller Canary, being named after part of the prescribed passages of song ('rolls') that these birds are taught, traditionally by a 'schoolmaster' canary at an early age. It was in the Harz Mountain region of Germany that the Roller Canary was first bred, being recognized before the end of the seventeenth century as an unrivalled songster. Indeed, these birds, with have also contributed to the bloodlines of other more localized breeds highly valued in their own countries for their singing prowess, such as the Belgian Malinois and the American Singer.

Plumage variations

Canaries also show more variation in the structure of their plumage than other finches. Apart from the crests of the Crested Canary and the Gloster Corona, more radical plumage modifications are apparent in the case of the various frilled breeds (as shown on page 76). These tend to have a localized distribution through much of mainland Europe, although now perhaps concentrated in Italy especially. Such birds are not appealing to everyone. Specific terminology has been evolved to cater for the various points of these birds, while posture is also considered an important feature for a good exhibition bird, as in other breeds.

Choosing a canary

Given the huge diversity of breeds and colours, it may seem difficult to decide on a particular choice. In the first instance, availability may be a determining factor. For a pet, the Roller Canary would seem to be the ideal choice because of its song. Since all cock canaries sing, you may wish to take other factors into consideration, such as size and colour. If you are seeking a specific breed, try to visit a show. It is here that you will see the largest selection of birds on display, and you can make useful contacts with breeders, who may have surplus stock for disposal.

Yet for the garden aviary, it matters little how closely an individual bird corresponds with an official standard for the breed concerned, providing it is healthy. Obviously, canaries that have been carefully bred over generations for show purposes will be more costly than those available in a pet store, for example, and you may feel that this additional expense is not justified unless you are keen to enter the exhibition side of the hobby. If you are interested in exhibiting, it is best to stick to one breed only, rather than having pairs of several breeds.

One sound reason for going to a breeder in order to obtain a canary is that the sex of the bird is more likely to be known for certain than when purchasing from a pet store. Breeders generally know their stock; it may be a different matter for a pet store assistant. Since it is not possible to sex canaries visually, the song is the most reliable guideline. Males out of condition, however, typically when they are moulting, will be reluctant to sing. Similar difficulties may arise with newly fledged birds. There is also no means of ageing a canary reliably once it is mature, but a breeder will probably have records available, which may not be the case in a pet store. As a general guide to age, however, look closely at the bird's legs. A thick, scaly appearance suggests an older bird. Always compare the canaries on offer from this point of view.

Above: **Clear Yellow Fife Canary**
This is one of the smallest breeds, having been bred in Scotland specifically with the intention of restoring the compactness once shown by the Border Canaries. This yellow form is the most popular of the Fife Canaries available at present.

songs reflecting the pure sounds of the mountain streams of their homeland, were exported throughout Europe in special craftsmen-built cages long before the serious development of either the type or New Coloured Canaries. Today, Roller Canaries are widely kept and

Above: **Yorkshire Canary**
This elegant and tall breed of Canary has retained an extremely wide popularity among enthusiasts.

Below: **Roller Canary**
Prized for its glorious song, the Roller is the most widely known of the Song Canaries. An excellent pet.

General care

Canaries will live quite happily in a spacious cage, and can occasionally be let out, provided there is someone on hand to supervise their activities. Canaries may develop sore feet from being kept on hard perches of constant diameter for any length of time, so provide some natural branches in the cage to give some variety. Occasionally, their claws do become overgrown and will need to be clipped back. Breeders usually inspect hens closely before placing them in breeding cages, since overgrown claws can damage eggs or even

pull young chicks out of the nest when the hen leaves her brood for a short period.

As members of a mixed garden aviary, canaries are far less aggressive than their wild counterparts. Keep cocks apart in separate accommodation whenever possible, however, to minimize the threat of fighting and the resulting disturbance to other members of the aviary. Canaries are relatively hardy birds, but be sure to provide adequate protection during the winter months, including heat if necessary. See also pages 44-47 for details of suitable aviaries.

Breeding and rearing

While it is possible to breed canaries in a garden aviary, they are more normally bred in cages, with a suitable nest-pan attached to one of the walls. Choose one of the larger cage designs on offer, or buy the cage front separately and construct the cage around its dimensions. Canaries, unlike budgerigars, are not destructive birds, and so the whole unit can be made almost entirely out of hardboard if desired, since this will be cheaper than plywood.

Two different breeding strategies are commonly used. In the first, cock and hen are introduced to the breeding cage simultaneously and remain together throughout the whole of the breeding period. Alternatively, the hen is placed in the cage on her own, with nesting material being provided, while a cock bird is close at hand. Once the hen has constructed the nest, she solicits the cock, who is introduced for several days to enable mating to take place. The hen is then left to lay, and rears the chicks on her own. This method means that one cock can be used to mate with several hens in fairly rapid succession and will not be able to disturb a sitting female. It does, of course, impose a greater burden on the hens concerned, and weaning can be more problematical, because this task is usually performed by the cock once the chicks have fledged.

The hen canary normally lays within two weeks of the cock being placed in the cage. The bluish green eggs, speckled with brown, are laid one a day, usually in the morning. Four eggs form a typical clutch. It is common practice for the first three to be removed and replaced with dummy eggs, the real eggs being stored carefully in a box lined with cotton-wool or tissue paper. On the morning that the fourth egg is anticipated, the dummy eggs are all removed and the real eggs replaced carefully under the hen. The idea behind this system is that the chicks will hatch together, and have a greater chance of survival, since there is no age gap between them. If you do decide to remove the eggs, always ensure that your hands are clean beforehand and that the storage area is in a cool location, out of sunlight.

The eggs should hatch after being incubated for about thirteen days, and the earliest sign is likely to be eggshells on the floor of the cage. Immediately before the anticipated date of hatching, provide the hen with the chosen rearing food in a plastic container. Increase the quantity offered as the chicks grow. Always ensure that the food cannot turn sour. Ideally, offer smaller quantities fresh several times throughout the day. Other items, such as greenfood and soaked seed, can also be included in the hen's diet to good effect, although domesticated canaries do not normally express any interest in livefood of any type.

There will be no need to interfere with the chicks if everything appears to be going well. If you intend to close-ring the chicks (i.e. put a closed band on the leg) be sure to do this by the time they are six days

Above: **Parisian Frill Canary**
This is one of the extraordinary frilled breeds that enjoy particular acclaim in mainland Europe. Breeding this type needs skill and patience. They are available in various colours.

Below: **Gloster Canary**
This Corona Gloster has the typical short crest that fringes the eyes. Coronas are not paired together because of genetical complications that prevent some chicks surviving.

old. After this, the procedure will not be possible as the individual toes over which the ring has to be slid will have grown too large. Chicks normally start begging for food when they are about ten days old, being clearly visible in the nest at this stage, and soon afterwards may start perching on the edge of the nest-pan. Some individuals tend to leave the nest rather prematurely at this stage, and - especially in aviary surroundings - you may have to place them back on the nesting site.

If the hen is to have a second round of chicks, reintroduce the cock bird approximately eighteen days after the first chicks have hatched, yet just before the weaning process starts in earnest. Make a second nesting pan available for the hen at this stage, along with additional nesting material. Continue feeding the rearing food throughout the whole time that the first chicks remain with the hen. They may even be seen feeding themselves, although they will continue soliciting food from their parent at every opportunity. Remove the first batch of young canaries to separate accommodation when they are about three weeks old, enabling the hen to focus on her second clutch.

The first youngsters are now entering the crucial weaning phase. Be sure to keep a close watch on the early youngsters to ensure that they are feeding themselves adequately. They are more likely to do so when several birds are housed together, rather than just one on its own. Supply the rearing food as before and sprinkle it with fine blue maw seed. Also provide an adequate supply of soaked seed. Good hygiene is vital at this stage, since perishable foods are on offer and canaries are notoriously wasteful feeders, scattering food all round their cage. Change the lining of the cage floor once or twice daily, so that there is no risk of the young birds succumbing to a digestive disturbance at the time when they are most susceptible. Offer hard seed to the canaries as they grow older, and they should be eating it readily by the time they are two months old. Gradually reduce the level of rearing food and soaked seed as the young canaries start taking dry seed.

Although canaries are domesticated, they have a fairly rigorously defined breeding period. They normally start breeding during late March or April in the northern hemisphere, depending on the weather, and will have two rounds of chicks as a general rule, before starting to moult in July and August. Ideally, give canaries a tonic during breeding to speed the birds through this debilitating phase. Canaries will breed in their second year, and can live well over ten years.

Very occasionally, a pet canary may learn to say an odd word, but they are essentially song birds and unlikely to become as tame as budgerigars. It is probably a combination of these reasons that led to the Budgerigar becoming the most popular pet bird, in place of the Canary, during the 1950s. Yet the Canary still has a justifiably strong following among pet owners.

Yellow-rumped Serin
Serinus atrogularis

- **Distribution:** Over a wide part of Africa from Arabia south-eastwards ranging to Angola and the Cape
- **Size:** 11.5 cm (4.5 in)
- **Diet:** A mixture of small seeds (including millet sprays), livefood and greenfood
- **Sexing:** No visible differences
- **Compatibility:** Keep pairs on their own, as cocks may prove aggressive, particularly when breeding
- **Pet appeal:** Attractive, lively songster

The singing ability of this serin has caused it to become known as the Black-throated Canary, although its song is certainly not as well developed as that of its domesticated counterpart. Individuals show considerable variations in plumage, but these are not reliable indicators of the sex of the birds in question. It is more likely that the serins are of different races; at least eight subspecies are recognized over the vast area of Africa where these birds occur. The most noticeable difference is likely to be in the throat markings, with some subspecies showing a significantly darker coloration in this region. The species is characterized overall by its yellow rump (seen in flight), a fact reflected in its other common name of Yellow-rumped Serin.

Breeding behaviour closely follows that of related species. With assistance from the cock bird, the hen constructs a cup-shaped nest. The clutch, typically composed of three eggs, is incubated by the hen alone, although the cock may briefly cover the eggs when she leaves the nest. The incubation period is about two weeks, being slightly longer for the first egg. (This is because the hen will not start to incubate the eggs in earnest as soon as she has laid, thus increasing the incubation period for the first egg.) Livefood is vital, particularly in the early stages of the chicks' development, and grass seedheads are another favoured rearing food.

The young birds fledge when two weeks old, and can be distinguished by the reduced area of yellow on the rump, which is also paler than in the adults. A hen often lays again rapidly once the chicks have left the nest, re-using the old nest and adding new material to it as necessary. Fighting is most likely to break out during the breeding period if the aviary is overcrowded. Providing the adults can establish a small territory around their nest, however, they rarely prove aggressive to other birds in the aviary.

Below: **Yellow-rumped Serin**
This bird's most characteristic feature - its yellow rump - is usually best seen when the bird is in full flight. An excellent aviary bird that will reward its owner with a tuneful song, vivacious nature and a willingness to breed in captivity.

Greenfinch

Carduelis chloris

- **Distribution:** Over much of Europe into Asia, from Ireland to the Ural Mountains, Russia, as well as Scandinavia
- **Size:** 15 cm (6 in)
- **Diet:** A mixed seed diet, including grain and oil-seeds such as rape and even sunflower. Fond of berries in season, as well as greenfood of various types
- **Sexing:** Hens are duller overall, being more brownish and lacking much of the yellow coloration seen in cock birds
- **Compatibility:** Best housed in individual pairs
- **Pet appeal:** Easy to maintain and keen to breed

In certain countries, such as the UK, only close-rung native greenfinches can be sold, since this confirms that they were bred in captivity. If you are concerned about the regulations governing the keeping of native species, consult the government department concerned for current information. In the UK, this is the Department of the Environment, whereas in the United States, the Department of the Interior, Fish and Wildlife Service is able to provide the necessary advice, as is the National Parks and Wildlife Service in Australia.

The Greenfinch is probably one of the easiest of the European finches to maintain and breed in captivity. Indeed, several colour mutations have even emerged in captive stock, the most striking of which is undoubtedly the lutino, which has

been known since the Second World War. Although greenfinches have nested satisfactorily in cages, they undoubtedly do best in planted aviaries, but they can prove rather destructive under these conditions. Plant hardy shrubs, therefore, including conifers, rather than flowering plants such as fuschias.

Greenfinches will breed quite readily in a variety of sites, ranging from nesting baskets to open-fronted nestboxes. They may even construct a nest in a bush, weaving a suitable structure quite rapidly. The typical clutch consists of about five eggs. The resulting chicks can be reared with only a minimum of livefood being provided: the adult birds hunt around the aviary for additional sources. Greenfood is an important item in the successful rearing of young greenfinches, and soaked seed can also be supplied.

Unfortunately, the major problem associated with greenfinches occurs when the youngsters have recently fledged. They are susceptible to the condition known as 'going-light', which describes the weight loss that is a feature of this illness. Early signs are likely to be slight ruffling of the plumage and a progressive lack of activity. The cause of the affliction is a subject of current veterinary investigation, but no reliable treatment is presently available. Some breeders claim that high doses of a vitamin and mineral preparation can lead to a cure, while others favour using antibiotics. It is likely that various different factors are involved. It is known, for example, that the bacterial disease pseudotuberculosis, caused by

Yersinia, can produce identical symptoms to those linked with 'going-light', but these bacteria cannot be isolated in every case. As a precautionary measure, however, remove any affected birds to separate quarters that can be easily disinfected. Leave recently fledged greenfinches with their parents for as long as possible, since premature weaning may be a predisposing factor. Then continue to offer the youngsters a wide range of foods, including greenstuff and soaked seed. Some breeders recommend altering the diet of adult birds through the year, keeping them largely on dry seed in the winter months, and then soaked and sprouted seeds for the remainder of the year. This feeding regimen may well help to stimulate breeding condition, with the protein level of the diet rising as the germinating seeds are gradually introduced to the diet during the spring. Greenfood should be available throughout.

Occasionally, other species of greenfinch from Asia are available, including the Himalayan Greenfinch (*Carduelis spinoides*) and the Chinese Greenfinch (*C. sinca*). These are similar in their requirements to the Common Greenfinch and need identical care. All species are quite hardy, but be sure to offer them some protection against the worst of the weather in temperate regions.

Below: **Greenfinch**
These are appealing birds with a lively character and a sweet song. To encourage breeding, maintain them in well-planted aviaries.

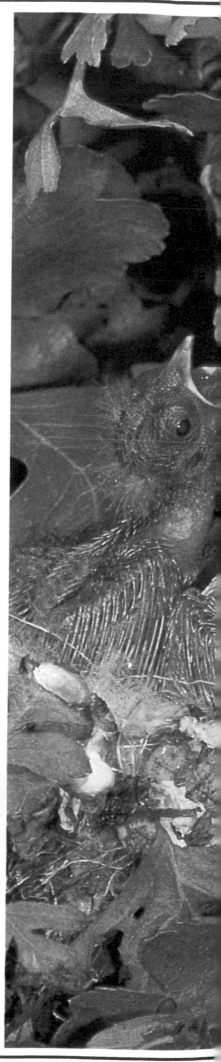

European Goldfinch
Carduelis carduelis

- **Distribution:** Over a wide area of Europe, from the UK eastwards into Asia, ranging south to northern Africa
- **Size:** 12.5 cm (5 in)
- **Diet:** A typical finch mixture, with small amounts of hemp added, plus greenfood and livefood
- **Sexing:** Sexes are alike, but hens may be duller, although this distinction does not always apply
- **Compatibility:** Can be kept safely in individual pairs or groups
- **Pet appeal:** Colourful and social by nature

Perhaps the most attractive of the European finches, the Goldfinch has long been prized as an avicultural subject. Breeders have invariably paired the most colourful of their birds together, in the hope of improving yet further on their birds' appearance. These finches are most suited to an outdoor aviary, which need not be an elaborate structure, providing it offers adequate protection against the elements.

If possible, include thistles as well as dandelions on the floor of the flight. Goldfinches delight in feeding on the seeds of these plants as they ripen. Their relatively long beaks are ideally suited for this task.

When breeding, these birds may build their nests either in the vegetation or adopt a nesting basket positioned in a secluded and sheltered spot. They will use a variety of nesting material, ranging from dried moss to grass and even moulted feathers. As in the case of other members of the genus, the incubation period is around two weeks, and a typical clutch consists of four eggs. The hen sits alone, and once the chicks hatch, be sure to provide a reliable supply of livefood, as well as greenfood and soaked seeds. Teazle, available from the specialist seed merchants, although expensive, is considered by many breeders to be a valuable rearing food for these birds. The young goldfinches grow quite fast and will fledge when they are around two weeks old. They are fed for a short time afterwards - largely by the cock bird - until they are independent.

Goldfinches occur in a variety of habitats through their range, and have proved highly adaptable. The birds are sent to the United States in particular, affording many more people an opportunity to keep these attractive birds.

There is a similar species found in North America, known as the American Goldfinch (*C. tristis*), but the capture of this species is forbidden. Races of the Goldfinch occurring outside Europe are also sometimes imported, notably the Himalayan Goldfinch (*C. c. caniceps*), which can be distinguished from native species by the absence of black markings around the head, and a greyish back and breast instead of the usual brownish plumage.

Left: **European Goldfinch**
Handsome and tuneful, these finches adapt well to captive conditions.

Common Bullfinch
Pyrrhula pyrrhula

- **Distribution:** Throughout Europe
- **Size:** Up to 19 cm (7.5 in)
- **Diet:** A canary seed mixture including rape, with added sunflower seed. Also provide berries, greenstuff and fruit
- **Sexing:** Hens are easily recognized by the overall brownish tinge to their plumage
- **Compatibility:** Pairs often become very territorial
- **Pet appeal:** Striking aviary occupants

These birds naturally frequent fruit orchards, where they are considered serious pests and persecuted accordingly. They not only eat fruit in season, but, more seriously, will damage the growing shoots just as the buds start to open in the spring. Not surprisingly, bullfinches will

greatly appreciate such twigs, and they also relish berries such as rowan, but be sure to collect them in areas where the fruit will not have been contaminated by chemicals. Unfortunately, these birds can also cause considerable damage in a planted aviary, and only hardy shrubs should be included.

Bullfinches are easy birds to cater for, although ensure that the oil-seed content of their diet, notably in terms of hemp, is kept relatively low. Apart from the risk of obesity, too high an oil-seed content can also promote abnormal feather coloration in the form of unusual areas of black plumage that appear at the subsequent moult. Colour food may be necessary in order to maintain the deep red body coloration of the cock bullfinch, although natural colouring agents present in berries can be valuable in this regard.

When breeding, bullfinches will

use a variety of twigs and other material such as moss and even horse hair. They may choose their own site, if the aviary is heavily planted, or use a wicker basket provided for the purpose. This can be disguised beneath suitable vegetation so it is not fully exposed in the open. Conifers and broom are popular nesting sites for these birds. The female is largely responsible for selecting the nesting area, and will ultimately lay a clutch of four or five eggs, which she incubates alone for thirteen days. Make a variety of rearing foods available, including suitable invertebrates, greenstuff and soaked seed. Depending on the time of year, it may be possible to supply seeding plantain heads, which bullfinches will greedily consume. Avoid areas where such plants could have been contaminated by sprays or soiled by animals. Insects are most crucial during the early

days of life, with the parent birds gradually adding other items to their offsprings' diet as they get older.

As in related species, there are various distinctive races of Bullfinch recognized over its wide range. There can be a significant difference in size and markings. The larger Northern or Siberian Bullfinch (*P. p. pyrrhula*), for example, has a greyer back, and cocks have dull red coloration compared with the European subspecies. In the Japanese Bullfinch (*P. p. griseiventris*), the red markings are confined just to the face, whereas no red is present in cocks belonging to the true Siberian race *P. p. cineracea*, which is thus known as the Grey Bullfinch.

The close relationship between the various finches and the domesticated canary has led to the development of another side to the hobby of keeping such birds. The

Common Hawfinch
Coccothraustes coccothraustes

- **Distribution:** Europe, extending to western parts of Asia
- **Size:** 20 cm (8 in)
- **Diet:** Able to crack a variety of seeds, including pine nuts, with its powerful bill. Provide a mixture of cereal seeds, sunflower and pine nuts, as well as livefood, fruit and greenstuff
- **Sexing:** Hens can be recognized by their duller coloration, being browner overall
- **Compatibility:** Best accommodated in pairs, in view of their powerful bills. Can become aggressive when breeding
- **Pet appeal:** Unusual and interesting

The hawfinches as a group are characterized by their immensely powerful beaks, and they are said to be able to exert a pressure of 60 kg (132 lb) or more; they can crack cherry stones, for example, with relatively little effort. The common name for these birds is based on their supposed liking for the seeds of the hawthorn tree. Handle these birds carefully, preferably with gloves, to lessen the effect of their vice-like grip. (For further advice on how to handle and catch birds, see pages 16-17 in Part One of the book.) Hawfinches generally are not suitable for indoor cages, but can become quite tame in a garden aviary.

These birds build a cup-shaped nest, often lined with feathers, with the cock bird being largely responsible for the collection of material. An aviary planted with conifers will encourage the birds to select a suitable nesting site. They will also adopt wicker baskets for the purpose, which provide more support. The hen lays a clutch of three or four eggs, which she incubates alone for two weeks; the cock bird feeds her during this time, and may sit for brief periods when his mate leaves the nest site. Livefood, softbill and rearing foods are all taken, along with seed when there are chicks in the nest.

Problems seem most likely to arise when the youngsters get older. It appears that cock birds often become increasingly aggressive at this stage, being keen to encourage the hen to lay again before the first round of chicks have fledged, causing them to be neglected. For this reason, it may be preferable to house these hawfinches in trios for serious breeding attempts, keeping two hens in the company of one cock bird.

Related species include the Yellow-billed Grosbeak (*C. migratorius*) and the closely-related Japanese species (*C. personatus*). In spite of its name, the latter is also found in China as well as in Japan. The Japanese Grosbeak is a significantly larger bird, however, being at least 2.5 cm (1 in) bigger overall. The black plumage on the head of cock Japanese Grosbeaks does not extend over the whole of the head region, and hens lack the reddish tint to the plumage present in the Yellow-billed Grosbeak. Once they are properly acclimatized, both species are relatively hardy.

Below: **Common Hawfinch**
A handsome bird with a relatively large and very strong beak. Keep it in separate pairs in an aviary. It is not suitable for keeping in a cage and should be handled with care.

Above: **Common Bullfinch**
This species makes a rewarding aviary subject. Here, a pair attend the nest, the brownish hen clearly distinguishable from the cock bird.

crossing of two different species of finches yields hybrids, whereas the mating of a canary with a finch is described as muling. Both mules and hybrids are frequently exhibited. Such birds, although usually sterile, are highly prized, not only for their appearance, but also for their singing prowess. Bullfinch mules are unusual, however, because they are produced by mating a cock canary with a hen bullfinch. In other instances, a hen canary is required. It is possible to produce mules from breeding stock housed in cages, especially where the hen is a canary. Supply a wide range of rearing foods for the maximum chance of success.

AUSTRALASIAN FINCHES

The Australian finches are well-known in avicultural circles throughout the world, having been domesticated over many years. They have proved generally keen to nest, either in cages or flights, and various mutations have been developed in some cases, notably the Zebra Finch. The Asian species tend to be duller in overall coloration than their Australian counterparts, and, with the particular exception of the Bengalese Finch, are not as suitable for breeding in cages. This is because they appear to need the close stimulus of others of the same species in order to encourage reproductive activity. They can be kept in mixed groups, but should not be housed alongside the smaller waxbills, which are liable to be bullied, especially in fairly confined surroundings. The following is a representative selection of the species available.

Zebra Finch
Taeniopygia guttata

- **Distribution:** Over much of Australia, except Cape York Peninsula, and south and south-eastern coastal districts, as well as Tasmania. Also occurs on islands of the Flores group, to the north-west of Australia
- **Size:** 10 cm (4 in)
- **Diet:** Millets and canary seed, with greenfood
- **Sexing:** Hens lack the zebra-like patterning on the cock's throat, and the chestnut flank markings
- **Compatibility:** Can be safely kept in groups, or as part of a mixed aviary
- **Pet appeal:** Keen to nest and available in a range of colours

The Zebra Finch is one of the most ubiquitous finches in avicultural circles, with huge numbers being bred both in cages and aviaries throughout the world. They are extremely easy birds to cater for, and prove prolific, not even requiring livefood during the breeding season.

Their only drawback, certainly in the close confines of the home, may be their fairly monotonous calls, although these are not far carrying.

The early history of the Zebra Finch is not well documented, although they were first described as long ago as 1805. These birds occur in quite large flocks in the wild, feeding on grass seeds, and various mutations have been established from wild-caught stock of this type. While the vast majority of Zebra Finches are captive bred, a few individuals of the northern race from the Flores Islands are occasionally imported. These are invariably costly, compared with the average price of a Zebra Finch.

Indeed, the relatively low cost of these finches means they are well worth considering as exhibition birds, where finance is an important factor. Even top quality winning stock is

Below: **Zebra Finch**
A male of the normal type, showing the characteristic zebra-like markings on the throat. These are excellent beginners' birds.

much cheaper to acquire than in the case of budgerigars, for example, although competition on the show bench will be no less fierce. Zebra Finches, unlike budgerigars and canaries, are invariably shown in pairs of the same colour variety, rather than individually. Again, there are official standards laid down for the various colour forms.

One of the earliest mutations to be recorded for the Zebra Finch was the White. Such birds are pure white in colour, so the characteristic barring and other markings that usually serve to distinguish a cock bird are absent. Nevertheless, hens usually still have a paler beak and can be recognized accordingly. While the White mutation was first bred in the aviaries of a Sydney breeder in 1921, the colour form now known as the Chestnut-flanked White was initially seen further north, in a flock of wild Zebra Finches in the state of Queensland. Cock Chestnut-flanked White Zebra Finches retain the typical markings indicative of their sex, but hens of this colour are predominantly white; nevertheless, their black tear stripes and barred tail serve to distinguish them from the White mutation itself. A rare Albino form is also known, but these birds can be distinguished from Whites by their red eyes.

Some Pied Zebra Finches may be predominantly white in colour, or may closely resemble normals. The effects of this mutation, as in the case of other species, are exceedingly variable. Originating during 1935 in Denmark, Pied Zebras are the hardest colour variety to exhibit as a result, especially in view of the need for well-matched pairs of birds.

Among the other colours available,

the Fawn has attracted a considerable following, with birds of this colour being of a warm brown shade. A paler form is known as the Cream. This arose by combining the Fawn and Silver mutations. The Silver is not really a colour, but exerts a diluting influence on whatever colour it is combined with. As a result of this diluting effect, Grey Zebra Finches then appear silver in colour, whereas the Fawn coloration becomes paler as well.

Other mutations are known but are generally scarce at present. The effects of mutations are not restricted to the birds' colour; Crested Zebra Finches, with a circular crest on the forehead, have been developed since the 1960s. In common with other crested mutations, it is necessary to mate crested and non-crested stock together, so as not to compromise the hatchability of the offspring (see page 73). The crested character can be transferred to any colour. A more unusual mutation seen in the Zebra Finch simply affects the beak coloration; this becomes modified from red to yellow. The plumage in certain instances may be slightly paler, but this is not usually noticeable. At present, the Yellow-beaked mutation remains uncommon, being viewed by established breeders as an oddity, rather than a trait to be encouraged.

The Zebra Finch has a great deal to offer as an introduction to the keeping of the smaller seedeaters in general. As childrens' pets, these

Right: **Zebra Finch in flight**
As elegant in flight as when perched, these lively birds can be safely kept in groups and are ideal subjects to include in a mixed aviary.

birds are inexpensive to buy and easy to maintain. Pairs nest very readily, and will rear their chicks quite satisfactorily without any livefood. A double-breeding cage can be used to house a pair indoors, with either a small nestbox fitted or a wicker nesting basket fixed in place. While this can be supported at the front of the cage on the bars, it is better positioned on the back or the side. Two netting staples tacked firmly in place will serve to anchor the wire supports from the basket and thus the structure itself. By this means, the birds can be easily seen on the nest from outside the cage. Ideally, use a foreign-finch front, so that there is no risk of these small birds becoming caught between the bars of a normal cage front. It is even possible to make a suitable breeding cage by fixing a front of this type on to a stout cardboard box.

Zebra Finches build a relatively bulky nest, and will use a variety of material, including pieces of greenfood. Try to encourage them to use aviary nesting material, by teasing it out and placing it between the cage bars. Once the hen has laid, withdraw all unused material; otherwise nest-building may continue and the eggs become buried. Chop any greenfood fed at this stage into very small pieces so that it cannot be incorporated into the nest.

Cock birds become more vocal when they are ready to breed, but it is the hen that is more likely to be seen carrying nesting material. Typical clutch size varies from between four and six eggs, and the hen shares the incubation duties with her mate. The eggs should start to hatch after twelve days. Provide a suitable rearing food or even bread and milk sop for the adult birds, taking care as always to ensure that it does not turn sour.

Fledging occurs when the young finches are about eighteen days old, and within two weeks they will be feeding independently. It is best to remove them from a breeding cage at this stage, as their parents are likely to be nesting again and may be disturbed by the presence of their earlier chicks, possibly harassing them as a result. Sometimes, some Zebra Finches appear to develop bald patches. This is the result of feather plucking and is likely to occur when a pair has been kept short of nesting material during the building phase, or alternatively, when the birds are overcrowded. Unlike parrots, however, Zebra Finches will rapidly desist from such behaviour as soon as their environmental needs are met.

Young Zebra Finches are usually recognizable by their dark brownish beaks. They mature quite rapidly, and are certainly capable of breeding by the time they are nine months old. The lifespan of these small birds may extend over a period of eight years or more. Although relatively hardy, Zebra Finches will benefit from the provision of artificial lighting during the short days of winter in temperate climates, even if heating is not available. Since these finches are not destructive, they are unlikely to damage any electrical cabling, but if the light source is located within their aviary, protect the bulb from them with a suitable screen. A box made from wire mesh is ideal for this purpose. When starting with Zebra Finches, try to obtain young stock if possible. The birds will soon settle in new surroundings, and their age should be known with certainty. In older birds, there tends to be a build-up of scales on the legs, resulting in a noticeable thickening in most instances.

Below: **Chestnut-flanked White**
This attractive colour form of Zebra Finch was originally seen in a wild flock. In this pair, the typically marked male is on the right.

Gouldian Finch
Chloebia gouldiae

- **Distribution:** Northern parts of Australia
- **Size:** 12.5 cm (5 in)
- **Diet:** Essentially smaller cereal seeds, with niger added in small quantities. Can be fed dry or soaked. Also provide greenstuff on a regular basis
- **Sexing:** Hens can be distinguished by their lighter overall coloration
- **Compatibility:** Can be kept together in groups
- **Pet appeal:** Unrivalled coloration

Undeniably the most striking of all the Australian finches, the Gouldian was named by the naturalist John Gould for his wife Elizabeth, who accompanied him on a marathon journey to Australia in search of wildlife. The birds were first seen alive in Europe towards the end of the nineteenth century, and since then arguments have raged over their care. Indeed, some feel that Gouldian Finches are extremely difficult birds to maintain, and in view of their relatively high price, beginners are advised to look elsewhere. Yet providing healthy stock is obtained in the first instance, there is no reason why these birds should present any particular problems in terms of their management.

The head coloration of the Gouldian Finch varies in the wild, with both black-headed and red-headed birds being observed. The yellow-headed form is rarest; this is simply a dilute variant of the red-headed. Various mutations have also occurred in captive stock. In the White-breasted mutation the usual lilac coloration of the breast is replaced by white. This characteristic can be combined with any of the three head colours, although the black-headed form is invariably most common, being genetically dominant to the red-headed form.

The Gouldian Finch is an ideal species to keep in the home, provided that it can have adequate flying space. Indeed, outside Australia, there is a tendency for breeders to house Gouldians in cages during the breeding period. Since these birds are reputed to be sensitive to low temperatures, keep them in a minimum temperature of 10°C (50°F).

Gouldians are quite undemanding in a choice of nest site, adopting either an open-fronted box or a nesting basket for the purpose. Nesting material should be available, but pairs vary as to how much they will choose to use. Up to six eggs may form the average clutch, and the sexes share the incubation duties. The chicks should hatch approximately sixteen days later, and suitable rearing foods, including soaked seed, must be supplied.

Right: **Black-headed Gouldian Finch**
Their stunning appearance has endeared these agile finches to birdkeepers throughout the world. In this pair, the slightly less colourful female is at the top of the picture.

Left:
Yellow and Red-headed Gouldian
Two colour forms that add superb variation to these exquisite birds.

Above: **White-breasted Gouldian**
In this colour form the lilac breast is replaced by white, here shown with both red and black heads.

Softfood and greenfood, especially chickweed, will be taken in increasing quantities as the young finches develop.

On fledging, Gouldians are drab in comparison with their parents, and, as with the Greenfinch, are at risk at this time from 'going light' (see page 78). In order to minimize the likelihood of losses, ensure that the birds are able to feed themselves before transferring them to separate accommodation, and provide an adequate range of the foods that they have been used to previously. The importance of vitamins, minerals and trace elements in the diet has long been a subject of controversy. Like the Budgerigar, Gouldian Finches may have relatively high requirements in certain instances. Apart from providing mineralized grit and oyster-shell grit, always supply cuttlefish bone and an iodine block. Breeders in continental Europe also favour the provision of rock salt to these and other Australian finches, as a further source of minerals. Pieces of powdered charcoal, said to reduce the risk of digestive ailments, may also be included in the grit pot. In some cases, possibly for the nest sanitation, pieces of charcoal are transferred to the nest but not actually consumed.

Birds which pass through their first moult are unlikely to succumb to 'going light', and can themselves be paired up during the following year. The colour of the beak is a reliable indicator of breeding condition in the Gouldian Finch. The tip of the male beak turns cherry red, whereas that of the hen takes on a darker hue. It is advisable to restrict Gouldians to rearing two round of chicks in a year, although some breeders, relying on Bengalese Finches as foster-parents, will encourage their birds to lay again.

The widespread use of Bengalese in rearing Australian finches, particularly Gouldians, may have contributed to weakness in certain bloodlines and helped to create the impression of the Gouldian as a rather delicate bird, which is reinforced by its exotic coloration. Certainly, much of the early stock that reached Europe from Japan – where these finches were effectively farmed using Bengalese – was weak and did not thrive out of doors. Another possible contributory factor was the Gouldian Finch's apparent susceptibility to air-sac mites, which live in the bird's airways and can cause severe respiratory distress. This is manifested by heavy gasping after a period of exertion, as often occurs just before catching. These mites, although not directly fatal, can contribute to an overall state of malaise. It is now possible to overcome such infections by an injection of an antiparasitic compound called ivermectin administered by a veterinarian. The mites are probably passed from adults to their chicks while they are being fed in the nest, or during the weaning period. Some breeders rely on dichlorvos insecticidal strips hung in the birdroom, but these may have toxic effects on the birds in a confined, poorly ventilated space.

Diamond Sparrow

Emblema guttata

- **Distribution:** Eastern Australia
- **Size:** 11.5 cm (4.5 in)
- **Diet:** A mixture of small cereal seeds, including spray millet. Also provide greenfood and possibly some livefood
- **Sexing:** Virtually impossible by visual means, but hens may be smaller and slightly duller, notably around the head
- **Compatibility:** May be kept satisfactorily in groups
- **Pet appeal:** Attractive and keen to breed

The Diamond Sparrow or Fire-tail has been kept and bred in Europe since the late 1800s. In the wild, these birds are often found close to houses and, perhaps for this reason, they are usually quite tame by nature. Unfortunately, in the confines of a cage they tend to become obese. If possible, therefore, house them for at least part of the year in flights. The Diamond Sparrow can show a tendency to breed during the winter months in the northern hemisphere, so you may need to keep them indoors in warm surroundings as a result.

In an aviary, these birds will spend much of their time on the floor, foraging for spilt seeds and other edible items. Typically they construct a nest in a low shrub, or in a small nestbox supplied for the purpose. Both members of the pair actively contribute to the building process, preferring to use stems of green grass for the purpose, if these are available. The interior is lined with soft material, such as feathers. The hen lays between four and six eggs, with both birds taking it in turn to incubate them. The eggs start to hatch after a period of about thirteen days. While some pairs will rear their offspring satisfactorily without any livefood being offered, the chances of success are increased if you provide the adult birds with small invertebrates, softfood, an insectivorous mixture, soaked seed and greenstuff. Diamond Sparrows can prove quite prolific, rearing three broods of chicks in rapid succession, but prevent them from having any more. The young birds often do not fledge until they are nearly four weeks old, and then enter a rapid moult.

These finches are relatively hardy, and can live for over a decade, but not all breeders are successful with them. It is certainly best if the birds can pair off themselves, when they appear to develop a strong pair bond. Occasionally, cocks in breeding condition may become very aggressive and should be removed from a mixed collection. Avoid unnecessary interference with a pair with eggs or chicks; this may cause the birds to desert, although generally they are reliable parents.

Below: **Diamond Sparrow**
House these appealing birds in an aviary, where they will keep active enough to avoid becoming overweight.

Painted Finch

Emblema picta

- **Distribution:** Ranges across the western and central areas of Australia, extending to the western borders of Queensland, being found in arid areas
- **Size:** 11.5 cm (4.5 in)
- **Diet:** Typical mixture of smaller cereal seeds with greenfood
- **Sexing:** Hens have reduced areas of red on the head compared with the cock, with such plumage being restricted to the lores (in front of the eyes)
- **Compatibility:** Usually quite tolerant occupants of a mixed aviary
- **Pet appeal:** Will add colour and interest to the floor of an aviary

The Painted Finch was first introduced into Europe as long ago as 1869, and has since been bred on numerous occasions, although it is perhaps not as well known as some other Australian finches. This

is unfortunate, because apart from disliking damp surroundings, it is very hardy in captivity. They feed essentially on the ground, and should have adequate cover provided on the floor of the aviary. Painted Finches will not thrive in cages, although they can be kept in indoor flights. For breeding purposes, these birds prefer to construct their own nest in a tussock of grass. You should provide suitable screening with this in mind. They can be persuaded to use a nest-basket, but you will need to disguise it close to ground level for them to accept it. Also provide a ready supply of nesting material to encourage breeding. Unusually, these birds may prepare a raised area of stones and other similar debris on the ground and build their nest on top.

Right: **Painted Finch**
Bright, agile and colourful, these Australian finches will thrive in an aviary or spacious indoor flight. They will nest fairly readily in captivity.

The incubation period is about fifteen days, and the task of caring for the eggs and then the chicks is shared by both adult birds. They may take some insects once the youngsters have hatched. A shortage of suitable rearing foods will lead to young birds being ejected from the nest. As with other related species, the post-weaning period can be a difficult time. It is advisable to leave them in the company of their parents for as long as possible, and maintain a varied supply of foodstuffs, including soaked seed, throughout this period.

Australian finches generally are attractive birds, and aviary-bred stock of other species is quite readily available. If possible, purchase home-bred stock. A number of these birds are imported to the UK, the United States and elsewhere each year from mainland Europe, where they are bred in large numbers, but imported birds are liable to require more careful management. They are generally kept in heated surroundings, and should not be transferred immediately to an outside aviary or birdroom, as is possible with stock bred and housed under such conditions. Among other species that are available and that have similar requirements to those outlined above are Bicheno's Finch (*Poephila bichenovii*) and the Long-tailed or Heck's Grassfinch (*Poephila acuticauda*). The closely related Parrot-finches (*Erythura* sp.) also do best when housed in planted flights.

- **Distribution:** Does not occur in the wild
- **Size:** 10 cm (4 in)
- **Diet:** Smaller cereal seeds, including millet sprays, and greenstuff
- **Sexing:** No visual plumage distinctions between the sexes
- **Compatibility:** Very docile
- **Pet appeal:** Provides an ideal introduction to keeping finches

It is generally agreed by zoologists that the Bengalese Finch is a domesticated strain of the White-backed Munia, which originated in the East, either in China or Japan. One account suggests that these birds were first bred in China, and then introduced to Japan about two hundred and fifty years ago. From

Sharp-tailed Munia

Lonchura striata

- **Distribution:** India and Sri Lanka; Nicobar and Andaman Islands
- **Size:** 11.5 cm (4.5 in)
- **Diet:** A mixture of cereal seeds, to which paddy rice can be added, and greenstuff
- **Sexing:** No clear visual distinction between the sexes
- **Compatibility:** Social by nature and best kept in groups
- **Pet appeal:** Lively, usually keen to nest

The classificatory position of this finch is rather confused, with a number of distinct subspecies being recognized over its large range. The Sharp-tailed Munia itself is one of the duller races and is sometimes considered to be a distinct species in its own right (*L. acuticauda*), with other forms being described as White-backed Munias. These birds are usually encountered in flocks, frequently in the vicinity of

cultivated crops, which has led to them being persecuted in certain areas. They have been seen alive in Europe since the seventeenth century, and make lively if not spectacular aviary occupants. Like other munias, the White-backed is best kept in small groups in an aviary or an indoor flight, rather than a cage, enabling the birds to pair off naturally.

The Sharp-tailed Munia has been bred successfully on many occasions when kept under such conditions. They build a nest, which can be quite bulky, often adopting a partially open-fronted nestbox for this purpose. As many as eight eggs can form the clutch, with both birds taking it in turns to incubate the eggs. The chicks normally hatch after about two weeks. They can be reared without livefood, if a selection of other items such as egg-food, soaked seed and greenstuff are supplied on a daily basis. The fledging period is nearly three weeks, and the young birds will be

Above: **Sharp-tailed Munia**
Keep these active munias in groups to satisfy their social nature and allow them to pair off naturally.

independent about ten days later. They can usually be left safely alongside the other birds in the aviary if required.

It can be difficult to recognize recently fledged munias, since they closely resemble adults in appearance and soon moult into mature plumage within three months of hatching. As a general guide, they may appear duller than the adults, with buff-coloured underparts. The tolerant nature of these birds - even when breeding - and their lack of dependence on livefood compensate for their fairly drab appearance. Once acclimatized, Sharp-tailed Munias are quite hardy, but be sure to provide additional lighting during the winter months if they are housed in an outdoor aviary. Heat may also be required in adverse weather at this time of year.

Japan they were dispatched to Europe, with the first examples being exhibited at the London Zoo in about 1860. Since that time, these finches have become widely appreciated, not only in their own right, but also as foster parents for the eggs and chicks of species that are less reliable in cage or aviary surroundings. One of the great virtues of the Bengalese is that it will breed readily in cage surroundings, although, unfortunately, it is not possible to distinguish the sexes until the male is in breeding condition. At this time, the song of the cock bird is a clear pointer to its sex. Again, once identified, the finches in question can be rung with differently coloured split celluloid rings, which serve to act as permanent markers for future reference.

When breeding, Bengalese Finches are extremely undemanding.

They will readily adopt nesting boxes or baskets as breeding sites, or may even build their nest in a shrub in a planted aviary. Always make available a suitable variety of materials to ensure that a solid structure results. The clutch size may vary from two to nine eggs, with an average being five. Incubation lasts for about thirteen days, and the adult birds may consume the eggshells of their newly hatched offspring. They are extremely devoted parents and tend to tolerate more interference than other finches, although obviously this should be avoided if possible. Bengalese are able to rear their chicks on soaked seed and egg-food, but difficulties can arise if the young of more naturally insectivorous species are fostered to them. Try to encourage them to take a high-quality softbill mixture under these circumstances,

which should help to overcome the need for insects.

Their own chicks may not fledge until nearly four weeks old, and they are usually dependent on the adults for a further two weeks. If the youngsters are cage-bred, remove them to separate accommodation so as not to overcrowd the adult birds, which are likely to be nesting again. Restrict them to a maximum of three clutches per year. Young Bengalese can be bred from the age of approximately nine months onwards. Bengalese are much steadier than related species, but equally hardy, and invariably keen to go to nest.

It is not perhaps surprising, therefore, that a variety of colour forms have been developed. Darker coloured birds are described as chocolate, in contrast to fawn individuals. They can be self-coloured, or combined with irregular

white markings, creating a pied appearance. A rarer, pure white form is also known, as is a crested variety, which needs to be bred in the same way as recommended for the Gloster Canary (see page 73). Other mutations have also been reported, but remain scarce. Some such birds may prove to be hybrids; for example, crosses with the Bronze-winged Mannikin (*Lonchura cucullata*) have yielded offspring that are almost totally black in coloration.

Below: **Bengalese Finch**
Universally acclaimed for its friendly disposition and enthusiasm for breeding, this finch is an excellent beginner's bird. It is often used as a foster parent to raise the chicks of other species. This is a fawn and white Bengalese Finch, one of several colour forms that range from dark chocolate to a rare pure white.

Spice Bird
Lonchura punctulata

- **Distribution:** Over a wide area of Asia into Indochina, from India eastwards to Formosa, and southwards over many islands, including Java, parts of the Celebes and Philippines
- **Size:** 12.5 cm (5 in)
- **Diet:** Small cereal seeds, including paddy rice, plus greenstuff
- **Sexing:** No external distinctions between the sexes
- **Compatibility:** Can be kept safely in groups or with other birds of similar size
- **Pet appeal:** Attractive and easy to cater for

Although the munias or mannikins also occur in Africa, it is the various Asian forms that are most commonly available in aviculture. This species occurs over a large area, whereas other related birds tend to have a much more restricted distribution. Again, various distinct races are recognized on the basis of plumage differences, and the only straightforward means of sexing these birds is on the basis of the cock bird's song. When singing, the cock will stand quite vertically on the perch and may also display to an intended mate by proffering a stem of grass as an initial gesture. If she responds in a similar fashion, holding a piece of nesting material in her beak, the cock will continue displaying until the hen indicates a willingness to mate. The song in fact is extremely quiet, being less audible than the normal call note of this species.

Breeding follows the typical pattern for members of this genus. A nestbox will be filled with suitable material, creating a bulky nest within, and then both sexes incubate the eggs for approximately two weeks. The chicks will be reared simply on a suitable rearing food, augmented with greenfood and soaked seed. Some pairs may prove more insectivorous than others if supplied with livefood. The fledging time is about three weeks, but the young birds will still return to roost in the nest alongside their parents at night.

Spice Birds are docile by nature, even when breeding, although cocks have a tendency to squabble if housed in cages alongside hens. Breeding results are more likely to be successful under aviary conditions, where the birds will probably be less disturbed.

Right: **Spice Bird**
Also known as the Nutmeg Finch, Spotted Munia and Spice Finch, this jaunty bird makes a fine, easy-care subject for a mixed aviary. The cock bird's quiet song and distinctive breeding display form the simplest way of distinguishing the sexes in this handsome species.

Java Sparrow
Lonchura (Padda) oryzivora

- **Distribution:** Thought to have originated on the islands of Java and Bali, but has since spread over a much wider area, ranging to Malaya, the Moluccas, the Philippines and other Asian localities
- **Size:** 14 cm (5.5 in)
- **Diet:** Small cereal seeds, including paddy rice plus some greenstuff and possibly livefood
- **Sexing:** The sexes are alike in appearance
- **Compatibility:** Keep members of this species in groups, or in the company of munias
- **Pet appeal:** Invariably sleek

The Java Sparrow often occurs in close proximity to agricultural areas. and, because of the damage that flocks can cause to the growing crops, it is also known as the Rice Bird. These finches have been kept in Europe since the nineteenth century and possibly earlier, with the first definite breeding success taking place during 1890 in Switzerland. Although they can be kept in cages, these birds do best in groups in indoor flights or outside aviaries.

Java Sparrows tend to breed better on a colony basis, where they can pair off themselves. They will adapt a budgerigar nestbox for their purposes, lining it with suitable material. Up to eight eggs may be laid, although four to six is more usual. Incubation is shared by the adult birds, and the chicks hatch in about two weeks. The usual foods should be available to them at this stage, and within a month, the young Java Sparrows will leave the nest. A further three weeks or so later they become fully independent. At this stage, they can be distinguished by their blackish beaks and the yellowish tinge to the white plumage on their heads. The youngsters will have moulted for the first time by three months of age, and it may then be possible to identify cock birds by their song.

Although Java Sparrows are not so widely bred as some finches, several mutations have emerged and are now successfully established. Indeed, the mutant forms appear to nest more readily in some cases than the native Grey Java Sparrow. The original mutation is believed to have occurred in China, and was then introduced to Japan several centuries ago. This is the White form, although, in most instances, there will be flecks of darker plumage still present on such birds, rendering them pied. Young birds of this colour invariably fledge with grey markings on their backs.

The other mutation commonly seen today is of much more recent origin. It is thought that the Cinnamon or Fawn Java Sparrow was first bred in Australia in the late 1950s. It has since become quite widespread in Europe. Such birds have the grey areas replaced by a warm shade of brown. The requirements of these mutations do not differ from those of the normal Grey. Once acclimatized, all are hardy and remain in immaculate plumage throughout their lives.

Below: **Java Sparrow**
This is the normal grey form. Colour mutations may breed more readily.

Left: **Red-crested Cardinal**
*Their striking coloration and natural
vivacity make these cardinals
attractive birds to keep in an aviary.
The colour may fade in captivity
over a period of time.*

Right: **Black-crested Finch**
*A male specimen of this strikingly
marked species. Pairs will nest fairly
readily in a planted flight. Provide
plentiful supplies of livefood during
the rearing period to ensure that the
chicks grow into sturdy youngsters.*

Black-crested Finch
Lophospingus pusillus

- **Distribution:** Bolivia, Argentina
  and Paraguay
- **Size:** 12.5 cm (5 in)
- **Diet:** A diet of mixed canary seed,
  to which millet has been added.
  Greenfood and livefood should
  also be supplied on a regular
  basis
- **Sexing:** Hens can be
  distinguished by their grey rather
  than black crests. They also have
  whiter throats
- **Compatibility:** Can prove
  aggressive, especially when
  breeding
- **Pet appeal:** Unusual appearance

The various perching birds found in
Central and South America are
generally not well known in
aviculture. This particular species of
bunting – also known as the Pygmy
Cardinal – has never been common,
yet pairs, when available, have
usually proved quite ready nesters.
They require a planted flight when
breeding, as this will afford them a
high degree of security. The hen
alone is responsible for constructing
the nest, and may even adopt a
canary nest-pan for the purpose. A
range of suitable supports should be
available, as the nest itself may tend
to be rather loose. They have even
used nestboxes for the purpose. The
hen sits alone, with the chicks
hatching after an incubation period
of about twelve days. The young
birds grow rapidly and should then
fledge in a similar period of time.
Supply livefood during the rearing
phase, along with other items, such
as soaked seed and insectivorous
food. Clutches usually consist of only
two or three eggs, but the hen lays
repeatedly during a breeding season,
often before the earlier chicks are
fully independent.

The fledging time can be a difficult
period since the young birds are still
quite immature at this stage. They
may succumb to cold or become
saturated in a shower of rain, and
need to be watched accordingly.
Unfortunately, cock birds also
become aggressive towards their
offspring at about the time they
begin to eat independently.
Therefore, transfer young Black-
crested Finches to separate
accommodation as soon as
possible. These birds live quite
satisfactorily in indoor
accommodation, and have nested
successfully under these conditions.
Pairs are best housed on their own
in any event. Although the song of
cock birds is not spectacular, it is
nevertheless quite appealing.

Red-crested Cardinal
Paroaria coronata

- **Distribution:** From Southeast
  Brazil to Paraguay, Bolivia,
  Uruguay and northern Argentina
- **Size:** 19 cm (7.5 in)
- **Diet:** A mixed diet of seeds, with
  softbill food and livefood, as well
  as some fruit and greenstuff
- **Sexing:** Impossible to distinguish
  the sexes reliably by plumage
  distinctions. Hens may be smaller
  in some cases
- **Compatibility:** Likely to prove
  aggressive, especially when
  breeding
- **Pet appeal:** Unusual appearance
  and lively by nature

First bred in Europe as long ago as
1836, the Red-crested Cardinal is an
easy bird to maintain, taking a wide
variety of foodstuffs. Although often
proving quite social in a mixed
collection, it is preferable to house a

breeding pair of these birds on their
own in an aviary, providing adequate
cover to encourage breeding. They
tend to prefer using a bush or other
vegetation as a site for their nest,
incorporating whatever material they
can find in the aviary for the
purpose. The female is largely
responsible for the construction of
the nest, although the cock bird will
help his mate by gathering material.

A clutch typically consists of three
or four eggs, and the hen will sit on
her own for about two weeks until
the eggs start to hatch. At first, the
parents feed small livefood almost
exclusively to the chicks, which, like
the young of other buntings, grow
rapidly and often leave the nest
when they are only two weeks old.
The cock is then responsible for
their care until they are independent,
about two weeks later. Remove the
youngsters – easily distinguishable at
this stage by their dull greyish heads
– as soon as possible, since the hen

is likely to be nesting again for a
second time.

Red-crested Cardinals are not
especially talented songsters and
can prove nervous when first
acquired, but will soon settle in their
surroundings. Although it is possible
to keep them in an outdoor aviary
throughout the year, they must have
adequate protection and be fully
acclimatized beforehand. Avoid
mixing these birds; they can prove
surprisingly aggressive with little
warning. In order to maintain the
bright red head coloration of this
species, it may be necessary to use
colour food. Other related species,
such as the Pope Cardinal (*P.
dominicana*) and the Yellow-billed
Cardinal (*P. capitata*) need similar
care. The latter species – slightly
smaller at 16.5 cm (6.5 in) in length –
is said to be less aggressive, and
can be sexed without difficulty. Hens
have duller heads and grey rather
than black backs.

Red Avadavat
Amandava amandava

- **Distribution:** Distinct populations range over western Pakistan to India; Burma, Nepal, Indochina, Java and islands to the east
- **Size:** 10cm (4 in)
- **Diet:** Small cereal seeds, including millet sprays, greenstuff and suitable livefood
- **Sexing:** Hens can be recognized by their duller body coloration, compared with cocks in breeding condition
- **Compatibility:** Quite social. Can be housed in the company of waxbills
- **Pet appeal:** Easy to cater for, and breeds quite readily

Few birds are known under such a wide variety of common names as this species: these include Strawberry Finch, Red Waxbill and Tiger Finch. Belonging to the same genus as the Golden-breasted Waxbill of Africa (*A. subflava*, see page 57), this species is the only waxbill in which the cock has a distinctive breeding plumage. Now less often available than formerly, the Red Avadavat can be bred quite satisfactorily in a cage. Indeed, one aviculturist developed a strain of ten generations from stock housed in breeding cages. However, birds kept indoors over a long period of time and fed essentially on hard seed only are likely to develop abnormal black areas of plumage. Although this in itself does not appear to harm the bird, it is an indication that environmental conditions could probably be improved. Such changes can be transitory, appearing at one moult and then disappearing again at the next. Cock birds are most likely to show signs of this complaint, known as acquired melanism.

When breeding, the cock bird is largely responsible for collecting material that the hen uses to construct the nest. Up to seven eggs may be laid, and these should hatch after an incubation period of about twelve days. Fledging occurs approximately three weeks later. Unlike some waxbills, the Red Avadavat appears less dependent on livefood when there are chicks in the nest, although a supply should be maintained if at all possible. It is best to house these particular finches in an outdoor aviary during the warmer part of the year, and then overwinter them in an indoor flight. Especially when first obtained, they can be delicate; do not keep newly imported stock out of doors, certainly for their first winter.

Below: **Red Avadavat**
An excellent bird for cage or aviary, this species will breed readily and reward its owner with beauty and a tuneful song. Ideal for beginners.

PARROTS

The Order Psittaciformes consists of approximately three hundred and thirty species, which are mainly confined to the tropical regions of the world, although there are a few notable exceptions, such as the Kakarikis (*Cyanoramphus* sp.) that occur on islands to the south of New Zealand. The majority of parrots occur in Central and South America, with the most southerly species being the Austral Conure (*Enicognathus ferrugineus*), which ranges to Tierra del Fuego at the southern tip of South America.

A number of distinctive features set parrots apart from other birds. They have a sharply curved upper beak that fits over their lower bill. This arrangement has led to these birds being described as hookbills in the United States. The degree of curvature depends on the species concerned, and this in turn is a reflection of its function. The Long-billed Corella (*Cacatua tenuirostris*), for example, uses its elongated upper mandible to dig for roots. In some instances, the fleshy tongue within a parrot's beak is also modified to assist with feeding habits, as in lories and lorikeets.

The perching arrangement of parrots is also unusual, but not unique in the avian kingdom. Their zygodactyl grip, with two toes pointing forwards and two behind the perch, is shared with some other birds, notably toucans and barbets, but parrots also use their feet to hold food up to their beaks. There are exceptions to this behaviour, however, notably in the case of budgerigars and other parrots that tend to feed on the ground. Studies show that the majority of parrots have a tendency to use one foot in preference to the other. This can be seen in pet birds, with the left foot often being preferred.

Another well-known characteristic of parrots is their potentially long lifespan, although this varies according to the species concerned. The longevity of most parrots is measured in decades, however, with some individuals living into their seventies. Clearly, they are more likely to achieve this age when kept as pets; mortality in the wild will account for birds long before they have reached their maximum natural lifespan.

Above: *An Amazon Parrot nestling developing its first feathers. Hand-raising a parrot demands patience and perseverance.*

Right: **Rainbow Lorikeet**
These superbly coloured parrots from Australasia make playful and lively subjects for a garden aviary.

Parrots in the home

The popularity of parrots stems partly from their ability to mimic sounds, including that of the human voice. Yet not all species are as talented as others in this respect and some can be extremely noisy. Parrots, providing they are obtained young, can also become extremely tame and devoted to their owners. Strangers may be viewed with suspicion, however; never try to pet an unfamiliar bird, as you may well end up with a bad bite on your finger. Indeed, the larger parrots especially have very powerful beaks, and this can be a deterrent to keeping them in a home with young children. In these circumstances always provide close supervision, even with a tame bird. As some parrots mature, they can develop unreliable temperaments, remaining tame for the majority of the time and then suddenly biting without provocation. Cockatoos can be a particular liability in this regard. A parrot may give some indication before launching into an attack of this kind, by constricting its pupils. This makes the eyes, in Amazon Parrots especially, take on a more colourful appearance for a fleeting moment. This response is a sign of sexual arousal, normally preceding mutual feeding in a compatible pair.

When seeking a parrot of any species as a pet, do not be in too much of a hurry to obtain a bird. Remember that the parrot will be part of the family for many years, and the high cost of acquiring an unsuitable bird makes the purchase an expensive mistake. In the first instance, decide on the particular species that you want. Bear in mind that the larger parrots are probably the most demanding of all pet birds, certainly in terms of the time you must give them on a daily basis. Gregarious by nature, many pet parrots will often pine if deprived of human company and may resort to feather-plucking, which will prove almost impossible to correct on a permanent basis.

Try to get some idea of the likely cost of obtaining a bird of the particular species you have in mind. Availability is likely to vary, depending on the country concerned and the stock held by aviculturists. For example, it is virtually impossible to obtain macaws in Australia, at present, because of a total ban on importation of such birds and the tiny number of macaws still kept in Australian collections. Conversely, in the United States, relatively large numbers of macaws are both imported and bred annually, so that there will be little difficulty in acquiring a suitable bird.

The key factor in obtaining a parrot that will develop into a good pet is to select a young bird of the chosen species, preferably one that has just started to feed itself. Clearly, a hand-raised bird is likely to be the best proposition, as it will have no fear of humans, having been reared in a domestic environment. There is, of course, a considerable amount of work involved in rearing chicks by hand from the egg, and hand-raised parrots are usually relatively expensive. In the long term,

however, they are likely to be the most satisfactory pets.

Make contact with a breeder by studying the columns of the various pet bird magazines. Alternatively, seek out your local bird club; there is almost certain to be someone there who keeps parrots and may be able to put you in touch with a friend, even if they cannot help you directly. Certain pet stores, especially in the United States, also stock domestically bred, hand-raised parrots, while large-scale specialist breeding units are becoming more common. The added bonus of obtaining a baby parrot from a breeder is that it will not have been subjected to the sudden changes in environment that an imported parrot will have experienced. Nevertheless, always obtain a diet sheet when you purchase your parrot, and avoid any dramatic change to the feeding regimen as far as possible.

The majority of parrots kept as pets are fed on a diet consisting largely of seeds, augmented with some greenstuff and fruit. There are exceptions, however, since lories, lorikeets and Hanging Parrots need to be given a nectar solution on a daily basis. It is likely that many of the cases of feather-plucking and poor breeding results could be improved if owners offered a better diet to their birds.

Prepare everything before getting your parrot home. Wash the cage, as dirt can accumulate while it is being stored at the shop, and ensure that it is as clean as possible before you place the new parrot inside. In budgerigar cages with hooded feeders, sprinkle seed on the floor close to the full feeders to encourage birds that may not be used to feeders of this type.

Use a closed box with ventilation holes to transport your parrot home. Avoid using a cage, in which it is likely to become distressed, clinging to the bars and damaging its plumage. Do not leave any parrot unsupervised in a box for any length of time, however, if it can reach the ventilation holes. These will provide a starting point for the bird to chew its way out of the container. For this reason, punch ventilation holes near the top of a relatively deep cardboard box. A plywood box is undoubtedly a safer option, however, and essential if the parrot is being moved by public transport.

Do not be surprised if at first a young hand-reared parrot begs for food, and then proves reluctant to eat when offered it. The weaning process in young parrots can prove protracted; in extreme cases, it may last for a year, although this is exceptional. Generally, however, as the bird starts to feed itself, often on soaked seeds, it will continue to call for food, which it then largely rejects. Always keep a close watch on the amount of food that a newly acquired parrot is eating, and its droppings. Young parrots are relatively soft-feathered and do not have the sleek appearance of an adult in most cases. They also tend to sleep for longer periods, which should not be confused with illness, the most likely sign of which will be a loss of appetite.

Budgerigar
Melopsittacus undulatus

- **Distribution:** Over most of Australia, but notably absent from the eastern seaboard and Tasmania. Nomadic by nature
- **Size:** 18 cm (7 in)
- **Diet:** A basic mixture of cereal seeds - millet and canary seed, with oats occasionally. Also greenfood and carrot
- **Sexing:** Hens develop brown ceres, most noticeable when they are in breeding condition. Those of cock birds are blue or purplish in colour
- **Compatibility:** Can be kept in groups, and also in the company of cockatiels. May live in harmony alongside larger finches, notably whydahs, weavers and java sparrows, but can tend to prove aggressive towards such birds
- **Pet appeal:** Still the most popular pet bird in the world, and justifiably so

When the naturalist John Gould returned to the UK from Australia with the first live budgerigars seen in Europe, it is unlikely that he could have foreseen the dramatic impact that these parakeets would create over the course of a few decades. Gould's pair nested while in the care of his brother-in-law, Charles Coxen,

Above: **Cobalt Blue Budgerigar**
Two features show this to be an immature bird: the barring pattern on the head extends down to the cere and the eyes are of a solid colour, without the white irises.

and subsequently, others were imported from Australia. By the 1880s, forty years later, commercial breeding units catering for as many as 100,000 budgerigars were established in Europe to meet the demand for these birds.

In the wild the Budgerigar lives a nomadic lifestyle, ranging across the interior of Australia, seeking out the grass seeds on which it feeds. Huge flocks can congregate in suitable areas, moving on again as soon as the food supply becomes exhausted. These parakeets are well adapted to live in this arid environment. It is said that they can exist for days without water, but, nevertheless, a fresh supply should always be available to domesticated stock.

Captive breeding over the course of generations has radically altered the appearance of the budgerigar, and, simultaneously, has helped to maintain its popularity. No other psittacine has achieved such a strong international following.

Left: **Blue and Gold Macaw**
This is one of the most familiar of the large parrots, being seen widely in zoos and bird gardens throughout the world. This rear-view shows the full majestic sweep of the bird.

Above: **Light Green Budgerigar**
This is the wild colour from which all other colours have developed.

Mutations and colour forms

One of the factors that has contributed to the widespread interest in the budgerigar is the wide range of colours that have been developed. The wild budgerigar is light green, although occasionally, a few mutant individuals have been seen in wild flocks. One of the earliest sightings was of a yellow form. This colour was subsequently produced in Belgium, during 1872. Such birds have black eyes and mauve cheek patches, which serve to distinguish them from the Lutino mutation that also first appeared in Belgium, seven years later. Lutinos have white markings on their face, with reddish eyes, and are in intense deep buttercup yellow overall.

Since relatively little was known about the mode of inheritance of such colours, the early Lutino bloodline faded into obscurity as the mutation was lost. A separate strain, from which today's Lutinos are derived, emerged in Germany during 1936. Albinos, which are pure white with red eyes, occurred just beforehand, in 1931. These birds were in fact used to develop the Lutino by careful pairings, as the genetical principles became more completely understood.

The Blue mutation of the budgerigar appeared in 1878, but disappeared, re-emerging in 1881. It was first shown in England during 1910 at the Horticultural Hall, London, where it created a sensation at the time. Indeed, such was the great international interest in budgerigars that some were sold to Japan for fantastic prices that seem high even by today's standards. Modification to the basic light green coloration was then achieved when the dark factor mutation occurred in 1915. This led to the emergence of first the Dark Green and then the Olive, which has two dark factors in its genetic make-up. In the blue series budgerigars, the equivalent colours became known as Cobalt and Mauve respectively. Then, by

Above: **Opaline Budgerigar**
A pair showing the typical alteration of the markings on the head.

the early 1930s, the violet factor emerged, and this, when combined with dark and blue characters, led to the appearance of the deep visual violet, which has remained a popular, although rare, colour ever since.

Also during the 1930s, the previously solid colours of the budgerigar became split into blue and white, and green and yellow forms for the first time. Such birds became known as Pieds, and two genetically and visually distinct mutations are now recognized. The Danish Recessive Pied was first bred about 1933, while in Australia, the Dominant variety appeared. These two forms can be separated visually, not only on grounds of size – the Dominant Pied is significantly larger than its Recessive counterpart – but also by their eyes. Those of the Recessive Pied are a deep plum colour, while those of a mature Dominant Pied have white irises and black pupils. The cere colour of adult cock birds provides another means of distinguishing between the two mutations; those of Dominant Pieds are blue, whereas in the case of Recessive Pieds, the cere always remains purplish, as in an immature bird. In this particular instance, there is also a slight difference in temperament, with Recessive Pieds tending to be more flighty by nature.

Among the other colours bred during the 1930s was the Grey form. As in the case of the Pieds, both recessive and dominant forms were developed, but the former type was then lost during the Second World War. The Grey mutation now widely kept is derived from Australian stock, although it may also have occurred separately in Germany during 1936. Before this time, it had been assumed that yellow could not occur on a blue budgerigar, being replaced by white plumage. The emergence of the Yellow-faced Blue mutation,

Above: **Violet Budgerigar**
A cock bird of this highly prized colour. The violet factor arose during the 1930s and was combined with dark and blue characters.

Below: **Lutino Budgerigar**
The deep yellow of this elegant colour form has made it a firm favourite. The red eyes and white facial markings are typical.

Above: **Recessive Pied Budgerigar**
An attractive hen bird. The proportions of each colour can vary from one bird to another. The eyes of Recessive Pieds are dark plum.

also in about 1936, was therefore sensational, and this trait was soon transferred to Grey budgerigars.

Apart from changes to the basic body coloration, mutations affecting the markings, notably on the wings, are also now well established. The Cinnamon has the effect of diluting the natural black patterning on the back, to create brownish markings. In addition, the eyes are also reddish. Yellow-wings, White-wings and Grey-wings are also known, while the Opaline has altered the distribution of the markings on the head, lightening the patterning and creating, in a good exhibition bird, a clear V-shaped area at the top of the wings. The Opaline characteristic can be combined with any colour, with such birds being described as Opaline Light Greens, for example.

Feather variants have also occurred, the most notable of these being the three crested mutations. Birds of this type were first bred during 1935 in Australia, while separate strains were evolved in France and Canada. The Tufted mutation has raised plumage, creating a tuft on its forehead, while the full circular mutation is characterized by a complete fringe of feathers around its head. In the case of the half-circular, the crest is restricted to the front of the head. Again, the crested mutations can be combined with any colour.

Numerous other budgerigar mutations are recognized, apart from the common varieties listed above, and new colours are likely to emerge in the future. The most recent mutation, which has become widely distributed since being bred in Australia during 1978, is the Spangled. The markings on the back are altered so that they become rather like those of the Pearl Cockatiel, with the dark feathers having a central paler area. The throat spots are similarly affected.

Buying budgerigars

There appears to be no significant difference between the talking abilities of budgerigars of varying mutations, but it may be difficult to obtain a bird of a particular colour or combination, such as a Crested Violet. The asking price is likely to be influenced by the colour of the bird in question to some extent, as well as its type. This is a reflection of the bird's pedigree; exhibition breeders aim to produce budgerigars which conform as closely as possible to the prescribed standards for the particular variety concerned. As a general rule, such birds are significantly larger than the average budgerigar kept in a garden aviary, and certainly bigger than their wild counterparts. This is not to say that they are necessarily healthier. Many exhibition birds tend to put on excessive weight, particularly if housed in cages indoors, where there will be less opportunity to exercise than in aviary surroundings. Furthermore, relatively little of their food intake is used to maintain their

body temperature and is thus likely to be stored as body fat. The average lifespan of such birds tends to be shorter, and they are more at risk from fatty tumours, known as lipomas, than budgerigars of less illustrious origins.

Since budgerigars are so widely kept, it is not usually difficult to contact a local breeder. In order to obtain a budgerigar that will settle well as a pet and become hand tame, you will need to acquire a youngster as soon as it is independent of its parents, at about six weeks of age. There is a popular view that only cock birds will talk, but no real difference exists between the sexes in this regard. Behavioural difficulties may be apparent in single birds of either sex kept on their own, once they mature. Since hens usually become destructive before laying, and can inflict damage on wallpaper and plants in the room if they are flying free, many owners prefer to opt for a young cock budgerigar in the first instance. Nevertheless, male birds are also capable of using their beaks for destructive purposes, and may feed toys in their cage, as well as attempting to mate on their owner's finger when the opportunity arises

There are various key indicators that will enable you to recognize a budgerigar of around six weeks of age. In most colours, the barring pattern on the head extends right down to the cere, immediately above the beak. The cere itself is purplish in colour in both sexes at this age, but tends to be darker and more prominent in young cock birds. By the age of about nine weeks onwards, the white irises surrounding the black or red pupils start to appear; up until this point, the eyes will be of a solid colour. A final note should be made of the appearance of the beak; in most cases, there will be a dark tip in a recently fledged budgerigar, although this does not apply in the case of yellow and

Above: **Recessive Pied Budgerigar**
This is the other colour combination commonly seen in Pied Budgerigars. There may be two shades of yellow.

white budgerigars. Check that the upper part of the beak fits properly over the lower – abnormalities may be apparent in young birds.

While a breeder is likely to have records of when a particular group of budgerigars was hatched, this is not likely to be the case in a pet store. The points listed above therefore assume much greater significance. Ask the assistant if the birds are finger tame. As a general rule, it is normally possible to approach a recently fledged budgerigar quite closely, being able to touch its feet in most instances without it appearing frightened.

If you are buying budgerigars for an outdoor aviary, their age is less significant, although young adult birds are to be recommended for breeding purposes. This applies especially to hens, whose optimum breeding life may not extend much beyond six years, whereas cocks can remain fertile for much longer. If a bird is rung with a closed circular band, this will be a reliable indicator of its age, with the year normally being indicated on the ring. Otherwise, there is no means of assessing the bird's age accurately.

Check specifically that there is no sign of scaly face on any adult budgerigar that you are thinking of buying. This ailment shows as whitish encrustations, usually on the beak bordering the cere. It results from a mite infestation and, although scaly face can be treated easily, affected birds need to be kept separate, so as not to spread the mites to other budgerigars. The parasites may be transferred by direct contact or via perches. Cock budgerigars in breeding condition will tap their beaks repeatedly on a perch as a display gesture, and could acquire such mites in this way.

Breeding budgerigars in aviaries

If you are keeping budgerigars together in breeding groups, take several precautions in order to minimize the risk of fighting occurring. In the first instance, ensure that all the budgerigars are paired, and especially that there are no odd hens in the aviary as they can be especially aggressive during the breeding period.

Position all the nestboxes at the same height in order to prevent hens fighting to secure the highest location. Space the nestboxes under cover around the aviary, and include more boxes than pairs of birds. This will ensure that there will be an adequate choice available to the budgerigars, which again serves to minimize the risk of territorial aggression. Never introduce new birds to an established colony during the breeding season, as this is almost certain to upset the group, and can lead to losses in the nest, quite apart from adult birds.

Budgerigars are extremely prolific, and will breed over most of the year, if given the opportunity so to do. In cold weather, however, there is an increased risk of hens succumbing to egg-binding and losses of both eggs and chicks as a result of chilling. In any event, overbreeding of budgerigars is not to be recommended; an increased incidence of the feather disorder French Moult, for example, is likely to become apparent. As a result,

Above: A hen Budgerigar feeds her young with partly digested seed and crop milk in the nesting box.

therefore, it is usual to confine the breeding period out of doors to the warmer months of the year, placing nextboxes in the aviary during early spring and removing them in the autumn. This should enable the birds to rear a maximum of two or three rounds of chicks during the year.

The most reliable indicator of the budgerigar's condition is its cere, which in the hen will become increasingly brown as the time for breeding approaches. She is likely to consume more cuttlefish bone, and, immediately before laying, her droppings may be noticeably larger and take on an unpleasant pungent odour. The number of eggs laid in a clutch is usually about four or five, although up to ten is not unknown. When breeding budgerigars communally, it is always possible that hens may occasionally share a nestbox, with a correspondingly large number of eggs being laid. The cock often joins his mate for periods in the nestbox, or remains outside, keeping away potential rivals. She will sit alone throughout the incubation period, with the eggs being produced on alternate days. They should start to hatch after a period of eighteen days, although it may be slightly longer in the case of the first egg. The hen does not always start incubating in earnest until the second egg is laid.

Above: Plucking the mask feathers to achieve the accepted pattern of throat spots for an exhibition bird.

Below: The desired result, six evenly spaced round throat spots, two merging with cheek patches.

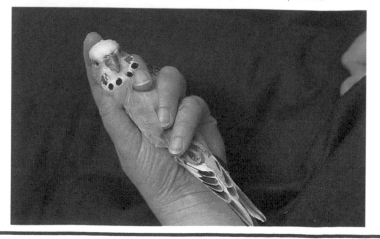

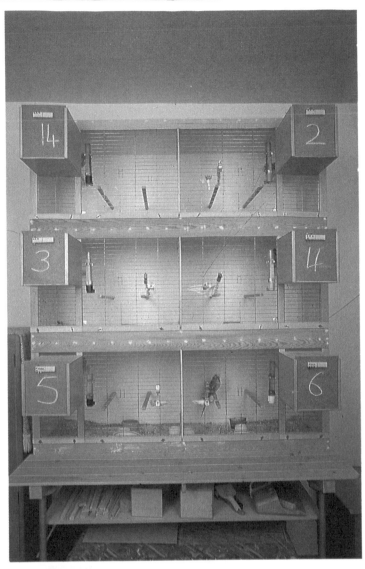

A high protein rearing food or even brown bread soaked in milk will be useful once the chicks hatch, assuming that the adult birds will take such items. Chopped greenfood placed on top of the dish can encourage reluctant individuals to sample such items. Be sure to remove any perishable foodstuffs at the end of each day, before they can sour. The chicks grow rapidly, and so be sure to inspect the nestbox regularly. Hens rarely resent this interference, providing they are warned in advance. If the hen is within, tap gently on the outside of the nestbox before opening the door. Once the chicks are about a week old, change the material lining the concave in the nestbox regularly. This applies particularly to pairs described as 'wet feeders', since their nests become badly soiled with the correspondingly watery droppings of their offspring.

There is a danger in allowing droppings to accumulate in the nestbox. If the chicks' feet become caked with droppings that harden, this can lead to malformation of the claws, and even restrict the blood supply to the toe, unless the dirt is removed. Always soak a chick's foot for a few moments in a small pot of tepid water before attempting to remove the nest dirt. This will serve to soften the deposit, which you should then be able to chip off carefully with your finger nail. In order to prevent damage to a claw, chip the debris longitudinally, running

parallel to the foot, rather than attempting to pinch across it. Check the inside of the beak also, and remove any deposit of food that collects beneath the tip of the upper mandible with a blunt matchstick.

It is likely that the hen will have started laying a second clutch of eggs before the original chicks leave the nest. Good hygiene is of particular importance at this stage, since if the fresh eggs become heavily soiled, they will be less likely to hatch successfully. Remove the chicks as soon as they appear independent, so they will not interfere with the next round of youngsters nor attempt to enter the nests of other breeding pairs. Budgerigars can be mature by the time they are six months of age, but do not allow them to breed until they are about a year old.

Indoor breeding
It is possible to breed budgerigars indoors, but you will need a special box-type cage equipped with a nestbox for this purpose. Keeping more than one pair in the same area is likely to yield the best chance of success, as these birds appear to need the stimulus of at least hearing others of their kind if they are to breed successfully. Unlike other members of the parrot family, budgerigars do not form a strong pair bond, and indeed, in a mixed aviary, a cock may mate with several hens. It is partly for this reason that exhibition breeders prefer to accommodate their birds in separate breeding cages to ensure the parentage of the progeny, which can be vital when attempting to produce specific colours.

Left: A typical set-up for breeding budgerigars. The arrangement of cages is ideal; they will breed readily in sight and sound of other pairs.

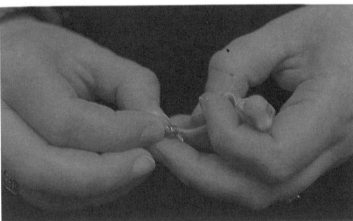

Above: *Putting a closed ring (band) on a 5-7 day old chick. Ease the ring over the front three toes.*

Below: *Fold the fourth toe up the leg towards the knee and push the ring carefully over it.*

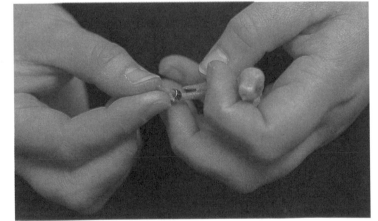

Above: *Release the fourth toe from the ring and allow the ring to fall back against the ball of the foot.*

Below: *The ring is year-coded, has a breeder's registration number and a sequential number to identify chick.*

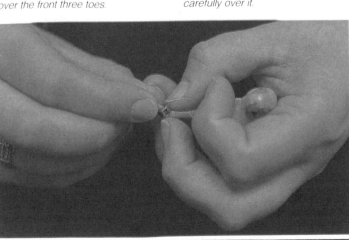

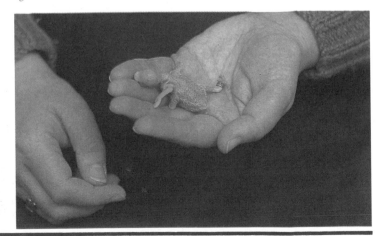

Cockatiel

Nymphicus hollandicus

- **Distribution:** Over much of Australia, apart from coastal areas, notably on the eastern side of the country. Also absent from Tasmania
- **Size:** 30 cm (12 in)
- **Diet:** A mixture of cereal seeds, notably canary seed and millets, with sunflower seed as well. Provide greenstuff regularly
- **Sexing:** Hens are duller overall, lacking the yellow facial patches of mature cock birds, and the undersurface of the tail is barred with yellow
- **Compatibility:** Very compatible with other birds, even finches. Will not interfere even during the breeding season
- **Pet appeal:** All the obvious appeal of cockatoos, without any of the drawbacks

Another member of the parrot family from the arid interior of Australia, the Cockatiel was also first seen alive in Europe about the same time as the Budgerigar, around 1840. Their crested appearance led to them being known as Cockatoo Parrots at first, and the term 'Cockatiel' did not come into fashion until towards the end of the nineteenth century. It was derived from the Dutch description *Kakatielje*, which originated from the Portuguese word *Cacatilho*, translating as 'little cockatoo'.

Indeed, the Cockatiel has a number of features in common with the cockatoos. Both parents sit during the incubation period, rather than just the hen, as occurs in other parrots. The distinctive crest of the Cockatiel can be held erect or lowered, which is a feature otherwise peculiar to the cockatoos. Nevertheless, unlike Cockatoos, the Cockatiel has evolved a long tail and is of slimmer proportions overall. They also have very different call-notes; cockatiels possess an inoffensive voice, compared with the harsh screeches of the cockatoos. The compatibility problems associated with cockatoos are not encountered in cockatiels, and thus cockatiels are ideal as pet or aviary birds. Furthermore, their inoffensive natures make them ideal occupants of a mixed aviary, although they are likely to destroy any plants growing in the enclosure. The calls of cockatiels are unlikely to be offensive to near neighbours, and they are hardy aviary occupants.

Colour forms

Cockatiels are widely bred throughout the world, and it is not surprising that a number of attractive colour forms have been developed in captive stock, although none has been reported from the wild. The most striking is undoubtedly the Lutino, which has a pale lemon body colour overall while retaining the orange cheek patches associated with the normal Grey. First described as 'Moonbeams' - being bred in America by an aviculturist called Mrs Moon during the 1950s - these cockatiels originally sold for fantastic prices, but are now freely available, and cost little more than the Grey.

they will settle quite rapidly in the home at this stage. Unfortunately, it is virtually impossible to sex cockatiels by sight until they start moulting for the first time, at about six months of age. Before this, however, some young cock birds may be recognized by their song. Cockatiels of either sex can become very tame, and will mimic equally well, so that the gender of a young bird is not necessarily significant.

Breeding

Several pairs of cockatiels can be kept together in an aviary, but breeding results are likely to be better if pairs are housed on their own. They will breed at a year old, although young pairs do not always make the best parents. The average clutch consists of about five eggs, but much larger numbers are not unknown. The cock bird incubates for much of the day, with the hen taking over in the late afternoon. The chicks, covered in a thin coating of yellow down, should start to hatch after a period of about nineteen days.

Avoid disturbing the sitting birds if possible, especially around the time that the chicks are due to hatch. Cockatiels on the nest will sway back and forth, and hiss menacingly at any potential intruder. If disturbed, there is an increased risk that eggs or chicks may be injured as a result. The presence of newly hatched birds will be evident from outside the aviary: young cockatiels have a loud easily discernible call. With a large clutch of eggs, hatching on alternate days, there is a risk that the youngest will not survive, particularly if the parents are kept short of suitable rearing foods. Bread and milk or a high protein insectivorous food may well be taken readily by a breeding pair of cockatiels.

These birds are so prolific that they will lay throughout the year if the opportunity presents itself. Restrict breeding activity to the warmer months only, however, by removing the nestbox as autumn approaches. Cockatiels will stop brooding their offspring through the day once the chicks are starting to feather up, and at this crucial period they will be very vulnerable in cold weather. The incidence of feather-plucking is not influenced by the accommodation provided for the parent birds. Affected chicks will need to be brought inside as soon as possible, however, particularly if the weather is cold. It will take several weeks for them to regrow new feathers, but they should not suffer any permanent harm. The vice may be inherited, however, and such birds are perhaps best regarded as pet rather than breeding stock.

It is possible to breed cockatiels satisfactorily in the home, but the birds will do best if you keep them in a small flight with a nestbox, rather than in a cage. Fledging can be anticipated when the chicks are about five weeks of age.

Cockatiels have a long potential lifespan, living well into their twenties, and are reproductively active for most of this time. Clearly, however, young stock is to be preferred for breeding purposes.

Left: Lutino Cockatiel
This most attractive colour form is justifiably popular throughout the world. The normal grey plumage is transformed into a lovely creamy yellow to set off the orange face. The colour intensity is variable.

Above: **Normal Cockatiel**
A pair, with the cock on the left showing the pronounced yellow face.

Below:
Pied Pearl Cinnamon Cockatiel
A blend of colour forms in one bird.

Among other mutations, the Pearl is unusual in that the markings are transitory in cock birds. The feathers of the Pearl Cockatiel retain grey borders, but have yellow centres: as a cock moults into adult plumage, however, this distinction is obscured. A European mutation first bred in the 1960s, the Pearl may have either relatively pale or dark yellow areas in its plumage.

The Cinnamon can also show a variable depth of coloration, with its warm brownish plumage serving to distinguish it from the normal Grey. Colour combinations featuring the various mutations all on the one bird, such as Pied Pearl Cinnamon Cockatiels, are now being bred with increasing frequency. The most recent development has been the breeding of White-faced Cockatiels, which lack any yellow or orange in their plumage. No doubt, new colour forms will emerge as breeding continues.

Cockatiels as pets

The gentle nature of the Cockatiel, and its ability to talk as well as to whistle simple tunes make it an ideal choice as a pet bird. Large numbers are bred in aviaries annually, with the biggest choice being available towards the end of the summer. It may be more difficult to recognize a young bird than in the case of the Budgerigar, so be guided by a breeder if possible. Young birds are very similar to adult hens in appearance, although the cere tends to be pinkish rather than grey and their tails are shorter than those of adult cockatiels. They are usually capable of feeding independently by seven weeks of age, and although young birds are often nervous when first obtained, unless hand-reared,

Lutinos can be sexed in an identical manner to normals, but you may need to hold a bird in the hand for a closer inspection to observe the characteristic darker yellow bars on the tail feathers of hens. The only drawback of the Lutino is that pairs often tend to pluck their chicks before they leave the nest. If this happens, ensure that the young cockatiels do not get chilled when they fledge in an outdoor aviary.

While the depth of coloration of the Lutino can be quite variable, the distribution of markings in the Pied mutation is also unpredictable. Some birds have predominantly grey rather than yellowish white plumage, yet the reverse may be seen in their offspring. Generally, cockatiels with larger areas of light plumage are preferred, and may sell for a slightly higher price. The Pied was the first cockatiel mutation to be developed, during the 1940s. It, too, emerged initially in American stock. In most cases, Pieds can be sexed by the characteristic difference in the coloration of the head or the tail. Alternatively, the cheerful warbling song of the cock bird will serve to distinguish the sexes.

LOVEBIRDS
GENUS AGAPORNIS

The lovebirds are a group of small, short-tailed parrots occurring in Africa and on certain offshore islands. Nine species form the genus, and all are characterized by their unusual breeding behaviour, which is almost unparalleled among parrot-like birds. Lovebirds collect nesting material, with which they line the nest site, carrying it either in their beaks or tucked in among the feathers of the rump, depending on the species concerned. In spite of their name, however, lovebirds can prove extremely aggressive, especially when breeding, and for this reason it is safer to keep pairs on their own. They are highly attractive and rewarding birds to keep.

Peach-faced Lovebird
Agapornis roseicollis

- **Distribution:** Southwestern Africa
- **Size:** 15 cm (6 in)
- **Diet:** Sunflower, safflower, millets and canary seed. Some greenstuff plus fruit
- **Sexing:** No visual differences between the sexes
- **Compatibility:** Risky
- **Pet appeal:** Underestimated. Deserves to be as popular as the budgerigar for its personality and attractive colour range. An ideal pet bird

These lovebirds are popular worldwide, and large numbers are reared annually in aviaries throughout the world. Young Peach-faced Lovebirds, or 'Peachies' as they are known in Australia, can be easily recognized by the dark markings present on their beaks when they fledge at about six weeks old. Their pink facial coloration is also less conspicuous than that of the adult birds at this time. If you obtain them as soon as they are eating independently, these lovebirds will make ideal pets. Hand-reared individuals are likely to prove very confiding, having been brought up in a household with human company.

Peach-faced Lovebirds can be taught to talk, and are neither as expensive nor as noisy as the larger parrots, yet perhaps possess more character than a budgerigar. A number of exciting colour forms have been bred during recent years and, although more costly than the normal green in most instances, they are no more difficult to keep. These new colours are described under a variety of sometimes exotic names. The Cremino has a lemon body colour, yet still retains a pinkish face, whereas the Lutino is pure yellow, with a region of deeper red plumage on the head, and it has red eyes. Although some Peach-faced Lovebirds are offered as 'blues', they retain a greenish tinge to their plumage, offset against a salmon-pink face, and are normally described as being Pastel Blue. This mutation first appeared in Holland during 1963. The coloration of Pied Peach-faced Lovebirds is extremely variable. Some individuals may be largely green rather than yellow, although those in which yellow predominates are considered more desirable. Three shades of green and pastel blue are also recognized now (as in the Budgerigar with the emergence of the dark factor mutation), so that colour combinations such as Olive Yellow Pieds can be obtained. If Pastel Blue is combined with the Pied factor, then the resulting birds show very pale areas of yellow, set against Pastel Blue coloration. The Yellow form of the Peach-faced is often described as the Golden Cherry, with its white counterpart being known as the Silver Cherry.

One of the most recent developments has been the breeding of a yellow-faced variety. The development of these colours is certain to continue.

Right: Pastel Blue Pied
In this colour form, areas of pale yellow appear on the Pastel Blue coloration. A striking combination.

Far right: Pastel Blue
The body plumage of this form has an overall bluish tinge and the face is a subtle salmon pink in colour.

Bottom right: Peach-faced Lovebird
This is the normal coloration from which the many colour forms have been developed. The pink face is less evident in very young birds.

Below: Yellow Pied Lovebird
The proportion of yellow and green in this colour form can differ quite significantly from individual to individual. Those with more yellow than green are highly prized.

Fischer's Lovebird

Agapornis fischeri

- **Distribution:** Northern Tanzania
- **Size:** 14 cm (5.5 in)
- **Diet:** Sunflower, safflower, millets and canary seed. Some greenstuff and fruit
- **Sexing:** There are no visual differences between the sexes
- **Compatibility:** Risky
- **Pet appeal:** Colourful, lively and potentially can talk

Considered by some taxonomists to be a subspecies of the Masked Lovebird, Fischer's Lovebirds nevertheless differ significantly in coloration. They have a similar avicultural history to the Masked though, being first seen alive in Europe during the 1920s, with breeding successes following shortly afterwards. Fischer's may be considered more hardy, however, although newly imported stock should never be placed outside

immediately before the winter. Such birds need to be kept in a frost-free environment until the onset of spring, when they can be released safely into an outside flight.

Like all lovebirds, the incubation period is about twenty-three days, and some pairs may produce two rounds of chicks in a season. They generally look immaculate, but when kept inside, a daily spray with tepid water will help to keep their plumage sleek. Lovebirds are easy birds to

maintain in good health, and Fischer's prove no exception. They may live for fifteen years or so, although the age of imported birds is likely to be unknown. Mutations in this species have been recorded, but are extremely scarce at present.

Below: **Fischer's Lovebird**
These splendid lovebirds make excellent pets for beginners. Once acclimatized, they are reasonably hardy in temperate climates.

Masked Lovebird
Agapornis personata

- **Distribution:** Northeastern Tanzania
- **Size:** 14 cm (5.5. in)
- **Diet:** Sunflower, safflower, millets and canary seed. Some greenstuff and fruit
- **Sexing:** No visual differences between the sexes
- **Compatibility:** Risky
- **Pet appeal:** Handsome. Need to be obtained when young

The Masked Lovebird is a member of the 'white eye-ring' group, so-called because of the presence of fleshy white circles around the eyes. These birds differ from the Peach-faced Lovebirds not only in this physical characteristic but also in their nesting habits. They carry nesting material in their beaks, rather than in their feathers, and the resulting nest tends to be correspondingly bulky. If deprived of fresh twigs, such as elder, they will use virtually anything available to them, including old millet sprays and even strips of newspaper.

These lovebirds have not proved generally to be as prolific as the Peach-faced, however, although individual pairs may excel in this respect. Nevertheless, a blue form derived from a wild-caught mutant discovered in the 1920s is now well established. Although described as

Left: Blue Masked Lovebird
In this well-established colour form the black mask is unchanged by the development of blue plumage.

Above: **Masked Lovebird**
The white eye ring shows up vividly against the black face, or 'mask', of this notably handsome lovebird.

the Blue Masked, the black mask is in fact unaltered in birds of this colour, with the body plumage being modified to a combination of blue and white. A yellowish green strain, sometimes misleadingly described as 'yellow', has also been evolved but has never proved very popular. When combined with the Blue Masked, it has been possible to create a 'white' masked, which again is not pure white, being pale blue and white in coloration.

While Masked Lovebirds can be bred successfully indoors, it is more likely that chicks will result if they are housed outside. This particular species has gained a reputation among aviculturists for laying relatively large numbers of fertile eggs that subsequently fail to hatch. The relatively low humidity indoors may be a contributory factor to this 'dead-in-shell' problem.

Nevertheless, two of these lovebirds will live happily indoors in a suitable flight cage. Some pairs become rather too amorous towards each other, and may pluck feathers from around their partner's neck. If this happens, it can be a sign that they are keen to nest. In any event, always make a nestbox available in their flight, since lovebirds invariably will roost inside it if given a preference. A nestbox in the shape of a cube, with internal dimensions of about 23 cm (9 in), will suffice for all species of lovebirds.

AMAZON PARROTS
GENUS AMAZONA

This genus consists of twenty-seven species, which occur in Central and South America, as well as on some Caribbean islands. They are popularly known as Green Parrots, because of the predominance of green coloration in their plumage, especially in the case of the mainland populations. Amazons were first brought to Europe in 1492 by Colombus returning from the momentous expedition to the New World, and they have been popular as pet birds ever since. During recent years, these parrots have also been bred in collections on a regular basis, and hand-reared chicks are often available. Hand-reared birds make the most amenable pets.

Orange-winged Amazon
Amazona amazonica

- **Distribution:** Ranges over most of northern South America, as well as the islands of Trinidad and Tobago
- **Size:** 30 cm (12 in)
- **Diet:** A good quality parrot mixture, augmented with daily supplies of fruit, greenstuff and vegetables such as carrot
- **Sexing:** There are no visual differences between the sexes
- **Compatibility:** Best kept alone or in pairs
- **Pet appeal:** A talented mimic

These parrots rank among the most freely available of the Amazons, and are sometimes confused with the equally well-known Blue-fronted Amazon (*A. aestiva*). Both have blue plumage, which is variable in extent on the head above the cere, but the red speculum on the wings of the Blue-fronted Amazon is replaced by orange in this species, hence the common name. The red coloration on the tail feathers is also diluted to orange. Overall, Orange-wings are noticeably smaller than Blue-fronted Amazons, and their upper beak tends to be paler, being horn-coloured rather than grey.

The Orange-winged Amazon is one of the commonest species in the wild, with thousands of these parrots congregating at certain

Above: **Orange-winged Amazon**
Despite its loud voice, this is a popular and widely available Amazon parrot. Provide a varied diet and plenty of opportunity for exercise.

roosting sites. Young birds can be distinguished from adults by virtue of their darker eyes. Unfortunately, their calls can be as noisy as those of larger Amazons, and some may become temperamentally unreliable as they mature. If you decide to obtain a mate for an established bird, take care to supervise their introduction properly. Place them side by side in separate cages, but never so close that they could bite each other through cage bars. Some individuals may be very jealous of a newcomer, especially at first, and fighting is inevitable under such circumstances.

Like all parrots, these Amazons must have adequate exercise, which entails either letting them out of the cage for long periods each day or, alternatively, housing them in an indoor flight. If you are going to be out for most of the day, then it is preferable to keep these social birds in pairs. There is no truth in the story that having two birds together will prevent them talking, although clearly, they may be more inclined to resort to their natural calls. The members of a pair are more likely to withdraw from human company but, by way of compensation, there is always a likelihood that they will nest successfully in the home.

Mealy Amazon
Amazona farinosa

- **Distribution:** From southern Mexico southwards into northern South America, to Bolivia and eastern Brazil, being confined to the east of the Andes
- **Size:** 38 cm (15 in)
- **Diet:** Parrot food, fruit, greenstuff and vegetables such as carrots
- **Sexing:** No sexual differences are apparent
- **Compatibility:** Pairs should be kept on their own
- **Pet appeal:** A large, striking bird that should learn to talk and become tame

The Mealy Amazon is the biggest of the mainland species, although certainly not among the most colourful. The appearance of individual birds can vary quite considerably, in fact. This does not indicate a sexual difference, but reflects the large area over which the species occurs. The Blue-crowned race (*A.f. guatemalae*) is confined to Central America and is rarely seen compared with the nominate subspecies *A.f. farinosa*, which is frequently exported from Guyana.

It is vital to obtain a young bird when seeking a pet, even though immatures will appear duller than their adult counterparts, with reduced yellow markings on the head. In addition, the irises, encircling the pupils in the eyes, are dark brown rather than the reddish colour seen in adult birds. Look closely at the nostrils of any Amazon that you are

considering; newly imported birds frequently have blocked nostrils, sometimes linked with runny eyes. Although this may simply be a minor infection, possibly linked to a dietary deficiency of Vitamin A, it can also indicate more serious ailments.

Mealy Amazons, in spite of their relatively dull coloration, can nevertheless make attractive pets. Their main drawback is their loud voice; Amazons are generally prone to regular periods of screeching both morning and evening. For this reason, draw the curtains in a room housing your parrot; otherwise, you are likely to be awakened by the bird's calls at first light, which may also offend your neighbours at an early hour. It might be possible to encourage your pet to desist from such behaviour by simply covering the cage when necessary, but even in domestically bred stock the urge to call loudly at dawn and dusk remains strong.

In common with other members of the genus, Mealy Amazons can prove long-lived birds, and may live for fifty years or more. They are easy to cater for; boiled corn-on-the-cob that has been allowed to cool down beforehand is a favourite food, especially with newly imported individuals, and can provide a useful source of Vitamin A. A wide selection of fruit and even dry dog food soaked in water will be taken readily by many birds. Some will even sample cooked meat, which is a valuable source of essential amino-acids, but avoid offering any fatty or fried foods, which may cause digestive problems in such birds.

Above: **Blue-crowned Mealy Amazon**
This race, distinguished by the area of blue plumage, is relatively rare in birdkeeping circles.

Right: **Mealy Amazon**
This has the loudest voice of the Amazon parrots, but nevertheless can become a rewarding pet bird.

White-fronted Amazon
Amazona albifrons

- **Distribution:** Central America, from Mexico to Costa Rica
- **Size:** 25 cm (10 in)
- **Diet:** A parrot mixture, including pine nuts if possible. Fruit, such as pomegranates, apple and figs, along with greenstuff such as spinach and carrots
- **Sexing:** The only species of Amazon that can be sexed visually. Hens can be recognized by their green rather than red wing coverts
- **Compatibility:** Best kept alone or in pairs
- **Pet appeal:** Smaller and less raucous than other Amazons

These attractive Amazons are not available as often as the preceding species, which is unfortunate, since they can make good pets if obtained at an early age. Being easy to sex, a true pair can be recognized without difficulty. Compared to adults, young birds have a reduced area of red on the sides of the face, while the white plumage on the forehead is distinctly yellowish.

As with all Amazons, the White-fronted varies in temperament, some individuals tending to become aggressive as they mature. All can prove talented talkers, however. There is a tendency for all the larger parrots to become particularly attached to one member of the family, and this should be discouraged if possible. It is important to allow an Amazon the opportunity to bathe, either in an open dish or by giving a regular daily spray (see pages 42-3). Be sure to provide an adequate supply of perches so that the bird can exercise its beak.

With a pair of Amazons, do not be surprised if it takes several years before they make any serious attempt to nest, although they may well choose to roost in a nestbox if one is available. Most birds will be mature by four years of age, and the onset of breeding condition can be detected by observing their behaviour. At this time, the parrots will be noisier, and you are likely to see tail-flaring. The clutch usually consists of three or possibly four eggs, which are incubated by the hen alone for four weeks. The chicks will be about two months old when they leave the nest for the first time, and during the whole of the breeding period the adult birds may be aggressive to anyone approaching their aviary. Under normal circumstances out of doors, Amazons will lay only once a year, but indoors, they may nest twice in quite rapid succession. Eggs are unlikely to be laid by birds kept in an outside flight until April in northern temperate climates.

Right: **White-fronted Amazon**
In this elegant pair, the male is on the right, clearly recognizable by the red wing coverts. Obtained when young, these parrots can make attractive pets that will enjoy human company and learn to talk. In common with other Amazons, they will appreciate a regular bath or spray.

MACAWS
GENUS ARA

The characteristic feature of the common *Ara* macaws is the large area of essentially bare facial skin on either side of the head. In most instances, this is white or yellowish. The genus is represented in both Central and South America, and formerly occurred during quite recent times on some of the islands in the Caribbean, although exact details of the number of species and their appearance is not known with any certainty. Undoubtedly, macaws have been kept for centuries as pets in their native lands, as archaeological evidence has revealed.

In contrast to their fearsome beaks, macaws can prove very gentle, but never take any chances with an unknown bird. They are not usually talented mimics, but are certainly intelligent birds and will readily recall any mistreatment, making it very difficult to regain the confidence of such a bird. Macaws show a strong tendency to become one-person pets, and this can present a great problem when purchasing a tame adult bird that is used to its surroundings. They have a long potential lifespan and mature slowly, rarely breeding before four years of age.

Blue and Gold Macaw
Ara ararauna

- **Distribution:** From eastern Panama across a vast area of northern South America, to Bolivia, Paraguay and Brazil. Absent from western coastal areas and parts of eastern Brazil
- **Size:** 86 cm (34 in)
- **Diet:** Good quality parrot food, with larger nuts, such as brazils, included when in season. Offer fruit, carrots and greenstuff regularly
- **Sexing:** No reliable external means, although cock birds may have bigger, bolder heads
- **Compatibility:** Keep them in individual pairs rather than in groups in most instances
- **Pet appeal:** Can become very tame and will probably learn a few words.

Above and right:
Blue and Gold Macaw
The light iris shown above indicates a mature bird. These magnificent parrots can become very tame in captivity, but are not really suitable for beginners to birdkeeping.

The large size of these macaws can create considerable difficulties if you attempt to house them in the home. In addition, their beaks are extremely powerful and capable of dismantling all but the strongest cage. In the United States and mainland Europe, suitably large and robust accommodation for macaws is available. Elsewhere, you will need to build a cage or import a suitable one.

Macaws are active, sensitive birds. Never confine them in a small space, otherwise feather-plucking will be almost inevitable, particularly if the bird is left on its own for any length of time. Opt for 12 gauge wire when building a cage, and choose a small mesh measuring 2.5×1.25 cm (1 × ½ in) or similar. This should prevent the macaw exerting excessive leverage on the component strands of wire, and snipping them with its strong beak. Such mesh will also provide some protection for the framework if wood is used; ensure that all timber is protected on its inner surface with wire mesh to put it out of the macaw's reach.

These macaws are not really suitable for novice parrot owners. They are no more demanding than any other psittacine, but they must be handled with particular care - a bite can cause serious injury to a finger, for example - and their calls are raucous. It is possible to train these birds to use a stand, but this needs to be quite stable and able to withstand the onslaught from the macaw's beak. Take great care if you are contemplating chaining your macaw to a stand and leaving it for any length of time. Check that it cannot get caught up, possibly injuring itself as a result. Furthermore, ensure that it is unable to free itself; an unsupervised macaw loose in a room can wreak serious damage to the furniture, fittings and fabrics.

Some macaws have a particularly strong musky body odour. It is thought that this may emanate from the preen gland at the base of the tail, along with the waterproofing secretion normally produced there. The pungent smell is more noticeable in some individuals than in others and is particularly evident at certain times of the year, so it may be linked to breeding condition. In any event, this odour is quite normal; a similar smell may be noted with Amazons kept in the home.

Green-winged Macaw

Ara chloroptera

- **Distribution:** Extends from Eastern Panama into north-western Colombia and across most of northern South America, east of the Andes, extending to Bolivia, Brazil, Paraguay and northern Argentina
- **Size:** 90 cm (36 in)
- **Diet:** A good parrot mixture, including some peanuts and larger pine nuts. These macaws will even eat small cereal seeds, such as canary seed, and also need fruit and greenstuff. Brazil nuts are especially favoured
- **Sexing:** No obvious external differences; cocks may be bigger, but this is more likely to be a regional difference
- **Compatibility:** Keep singly or in pairs
- **Pet appeal:** A spectacular and striking bird, which should tame readily if acquired as a youngster

The Green-winged Macaw is sometimes confused with the Scarlet, since both are predominantly red in colour, but the former lacks any yellow on its wings, and has distinct feather traces over its bare facial area. These large birds are very similar to the Blue and Gold Macaw in their requirements. If you do decide to opt for one of these species as a pet, search for a hand-reared youngster, which will not resent human attention. They can be recognized by their dark eyes and maroon rather than red facial feathering.

In spite of their huge size, these macaws do not need spacious surroundings in order to nest satisfactorily, and successes have been recorded from pairs kept in small flights in various homes. Provide a large nestbox, such as a disused beer cask, and fix it firmly in place so that it cannot be dislodged accidentally by the birds. Place some wooden offcuts inside the nestbox so that the macaws can gnaw these to form nest litter. The usual clutch consists of two or three eggs, and the incubation period lasts about twenty-seven days, with the young birds fledging when they are about three months old. Pairs breeding for the first time may not always prove reliable parents, but once macaws start nesting, they usually breed regularly over subsequent years. Take particular care during the breeding period; some pairs may become very aggressive towards their owner and resent any interference. Breeding macaws are kept at liberty in some of the larger bird gardens and zoos, and make a spectacular sight swooping over the trees down to their nesting barrels.

Right: **Green-winged Macaw**
A large and powerful macaw that will nest successfully in fairly compact accommodation. The common name refers to the areas of green plumage confined to the wings of this otherwise basically red bird. Alternative common names for the Green-winged Macaw include Red and Blue, and Red and Green Macaw.

Severe Macaw
Ara severa

- **Distribution:** Extends from eastern Panama over a wide area of northern South America to Bolivia and Brazil
- **Size:** 51 cm (20 in)
- **Diet:** Parrot food with pine nuts when available. Fruit, such as apple, and greenstuff, such as spinach, the thicker stalks of which are usually preferred to the leaves
- **Sexing:** There are no external differences between the sexes
- **Compatibility:** House singly or in pairs. Fighting might occur if these birds are kept in groups in enclosed surroundings
- **Pet appeal:** Has the natural intelligence of the larger macaws, but is easier to accommodate successfully in the home

The Severe Macaw is one of several so-called dwarf macaws that are predominantly green in colour. They are less often seen than their larger relatives, however, possibly because they are less colourful. Nevertheless, young birds, characterized by their darker irises, settle well in the home and can become very tame. They may also learn to speak a few words, although macaws cannot be compared in this respect with Amazon Parrots, for example.

Once they are properly

Above: **Severe Macaw**
An excellent dwarf macaw that makes an intelligent companion. Young birds can become very tame.

acclimatized, Severe Macaws can be kept out of doors, provided they have adequate protection in the winter. When provided with a nestbox for roosting purposes, they are unlikely to need heat at this time. Supervise any introduction of macaws closely, however, particularly if a tame bird is involved. Serious fighting can develop unexpectedly over the first few days until the birds are used to each other; in the interim, the dominant individual may monopolize the food and water containers. Unfortunately, the calls of these smaller macaws are far-carrying, and may well lead to complaints from near neighbours if the birds are kept in an outside flight in a suburban area.
Young Severe Macaws can be recognized by their dark eyes, whereas those of mature individuals have pale whitish irises. The distinctive feature of these birds is the chestnut-coloured plumage directly above the cere and, for this reason, they are sometimes advertised as Chestnut-fronted Macaws. If a pair do nest, their clutch is likely to consist of two, possibly three eggs, which hatch in about twenty-eight days. Chicks fledge when they reach around two months of age.

Maximilian's Parrot
Pionus maximiliana

- **Distribution:** Occurs over a wide area of eastern South America, from northern Brazil to Bolivia, Paraguay and Argentina
- **Size:** 30 cm (12 in)
- **Diet:** Parrot food, with fruit and greenstuff. Will also take the smaller cereal seeds
- **Sexing:** No visual distinction between the sexes
- **Compatibility:** Keep singly or in pairs
- **Pet appeal:** Tends to be overlooked, but better for the average household than most Amazons

The *Pionus* parrots form a small genus of seven species, members of which are generally rarely available, although the Maximilian's ranks among the most common. To be fully appreciated, it really needs to be seen in an outside aviary, where sunlight can reveal the subtle hues in its plumage. Nevertheless, providing they are obtained as young birds, these parrots can develop into highly attractive pets and prove not untalented mimics. Generally, immatures have a reduced area of blue on the breast when compared with the fully mature adult birds, while their heads tend to be paler green overall, with a reddish forehead.

Above: **Maximilian's Parrot**
Although comparatively rare, this species can develop into a very reliable and rewarding pet bird.

Take particular care when buying one of these parrots. The genus as a whole is prone to the fungal disease aspergillosis, which is difficult to detect in its early stages. Any bird that appears slightly fluffed-up and has irregular breathing, as seen from its tail movements, may be afflicted with this ailment, for which there is no reliable cure. Watching the bird quietly for a period of time affords the best opportunity of noting such symptoms. Otherwise healthy birds may also wheeze noisily, if they are nervous and closely confined in human company.
The calls of these parrots are much less disturbing than those of Amazons, and they are also more reliable in terms of temperament. Maximilian's Parrots have been bred successfully on various occasions, but it may not be very easy to obtain a hand-reared youngster. Nevertheless, a pair may well attempt to breed if provided with suitable accommodation, but do not disturb them more than absolutely necessary. It is not unknown for *Pionus* parrots to mutilate their chicks, with some pairs proving worse in this respect than others. In extreme cases, the young birds may have to be removed for hand-rearing at an early age if they are to survive.

CONURES

The term 'conure' simply refers to various Central and South American parakeets, being derived from their old scientific name, *Conurus*, which has been preserved in popular parlance. Conures are medium-sized birds, often proving quite destructive and vocal; the largest member of the group is the Patagonian Conure (*Cyanoliseus patagonus*), which is more reminiscent of a dwarf macaw in terms of its overall appearance and noisy calls.

There has been a considerable increase in interest in conures as breeding birds during recent years, and relatively large numbers are now being reared by aviculturists each year. As pets, conures have several advantages over the larger psittacines. They are considerably less expensive in the first instance, and usually have trustworthy temperaments. Conures can become exceedingly tame, and will also learn to talk, although they are unlikely to develop the vocal repertoire of the bigger parrots. The lifespan of conures is probably around twenty years, although there are individual variations. It is impossible to judge the age of adult birds if no records are available when you buy one, but in some cases differences in the beak – those of immature birds may be paler – or iris colour can help to distinguish young birds.

White-eyed Conure
Aratinga leucophthalmus

- **Distribution:** Occurs over an extremely wide area of South America, although absent from the western side of the country. Ranges from the Guianas south to Argentina and Paraguay
- **Size:** 33 cm (13 in)
- **Diet:** Sunflower seed and other typical ingredients of a parrot mixture, plus fruit and greenstuff
- **Sexing:** No sexual differences
- **Compatibility:** Best kept individually or in pairs
- **Pet appeal:** Can become very tame and will talk

Within the genus *Aratinga*, there are a number of predominantly green species that have scattered areas of red plumage, notably on the head, as well as at the edge of the wings and extending across the wing coverts. The distribution of these markings are highly individual, and this can lead to difficulties over correct identification. The situation becomes further confused in the White-eyed Conure, where several subspecies are recognized. The distinguishing feature of the White-eyed Conure generally, however, is an area of yellow plumage across the greater wing coverts seen on the undersurface when the wing is held open. This distinction is not apparent in young birds, though, which are duller overall, lacking both the red and yellow wing markings. The area of bare white skin around the eyes is not significant in terms of identification since this characteristic is also apparent in other conures.

White-eyed Conures nest quite readily, either in an indoor or outdoor environment. It is likely that if kept inside, they may have two rounds of chicks; in a garden aviary, they tend to be single-brooded. At the onset of the breeding period they become increasingly destructive, so be sure to provide adequate supplies of softwood in the nestbox so they can create their own nest-litter. In

Below: Dusky Conure
Suitable for both indoor and outdoor accommodation, this conure is keen to nest and friendly to its owner. Provide shelter in a garden aviary for roosting during bad weather.

Above: White-eyed Conure
This conure, becoming increasingly available to birdkeepers, has an agreeable nature and tames easily. It is compact, not too noisy and can become a rewarding pet bird.

common with other conures, the White-eyed is hardy once acclimatized, but should have a nestbox available throughout the year so the birds can roost within, particularly during bad weather. Chicks will normally fledge around nine weeks of age and can develop into marvellous pets, becoming very affectionate towards their owner. The

red markings develop at the first moult

Among other conures with similar coloration are the Mitred (*A. mitrata*), Red-fronted (*A. wagleri*) and the Red-masked (*A. erythrogenys*). The red plumage on the head is most extensive in the Red-masked Conure, extending over the whole of the facial region. All need similar care to the White-eyed Conure.

Dusky Conure
Aratinga weddellii

- **Distribution:** Extends over much of the Amazon Basin into Brazil, Peru, Ecuador and Bolivia
- **Size:** 28 cm (11 in)
- **Diet:** A parrot mixture, with safflower and small pine nuts; millet and canary seed. Fruit and greenstuff
- **Sexing:** No visible distinctions between the sexes
- **Compatibility:** Keep individually or in pairs
- **Pet appeal:** Relatively small and highly personable

Although not as striking as some other members of the genus, the Dusky-headed Conure is an attractive bird. It has never been frequently available, but has been imported in larger numbers during recent years, and breeding stock is now established in numerous collections. Perhaps surprisingly, however, this species was not bred until 1978, when pairs nested in both Holland and the United States. This should not deter you from keeping these conures, though. Now, with surgical sexing, pairs can be recognized with certainty, and will nest as readily as other conures when provided with suitable accommodation.

As pet birds, Dusky-headed Conures can become very tame and are full of character. Youngsters are easily identifiable on the basis of their dark irises. Their calls are generally not as disturbing as those of other members of the *Aratinga* genus. In common with related species, Dusky Conures often show a distinct preference for fruit in their diet. Even newly acquired individuals will take a wide variety of fruit, from apple to grapes and even guava, which is a popular food in the wild. Conures will also eat canned fruit, but it is preferable to offer only fruits in natural juice, rather than in syrup, and to drain off the fluid beforehand.

Golden-crowned Conure

Aratinga aurea

- **Distribution:** Occurs through most of Brazil, ranging into Argentina, Bolivia and Paraguay
- **Size:** 25 cm (10 in)
- **Diet:** Sunflower seed, small pine nuts, some hemp and peanuts, as well as safflower and smaller cereal seeds
- **Sexing:** No sexual differences
- **Compatibility:** Best kept individually or in pairs
- **Pet appeal:** Lively and tames easily

The Golden-crowned Conure is sometimes confused with the Golden-capped Conure (*Aratinga auricapilla*), one of the group of predominantly fiery yellow coloured conures, which includes the Sun Conure (*A. solstitialis*). Apart from the characteristic orange band across the forehead, the plumage is predominantly green in the Golden-crowned. The extent of the orange markings can vary, but does not indicate the sexes; in some cases, hens may appear more colourful than cocks and vice versa. Such variations probably occur throughout the extensive natural range of these birds. Young Golden-crowned Conures can be easily recognized, however, since they have a distinct band of yellow plumage alongside the orange markings on the forehead. In addition, their beaks are paler than those of adult birds, notably on the sides in newly fledged youngsters.

The major drawback of conures as pets or aviary birds is their loud and sometimes persistent voices. In this respect, however, the Golden-crowned is relatively inoffensive compared with larger species such as the Red-masked Conure (*A. erythrogenys*), which also tend to be more destructive. Pairs of Golden-crowned Conures will nest in suitable accommodation, either inside or out of doors. Place the nestbox in a relatively secluded and dark locality. Before laying, it is not unusual for these conures to pluck themselves, but their feathering normally regrows perfectly well later on to restore their appearance.

Four eggs may form the clutch, and these hatch after an incubation period of about twenty-six days. Golden-crowned Conures normally make reliable parents, and the chicks will fledge at around seven weeks of age, being independent several weeks later. Brown bread soaked in milk is a popular and ideal rearing food. In the United States, the Golden-crowned Conure is often sold as the Orange-fronted (or Petz's) Conure, (*A. canicularis*), which in fact can be distinguished by its horn-coloured rather than black beak.

Below: **Golden-crowned Conure**
Vivacious and affectionate, this conure can be recommended to newcomers to this group of birds.

117

Above: **Canary-winged Parakeet**
This is the subspecies B. v. chiriri. These compact parakeets make attractive, if rather noisy, aviary occupants. They are not really free breeding in captivity, however.

Left: **White-winged Parakeet**
This is the subspecies Brotogeris v versicolorus, as is evident from its darker overall coloration. Both subspecies are popular as pets and should be kept in the same way.

Canary-winged Parakeet

Brotogeris versicolorus

- **Distribution:** This species has two main areas of distribution, one over the Amazon drainage basin and another more southerly one that includes a large area of Brazil, to Bolivia, Paraguay and Argentina
- **Size:** 23 cm (9 in)
- **Diet:** Sunflower seed and other ingredients of a parrot mixture, as well as cereal seeds. Fruit should feature prominently in their diet
- **Sexing:** There are no reliable means of distinguishing between the sexes, although sometimes cocks can be recognized by their larger heads

- **Compatibility:** Can be kept in groups, but newcomers will not be tolerated
- **Pet appeal:** Youngsters tame readily and will talk

There are two distinct subspecies of the Canary-winged Parakeet. The nominate race, *B. versicolorus versicolorus*, is known as the White-winged Parakeet, being significantly darker in coloration than the Canary-winged Parakeet (*B. v. chiriri*). Examination of the wings will resolve any confusion over the identity of a particular bird, with a large area of white plumage being apparent when the wing of a White-winged Parakeet is held open. This area is smaller in young birds and bright canary yellow in a Canary-winged Parakeet.

Although *Brotogeris* have proved highly adaptable in the wild, with liberty populations established in various parts of the world, they have yet to prove prolific avicultural subjects. It can be difficult to obtain a young bird, therefore, although some individual breeders, notably in the United States, have been very successful with these parakeets. Certainly more than one pair needs to be kept for the best chance of success, since they should be housed within sight and sound of other *Brotogeris* parakeets. Alternatively, they can be kept and bred satisfactorily in groups, but if a bird is removed from an established colony, it is unlikely to be accepted back into the group later on. The only safe means of altering a colony

is to remove all birds from the communal flight for a few days and then introduce the established birds alongside the new individuals at the same time. If a pair go to nest, the eggs should hatch after an incubation period of twenty-six days, and the chicks fledge about two months later, being fully independent several weeks later.

Young *Brotogeris* parakeets will tame rapidly, but older birds tend to remain shy. Unfortunately, these small parakeets can become so attached to their owners that they become jealous of other pets, and call noisily if ignored. Always provide them with a good supply of branches to chew. They are surprisingly destructive birds for their size, and need to exercise their beaks if these are not to become overgrown. Fruit is a vital ingredient of their diet, with banana often proving a particular favourite. Flocks in the wild frequently descend on banana plantations and can inflict considerable damage on the growing fruit in the fields.

White-bellied Caique
Pionites leucogaster

- **Distribution:** Occurs south of the River Amazon in northern Brazil to Peru and Ecuador, extending southwards to Bolivia
- **Size:** 23 cm (9 in)
- **Diet:** A parrot mixture, plus a variety of fruit. Walnuts are a particular favourite of many caiques
- **Sexing:** No visual distinction between the sexes
- **Compatibility:** Best kept in pairs
- **Pet appeal:** Become extremely tame and devoted to their owners

The caiques are considered to be closely related to the conures, in spite of their short-tailed appearance. Both species can be identified instantly by their white breast feathering, a unique characteristic in the parrot family. They are identical in their requirements; indeed, the only apparent distinction is that the White-bellied Caique has lost the black pigment evident in the Black-headed species (*P. melanocephala*). In young birds, however, the beak is dark, and odd black feathering may be seen on the head. The irises of immatures are again darker than those of adult birds, and the legs are greyish rather than pink.

Caiques are extremely sociable birds that, ideally, should only be kept in pairs. Never keep them on their own unless you can devote long periods of time to keep the bird amused. The natural curiosity of caiques may even be apparent in aviary surroundings, where they often become surprisingly tame, feeding from the hand without hesitation in some cases. The two main drawbacks associated with caiques are their destructive natures and relatively loud calls. Always provide adequate perches for these birds to gnaw, so they can keep their beaks in trim. They will delight in removing the bark from a fresh branch of elder, for example, before proceeding to demolish the wood itself, rather than attacking the aviary structure. Although highly social by nature, an established pair of caiques will not tolerate the presence of a newcomer, and a fatal outcome to such an encounter is almost inevitable in most cases.

Caiques can be extremely consistent if not prolific breeders. Pairs may produce four chicks in a nest, with the incubation period being around twenty-five days. One pair kept in Miami, Florida, produced an average of four youngsters every year over the course of a decade. The secret with breeding caiques appears to be to provide a nestbox in a dark, secluded locality. Young hand-reared caiques are truly delightful birds, but do not be misled; they are extremely demanding in view of their active, social natures, and will not thrive if kept in cages on their own. They are long-lived birds, with reliable records revealing that caiques have lived for forty years.

Right: **White-bellied Caique**
Keep these parrots in pairs to satisfy their highly social natures.

Vernal Hanging Parrot
Loriculus vernalis

- **Distribution:** From southwestern India, in a broad band along the coastal area to the Malay Peninsula and Indochina. Also occurs on the Andaman Islands
- **Size:** 14 cm (5.5 in)
- **Diet:** Fruit, berries, small seeds and a regular supply of fresh nectar. May occasionally take mealworms
- **Sexing:** Hens usually lack the blue throat markings and have brown irises
- **Compatibility:** Can be kept safely in the company of both small seedeaters and softbills
- **Pet appeal:** Small, inoffensive and interesting

The Hanging Parrots are an unusual group of birds found throughout Southeast Asia and neighbouring offshore islands, including the Philippines. They do have fairly specialist needs, however, and are unlikely to become tame or talk, so these parrots hold a limited appeal for the traditional petseeker. Hanging Parrots are named after their unusual habit of roosting upside down from a perch, with their head hanging towards the ground.

These parrots can prove excessively messy birds, especially when kept in a cage, since they will scatter pieces of fruit in all directions, which in turn may stick on the sides or bars of the cage as well as on neighbouring furniture. Apart from being unsightly, it can be

difficult to clean such deposits without removing the birds from their quarters almost on a daily basis and washing the interior thoroughly. Be sure to use an absorbent floor covering, such as paper towelling or a thick layer of newspaper, in order to cater for their fluid droppings.

The most satisfactory means of accommodating Hanging Parrots is in a relatively spacious flight, designed for ease of cleaning. They do best in a planted aviary, and can be kept satisfactorily out of doors during the warmer months of the year. Pairs may nest successfully under such conditions, with the female building a nest in a suitable box or log, using leaves which she carries to the nesting site tucked in among the feathers of her rump and

Above: **Vernal Hanging Parrot**
This fascinating and lively bird roosts in a head-down position.

breast. The leaves are normally cut into longitudinal strips, with green leaves often being preferred for the purpose.

The eggs, normally laid on successive rather than alternate days, which is probably unique in the whole of the parrot family, should hatch after about three weeks. Three or four chicks form a typical clutch, and fledge at around five weeks of age. They resemble their parents, but have paler beaks and darker feet. Be sure to provide adequate protein, such as a suitable rearing food, to ensure that the chicks are reared successfully.

Guiana Parrotlet
Forpus passerinus

- **Distribution:** Parts of Venezuela and Colombia, to the Guianas and northern Brazil. Also occurs on offshore islands, including Trinidad
- **Size:** 12.5 cm (5 in)
- **Diet:** Smaller cereal seeds, including millet sprays. Some sunflower and small pine nuts. Fruit and greenstuff
- **Sexing:** Hens can be distinguished by the absence of any blue plumage, and their more yellowish heads

- **Compatibility:** Keep pairs apart from other parrots since they tend to be savage
- **Pet appeal:** Do not need spacious surroundings, nor are they noisy

The parrotlets are a group of small short-tailed parrots confined to South America. It can be difficult to identify them correctly, because a relatively large number of subspecies exist with minor plumage differences. In spite of their small size, however, these birds need to be kept apart, because pairs are surprisingly savage towards other parrotlets.

They have been bred successfully in cages indoors, and there is even a record of a cock parrotlet eighteen years old fathering chicks, but some pairs prove very aggressive even towards their own offspring. The risk of fatalities is greatest when breeding parrotlets in cages, and newly fledged youngsters are most at risk. Remove youngsters to separate accommodation as soon as possible. The incubation period is approximately eighteen days, and up to eight chicks have been reared successfully by a pair at one time.

Provide foods such as bread and milk, and soaked groats in increasing quantities when there are chicks in the nest. They leave the nest at around six weeks of age, and, unlike larger parrots, may start nesting when only six months old.

Below: **Guiana Parrotlet**
The female – the right-hand bird of this pair – clearly shows a more yellow head than the male, and lacks the blue plumage evident in the male. Although small, these parrots can be hostile, even to their own youngsters in some cases.

COCKATOOS

F ive genera of cockatoos are recognized, but generally, those species belonging to the genus *Cacatua* are most often seen, whereas the various black cockatoos are scarce in avicultural collections. All cockatoos can be instantly recognized by their crests, which are raised when the birds are excited or alarmed. The shape and length of the crest feathers are variable, however; in the case of the Goffin's Cockatoo (*C. goffini*), the crest is relatively short, whereas the component feathers are both long and broad in the Moluccan Cockatoo (*C. moluccensis*).

Greater Sulphur-crested Cockatoo
Cacatua galerita

- **Distribution:** New Guinea and surrounding islands, north and eastern Australia southwards to Tasmania
- **Size:** 51 cm (20 in)
- **Diet:** Parrot food, fruit and greenstuff
- **Sexing:** Hens may be distinguished by their more reddish brown irises
- **Compatibility:** Keep individually or as pairs
- **Pet appeal:** Large, spectacular birds

These cockatoos are superficially similar to the Lesser Sulphur-crested, but are significantly larger and have pale rather than dark yellow ear-coverts. Various island subspecies are recognized in both instances, however; while the Citron-crested Cockatoo (*C. s. citronocristata*), with its orange crest and ear-coverts, is the most distinctive race of the Lesser Sulphur-crested, the Triton (*C. g. triton*) is the least typical of the forms of the Greater Sulphur-crested Cockatoo. Its bluish skin around the eyes and more highly developed crest is in fact more typical of the

Above:
Greater Sulphur-crested Cockatoo
A striking pet or aviary bird.

Blue-eyed Cockatoo (*Cacatua ophthalmica*). These island races are occasionally available, but invariably command a high price. Yet in Australia, the Greater Sulphur-crested Cockatoo is regarded as a pest species and treated accordingly, being killed in large numbers, although its exportation is currently forbidden.

Young birds are again most suitable as pets, although in view of their size they can be harder to accommodate than other smaller cockatoos. They appear to rank among the longest-lived members of the parrot family. One famous individual known as Cocky Bennett was said to have lived for 119 years, being almost totally bald for the latter years of his life. It can be difficult to distinguish an immature Greater Sulphur-crested Cockatoo, since the difference in eye coloration is not as marked as in the case of the Lesser species. It tends to be a lighter brown than that of an adult cock bird. The plumage on immature birds may have tinges of grey apparent, notably on the back and wings.

For breeding advice for cockatoos, see Umbrella Cockatoo.

Umbrella Cockatoo
Cacatua alba

- **Distribution:** Moluccan islands: Obi, Tadore, Termate, Batfan and Halmahera
- **Size:** 51 cm (20 in)
- **Diet:** Parrot mix, fruit and greenstuff
- **Sexing:** Hens invariably have reddish brown irises; those of cocks are black
- **Compatibility:** Best kept individually or in pairs
- **Pet appeal:** Become very affectionate and may learn to talk

The broad crest of the Umbrella Cockatoo is said to be responsible for its common name, curving backwards over the head. These cockatoos are very similar in appearance to the Moluccan Cockatoo (*C. moluccensis*), but are essentially white in colour rather than a variable shade of pink. The Umbrella is generally less expensive but no less noisy than its pink cousin. These rank among the most raucous members of an extremely noisy group of birds. They also possess correspondingly powerful beaks, and are not ideally suited to the average household as a result.

In common with related species, the Umbrella Cockatoo may display a tendency to pluck its feathers if conditions are unsuitable. The plumage on the breast is most likely to be the target, and resulting areas of baldness should not be confused with the appearance of Feather Rot. Such behaviour will rapidly become persistent, and a change of environment is to be recommended at the earliest opportunity. The diet may be inadequate; unfortunately, all cockatoos tend to be rather conservative in their feeding habits, but do try to encourage such birds

Below: **Umbrella Cockatoo**
A majestic, if noisy, cockatoo that develops into a devoted companion.

to sample foods other than sunflower seed. This is much easier to accomplish with hand-reared chicks, whose natural curiosity ensures that they will take more or less any item offered in the post-weaning period, and then will not be reluctant to eat a wide variety of foods in later life.

Umbrella Cockatoos make striking aviary occupants, but they are certainly not suitable for the average suburban garden, where their loud calls will almost inevitably become a source of complaint from neighbours. It is not always easy to obtain a compatible pair of these birds; this applies also to other *Cacatua* species. Males tend to be dominant, and may attack their mates, sometimes with fatal consequences. Provide a stout nestbox, such as a reinforced beer barrel, for breeding purposes and place some wooden offcuts inside, which the birds can whittle down to form their nest litter. Two eggs form the normal clutch, and these should hatch after an incubation period of twenty-five days. Both adult birds take turns at this task, as in the case of most other cockatoos. Even if both chicks hatch successfully, though, it is not unusual for the younger and weaker individual to be lost during the rearing period. The only option under these circumstances in hand-rearing, if one chick appears to be falling behind its sibling in terms of growth.

Take great care with an adult breeding pair of cockatoos, particularly if one or both birds are tame. They can become extremely aggressive at this time, and will not hesitate to attack their keeper, often without provocation. Similarly, pet birds can become temperamentally unreliable once they mature, and may bite the unwary. This is especially likely if the cockatoo has developed a strong bond with one member of the family and resents the apparent interference of others in its daily routine. (For handling, page 16.)

Lesser Sulphur-crested Cockatoo
Cacatua sulphurea

- **Distribution:** Sulawesi (Celebes) and neighbouring islands
- **Size:** 33 cm (13 in)
- **Diet:** A good parrot mixture, with fruit and greenstuff
- **Sexing:** Mature hens can usually be distinguished by their reddish irises
- **Compatibility:** Keep individually or in pairs
- **Pet appeal:** Lively character, and can become very tame

This species is probably the most commonly kept cockatoo, and has long been popular as a pet. Young birds can be easily recognized by their grey irises, and only a youngster should be obtained as a pet. Cockatoos by nature tend to be rather highly strung, and it will be impossible to tame a wild adult bird. Nevertheless, a young cockatoo, especially if it has been hand-reared, should become exceedingly tame and affectionate towards its owner, although generally these birds do not prove great talkers as pet birds.

Bear in mind that cockatoos are intelligent, and also possess strong beaks. For this reason, secure the door of the cage with a padlock, rather than with just a hasp or catch. The bird has a prehensile tongue and may well learn to undo simple catches without difficulty and, once free in a room, may cause damage to furniture.

Unfortunately, the Lesser Sulphur-crested Cockatoo seems to suffer more readily than other related species from an ailment known as Feather Rot. This is a progressive disease manifested by weak and stunted plumage. In the terminal stages, both the beak and claws may be affected, turning soft and brittle. There is no effective cure for the condition, although thyroid tablets available from a veterinarian may bring temporary relief. Its cause has yet to be explained, although attention is being focused on viral and toxicological investigations.

It can be possible to recognize the disease at an early stage in young birds, so always look closely at the plumage. As yet, however, Feather Rot does not appear to have been reported in domestically raised stock, nor, in spite of the suggestion that it could be a virus, does it appear infectious. An early indication of the disease is the appearance of twisted, brownish body feathers. The presence of any nest dirt on the predominantly white plumage of these birds will obviously show up clearly, and a brownish colour alone is not indicative of Feather Rot. If combined with broken (rather than moulted) and stunted feathering, then Feather Rot can be suspected. (See pages 26-31 for health care.)

For breeding advice for cockatoos, see Umbrella Cockatoo.

Left:
Lesser Sulphur-crested Cockatoo
This is the most widely kept cockatoo and justifiably prized for its intelligence, its vivacious character and its friendly nature.

Roseate Cockatoo

Eolophus roseicapillus

- **Distribution:** Occurs over much of Australia
- **Size:** 35.5 cm (14 in)
- **Diet:** Parrot mix and cereal seeds plus fruit and greenstuff
- **Sexing:** When viewed in a good light, hens have redder irises than cock birds
- **Compatibility:** Best kept individually or in pairs
- **Pet appeal:** Colourful and relatively quiet

The Roseate Cockatoo used to be the most common cockatoo kept as a pet, but following the ban on the exportation of these birds from Australia in 1960, the numbers overseas have declined (and the price has risen accordingly), although youngsters are produced each year from aviary strains. In Australia, where the Roseate, or Galah, remains a pest species in agricultural areas, these birds are freely available at low cost.

Young Roseate Cockatoos can be easily distinguished by their grey irises, and tend to be duller in coloration overall. Yet in a few instances, the traditional means of sexing adults on the basis of eye coloration has proved unreliable. Chicks fledge around seven weeks of age, and should be fully independent about one month later. Youngsters can become very tame and develop into talented mimics. Although easier to handle than the larger *Cacatua* species, they may still inflict a painful bite.

If you are considering keeping a Roseate Cockatoo as a household pet, you should take great care with the diet you provide. These birds are prone to a specific type of tumour known as a lipoma, which is non-cancerous accumulation of fatty tissue. A swelling, frequently near the sternum (breastbone), and an apparent inability to fly are the typical signs, although lipomas can develop anywhere on the body. Herein lies the danger – while it is possible in certain cases to remove the tumour by surgery, especially while it is relatively small, the likelihood of success is influenced by its location on the body. In some instances, this can render the tumour inoperable. It may well be that a relatively high level of dietary fat is a contributory factor in the development of lipomas, bearing in mind that Roseate Cockatoos normally feed in open country, foraging for cereal seeds rather than nuts. It is unlikely that their diet in the wild contains a significant amount of fat. In the domestic environment, where the birds expend relatively little energy, fat can accumulate quite readily in the body. As a preventative measure, therefore, attempt to persuade these birds to take cereal seeds, including boiled maize, on a regular basis, rather than being dependent exclusively on a conventional parrot mixture.

A white mutation of the Roseate has been recorded, with the typically grey areas being replaced by white plumage, leaving the pink body coloration otherwise unaffected. A pair of Roseates of this type were kept in the extensive collection of the Duke of Bedford, being obtained in 1928. Although they bred consistently for nearly twenty years, no similarly coloured offspring resulted. The cock of this pair, which was mature when acquired by the Duke, died after twenty-five years. Another British aviculturist who had this rare mutation found that such birds inevitably failed to hatch or died in the nest, and this may account for the apparent absence of such chicks from the Duke of Bedford's pair.

Below: **Roseate Cockatoo**
The splendid colour of this relatively docile cockatoo can vary in tone from bird to bird.

Grey Parrot
Psittacus erithacus

- **Distribution:** Across a wide belt of central Africa, from the Guinea Islands eastwards to Kenya and northwestern Tanzania
- **Size:** 33 cm (13 in)
- **Diet:** Parrot food, fruit and greenstuff
- **Sexing:** Hens may be a paler grey, most noticeable on the back and wings, but this is not entirely reliable
- **Compatibility:** Best kept in pairs or individually
- **Pet appeal:** Probably the best talking parrot

The Grey Parrot has been a cherished pet in Europe since the reign of Henry VIII during the sixteenth century, and possibly even earlier than this time. Young birds, easily distinguished by their grey irises, become tame and can develop an unparalleled vocabulary, although adult Greys have nervous natures and will neither talk nor settle well in the home. They are sometimes described as 'growlers', because of the characteristic noise that they make when approached closely. The irises start to change from grey to yellow when the bird is about five months old.

There can be considerable variation in the depth of the grey coloration. Lighter birds, often advertised as 'Silvers', are generally most expensive, whereas the duller Timneh subspecies (*P. e. timneh*) from the western part of the Grey's range, is often significantly cheaper. It is slightly smaller than the nominate form, with a pinkish upper mandible and a black tip. Instead of bright red tail feathers, those of the Timneh are almost maroon in appearance. Nevertheless, such birds can become as tame as any other Grey Parrot and can be taught to talk successfully. Occasionally, Grey Parrots with scattered areas of red in their grey plumage can be seen. This often occurs in older birds and the coloration may be transitory, disappearing at the next moult, or conversely sometimes increasing in area. There is even a report of a Grey Parrot that was predominantly pinkish in colour, being reminiscent of a flamingo in its overall coloration.

Grey Parrots need a considerable amount of attention if they are kept on their own indoors. They are extremely intelligent birds, as studies have shown, and need constant stimulation if they are not to become bored. This fact, coupled with their sensitive natures, is probably why many Greys become notorious feather-pluckers, denuding much of their body, starting on the breast and even moving to the back of the head and wings. New feathers are removed as they start to emerge through the skin. Rapid action is necessary to prevent the condition becoming habitual (see also page 28 for more on feather-plucking).

It is not unusual for a single Grey Parrot hen to lay a clutch of eggs in its cage, although of course these will not be fertile. If a cock bird is then acquired, the parrots may well nest successfully in the home. Unfortunately, many pairs do not prove reliable parents once their chicks hatch, after the incubation period of approximately four weeks. Hopefully, the young parrots should leave the nest when approximately three months old. Like other parrots of similar size, Grey Parrots may not attempt to breed until at least their fourth year, but once they start breeding they have a long reproductive life. There are reliable records of birds breeding well into their thirties. Again, tame individuals may display signs of aggression at this time of year. Not all pairs prove compatible, however, and thus make no attempt to nest, even though they are mature.

Grey Parrots appear to have a natural ability to mimic the human voice, and can be taught new words and even phrases throughout their lives. They are talented whistlers and imitators of household sounds, with whistling notes featuring prominently in their natural calls. Unfortunately,

Above: **Grey Parrot**
This is the 'classic' pet parrot beloved of its owners throughout the world for its intelligence and astounding talking ability.

however, even the most talented talking Grey is often reluctant to perform on demand in front of strangers. They are introverted birds in this respect; once they feel that they are no longer the centre of attention, they are likely to start talking without any prompting.

Senegal Parrot

Poicephalus senegalus

- **Distribution:** In a broad band of country from Senegal eastwards to Chad
- **Size:** 23 cm (9 in)
- **Diet:** Parrot mixture, with pine nuts. They often show a preference for peanuts, which can be useful for taming purposes
- **Sexing:** Impossible to distinguish the sexes reliably by sight
- **Compatibility:** Best kept alone or in pairs
- **Pet appeal:** Small, yet typical parrot appearance. Can become very tame and may learn to say a few words

The Senegal is the best-known member of a genus of nine square-tailed parrots confined to Africa. Three subspecies are recognized on the basis of the depth of abdominal coloration. This ranges from yellow through orange to red. Birds with the latter coloration should not be confused with the distinctive Red-bellied Parrot (*P. rufiventris*), which is confined to eastern Africa.

Senegal Parrots were once widely kept as pet birds in the home, but are now better known as aviary occupants. Youngsters can be distinguished by their black irises, as well as by the pinkish tinges to their beaks when newly fledged. The eye coloration becomes progressively lighter as they mature, turning grey and finally bright yellow in an adult bird. A newly fledged Senegal will develop into a marvellous pet, with all the attributes of the larger species, although being less costly to buy and easier to manage. The problem is likely to be acquiring a genuine youngster.

Pairs have been persuaded to nest indoors. Indeed, a Swedish breeder was successful with Senegals housed simply in a traditional wire parrot cage. The birds used a nestbox attached to the outside of their small enclosure, and were successful in rearing one youngster out of two that hatched. It fledged at nine weeks of age and was feeding itself within a week. Three or four eggs appear to form the usual clutch for this species, and the incubation period is four weeks.

Unlike many parrots, Senegal Parrots are ideal for a garden aviary in a relatively urbanized area. They are normally quiet birds and their calls consist largely of a series of high-pitched whistles, which are not very disturbing. The main drawback of some pairs is that they are highly nervous; they are likely to retreat to a nestbox or within the shelter of their aviary when disturbed or when anyone approaches.

It is not unusual for Senegal Parrots to start breeding activities during the colder months of the year. At this stage, the hen may display by tail-flaring close to the nestbox. In order to minimize the risk of egg-binding, position the box in the aviary shelter. This location will also be darker, which seems to encourage breeding behaviour in this group of parrots. They can prove quite destructive, however, especially when breeding, and their perches may need to be replaced frequently as a result of their chewing activities.

Below: **Senegal Parrot**
Once they settle down, these compact African parrots can become very rewarding pets full of personality. They will also breed fairly readily in suitable surroundings.

Ring-necked Parakeet
Psittacula krameri

- **Distribution:** Occurs over a vast area, in a band across northern Africa, and in Asia from western Pakistan through India to Burma. Introduced to many localities, including parts of Europe
- **Size:** 40.5 cm (16 in)
- **Diet:** Parrot mixture, pine nuts, fruit and greenstuff
- **Sexing:** Hens lack the characteristic black neck collar of the cock bird
- **Compatibility:** Can be housed individually, in pairs or in groups
- **Pet appeal:** Elegant appearance and ability to talk

This species has a wider distribution than any other member of the parrot family, and was probably the first psittacine to be seen alive in Europe.

During the days of ancient Rome, such birds were so highly prized that they fetched more than slaves, being kept in cages made of rare and precious metals ornamented with jewels. In India, these parakeets were regarded as sacred, because of their ability to reproduce the sound of the human voice.

It is possible to distinguish between the Indian and African races by virtue of their beaks and overall size. The Indian Ring-necked Parakeet (*P.k. manillensis*) is the larger form, and has a black lower mandible; that of the African race (*P. k. krameri*) shows dull red markings at the base of the beak.

Ring-necks are more often seen as aviary rather than pet birds, since they do not become very affectionate towards their owner in most cases. This is probably linked to the fact that there is no strong

natural pair bond in these birds, unlike other psittacines such as the Grey Parrot. Indeed, for most of the year, the hen is dominant to the cock, and there is no direct physical contact between the members of the pair, such as the mutual preening commonly seen in many other parrots outside the breeding period. Ring-necked Parakeets are also very active birds and require spacious surroundings in which to exercise, particularly if their elegant appearance is to be fully appreciated.

Below: **Ring-necked Parakeet**
This male displays the typical collar of dark feathers around its neck. Long popular as an aviary bird, and celebrated for its talking ability, the Ring-necked Parakeet has given rise to several colourful mutations in captivity, including Lutino, Blue and Albino forms.

A young Ring-necked Parakeet can become tame and will learn to speak a few words, even if it apparently resents being petted. Immatures resemble adult hens in appearance, but have shorter tails and grey rather than yellow irises. It is not uncommon for adult cock birds, showing a full pink collar, to be sold as youngsters, but this characteristic marking will not be apparent until they are at least three or four years old.

When housed in a suitably spacious outdoor aviary, a breeding group of Ring-necks can be kept together satisfactorily. Ideally, offer them a choice of nesting sites. They tend to nest earlier in the year than other parakeets, with eggs and chicks likely to be lost during a cold spell. The birds normally prove reliable parents, however, especially once the chicks hatch. For best results, house these parakeets in individual pairs. A clutch may consist of as many as six eggs, hatching on average about twenty-three days after being laid. Fledging normally takes place about seven weeks later.

As might be expected, these parakeets have a fairly rigorously defined breeding pattern, and rarely produce more than one round of chicks in a season, unless early chicks fail to hatch or die soon afterwards. Removing the offspring at an early stage for hand-rearing can also encourage an adult pair to breed again shortly afterwards.

Ring-necked Parakeets are frequently recommended for people who want to start keeping and breeding parrot-like birds. They are attractive, easy to sex and generally keen to breed. Their calls may be disturbing in close proximity to neighbouring houses, however, and they can prove destructive. Always leave the nestbox available to the birds throughout the year. Ring-necked Parakeets are prone to frost-bite if allowed to roost on perches in the outside flight during the winter months, and so should be encouraged to use a nestbox for the purpose. Some pairs prove less destructive than others, but any exposed woodwork in the flight is likely to be attacked by their strong beaks. Records show that Ring-necks are long-lived birds; one individual is known to have lived for a period of fifty years.

As a result of their popularity as aviary birds, it is perhaps not surprising that various mutations of the Ring-necked Parakeet have occurred in captive stock. Some are also known to have originated in the wild. The Lutino, a striking shade of yellow in which the cock's pink collar remains unaffected, is the most widely distributed at present, although the Blue form has fallen in price quite considerably during recent years and become more widespread. By combining these mutations, an Albino form has been produced, but has aroused little interest. Since it takes three years or so for Ring-necked Parakeets to mature, the development of mutations tends to be a relatively slow process compared with other parrots, such as lovebirds, which can breed during their first year.

Turquoisine Grass Parakeet

Neophema pulchella

- **Distribution:** Ranges through southeastern Australia
- **Size:** 20 cm (8 in)
- **Diet:** Small cereal seeds, with some sunflower, as well as greenfood and fruit, especially sweet apple
- **Sexing:** Cocks can be distinguished by their red wing patches
- **Compatibility:** Pairs must be kept apart from each other, but can sometimes be mixed with finches and even Cockatiels. Problems are most likely to arise during the breeding season
- **Pet appeal:** Quiet, attractive and often free breeding

The Turquoisine is one of the most colourful members of this genus of small parakeets, which will thrive in relatively small aviaries and nest quite readily. They are in no way true pet birds, however, as they will not talk, and remain flighty, particularly if closely confined. Because of their relatively thin skulls, injuries and even fatalities are not unknown under these circumstances. Grass parakeets, as their name suggests, frequently prefer to feed on seed spilt on the floor of their enclosure, and so good hygiene is vital if they are not to succumb to intestinal problems. For the same reason they are at risk from intestinal parasites, and newly acquired stock should be treated routinely with a deworming compound before being released into the aviary.

Although believed to be rare in the wild, this species is well established in aviaries throughout the world. Their calls are not disturbing, being almost musical to the ear, nor are these parakeets destructive in aviary surroundings. It is generally best to acquire young stock at the end of the breeding season, rather than buying adult birds. The youngsters will be mature by the following year, and their age will be known, while the vices encountered in certain adult birds are less likely to arise. Some cock birds, for example, can prove especially aggressive to their

intended mates at the onset of the breeding season.

Introduce the nestbox to the aviary in the spring. The hen will lay about five eggs in an average clutch, although double this number is not unknown. It is doubtful whether she will be able to incubate as many as ten eggs successfully, and it may be possible to foster a few under a pair of budgerigars. The incubation period is the same in either instance, being about eighteen days. Indeed, it is thought that the *Neophema* parakeets are the closest relatives of the Budgerigar.

The chicks grow quite rapidly, sometimes fledging before four weeks of age, and are soon independent. Indeed, it is best to remove them from the aviary as early as possible, in case they are attacked by the cock bird in particular, while his mate is laying a second round of eggs. Take extra care when catching the chicks, since they are usually extremely nervous and may fly hard into the aviary wire, with fatal consequences. If possible, hang sheeting around the flight at this stage, so as to create the impression of a solid barrier to the young birds.

Having been bred in captivity for generations, Grass Parakeets are quite hardy, although they can be prone to respiratory disorders during periods of persistently damp and cold weather. Other species with identical needs to those of the Turquoisine include Bourke's Parakeet (*N. bourkii*) and the Splendid Parakeet (*N. splendida*). The Redrump Parakeet (*Psephotus haematogaster*) also has similar requirements, but tends to prove more aggressive.

Below: **Plum-headed Parakeet**
The male bird of this Asian parakeet is clearly recognizable by the superb plum colour of its head. A colourful and relatively quiet species with a musical call.

Plum-headed Parakeet

Psittacula cyanocephala

- **Distribution:** Over much of the Indian subcontinent, including Sri Lanka
- **Size:** 33 cm (13 in)
- **Diet:** A parakeet mixture of sunflower, small pine nuts, groats, canary seed and millets, as well as fruit and greenstuff
- **Sexing:** Males have plum-coloured heads
- **Compatibility:** Can sometimes be kept safely in a mixed collection alongside finches, but breeding pairs certainly should be kept in separate accommodation
- **Pet appeal:** Lively and attractive

Left: **Turquoisine Grass Parakeet**
A striking male specimen, clearly showing the distinctive red wing patches. A vivacious species.

The Plum-headed Parakeet is probably more suitable than the Ring-necked Parakeet for an outdoor aviary in a built-up area. Certainly Plum-heads should not be kept in cages for any length of time, and will require a flight if they are to be kept indoors. They are not as noisy nor destructive as their more commonly seen relative, and usually prove keen to breed in suitable surroundings. Unfortunately, although Plum-heads normally lay later than Ring-necks, losses of chicks can be high because hens tend to stop brooding their offspring at night before they are fully feathered, and a cold spell may then be disastrous for them.

Under normal circumstances, the incubation period and fledging times are about the same as for a Ring-neck (see page 127), but if a nesting failure occurs, the Plum-

headed Parakeet is most unlikely to breed again that year.

Fruit is a particular favourite with these parakeets, as it is with the closely related Blossom-headed Parakeet (*P. rosa*). Many people consider that these forms should be grouped as subspecies. The Blossom-head can be distinguished, however, by virtue of the pinker forehead and cheeks in males, whereas hens have a small patch of maroon plumage on each wing. Young birds lack these markings, but otherwise resemble the hen. Perhaps surprisingly, a relatively high proportion of young birds of both species moult out to be cocks. Early signs are the appearance of a few sporadic purplish feathers on the head, sometimes before the final adult moult. Examining the bird closely in the hand may be the only way to spot this initial change.

Mealy Rosella
Platycercus adscitus

- **Distribution:** Northeastern Australia
- **Size:** 30 cm (12 in)
- **Diet:** Parakeet mixture consisting essentially of cereal seeds and a little sunflower, with plenty of greenfood (especially during the breeding season) and fruit, notably apple
- **Sexing:** Cocks lack any trace of the wing stripe present in hens and immature birds
- **Compatibility:** Keep in pairs
- **Pet appeal:** Attractive coloration

The eight species of rosella parakeet are naturally confined to Australia, although some have been introduced successfully elsewhere, notably to New Zealand. Like all the Australian parakeets, but with the

Above: **Mealy Rosella**
This beautifully marked parakeet will bring superb colour to any aviary. Keep pairs apart from each other to prevent the fighting that will inevitably occur. In calm and suitable conditions, these birds will breed reliably season after season.

notable exception of the Budgerigar, these birds are not suitable as home pets. They make striking aviary occupants, however, and usually breed quite readily. This particular group can prove exceptionally aggressive, and pairs should be watched closely to ensure that the hen is not being persecuted unduly. They can have a long and fruitful reproductive life, often rearing two clutches of chicks each year for more than twenty years. Pairs differ significantly in this respect, however, and not all will breed so freely. Best

results are likely if these parakeets are kept away from each other, with pairs never being housed side by side since they will squabble persistently under these particular circumstances.

The Mealy Rosella was first seen alive in Europe during 1863, at the London Zoo, and bred successfully in Belgium nine years later. They can have up to eight chicks per clutch, and may rear them all without difficulties. In an emergency, however, a co-operative breeding pair of Cockatiels can be used as foster-parents. Unlike related species, including the Golden-mantled Rosella (*P. eximius*) and Pennant's Parakeet (*P. elegans*), this particular species is often only single-brooded. The incubation period is approximately twenty-six days, with the young fledging at about five weeks of age.

LORIES AND LORIKEETS
FAMILY LORIIDAE

These parrots form a distinctive group in terms of their feeding habits, and are usually extremely colourful in appearance. They have a lively, jaunty manner and many species are quite noisy, with high-pitched and far-carrying calls, although they do not rival the larger parrots in this respect. The term 'lorikeet' is usually applied to species with long tails, contrasting with the short-tailed lories. The most significant common feature of these birds is unlikely to be immediately apparent, however, unless they are watched closely. They feed largely on nectar and pollen gathered from flowers, and their tongues are tipped with brushlike protrusions known as papillae that serve to gather their food efficiently. Particles of pollen are effectively rasped from the flowers and accumulated on the tongue, where the microscopic granules are compressed into pellets of a suitable size to be swallowed. They are also known as 'brush-tongued parrots'.

The dietary habits of lories and lorikeets tend to render them unsuitable for close confinement in the domestic environment. Their droppings are extremely fluid, while the predominantly sticky nature of their foodstuffs is a further problem. In an outside aviary, a pair of these birds will be seen to good effect, however, and most species prove keen to nest in aviary surroundings. Provide an enclosure that is easy to clean, with a solid floor that can be hosed down regularly. Two typical species are listed here.

Green-naped Lorikeet
Trichoglossus haematodus

- **Distribution:** Populations of this species occur on many islands to the north and east of Bali, extending to New Caledonia and the Loyalty Islands, off the east coast of Australia. These lorikeets are also found in northern and eastern parts of Australia, ranging down to Tasmania
- **Size:** 26 cm (10.25 in)
- **Diet:** Nectar and fruit should form the basis of the diet, although these birds may also take a small quantity of seed and greenstuff
- **Sexing:** There are no visual distinctions between the sexes
- **Compatibility:** Pairs are best kept alone
- **Pet appeal:** Colourful, lively and playful

These lorikeets are often available, and pairs nest readily when kept in suitable surroundings. Indeed, they may have reared chicks as long ago as the 1780s, in the aviaries of the Governor of the Cape of Good Hope. The discontinuous distribution of the Green-naped Lorikeet has led to the development of many distinctive races. Some taxonomists

recognize no less than twenty-one subspecies, each of which vary slightly in their appearance. Considerable confusion exists over the correct identification of these birds. (If you would like to pursue this further, consult one of the specialist texts listed in the Further Reading list on page 198.)

While the island races, such as the Green-naped (*T. h. haematodus*) and Edward's Lorikeet (*T. h. capistratus*), are most commonly seen in Europe and the United States, the Rainbow or Swainson's Lorikeet (*T. h. moluccanus*) is more widely kept in Australian collections. The naturally tame nature of these birds is seen to good effect at the Currumbin Bird Sanctuary close to Brisbane, where large flocks congregate to feed on trays of bread soaked in honey, much to the delight of visitors. Similar scenes, albeit on a smaller scale, can be seen at campsites and other localities elsewhere in Queensland.

A very wide range of nectar mixtures are used for lories and lorikeets, although there is a growing trend towards using one of the proprietary brands, which simply need to be dissolved in warm water as directed. These contain all the necessary ingredients to keep these birds in good health. Do not change

Left: Green-naped Lorikeet
These delightful birds will bring colour and movement to an aviary.

the diet suddenly, however, for fear of precipitating a sudden and possibly fatal digestive disturbance. When you first acquire a lory or lorikeet, keep to the nectar mixture that it has been fed on and gradually introduce the new solution in a separate feeder. Using a proprietary lory nectar also saves considerable time, rather than having to mix various foodstuffs together.

Good hygiene is particularly essential with this group of birds, since moulds and bacteria can develop rapidly on their feeding containers. Preferably, use a tubular drinker rather than an open pot. There is less risk of the nectar mixture becoming contaminated and the birds will not get immersed in the sticky solution, as may happen with an open pot. Use a special bottle brush to clean drinkers properly, ensuring that no trace of a previous feed remains when a new solution is added to the container.

Nectar mixtures need to be prepared fresh, although it is possible to store them for a short period in a refrigerator, allowing the solution to warm up to room temperature before use. In any event, discard a solution after a twenty-four hour period. Diced fruit can be provided either in a plastic pot that hooks on to the cage or aviary mesh, or in a heavy earthenware container which the birds cannot overturn. Provide a selection of fruit if possible, with

apples, grapes and even bananas proving popular. In order to mimic the natural diet of these brush-tongued parrots, sprinkle pollen granules lightly over the fruit; these granules are available from health food stores.

Green-naped Lorikeets usually produce clutches consisting of two eggs, with the incubation period being about twenty-six days. They may lay two or three times a year, with the chicks fledging at about eight weeks old. It is not unusual for the young birds to be plucked before they leave the nest. Take particular care to ensure that they do not become chilled at this stage, until their plumage regrows.

Red Lory
Eos bornea

- **Distribution:** Occurs on various islands to the west of New Guinea; Ceram, Goram, Ceramlaut, Amboina, Saparua. Also on Watubela and the Kai Islands of Indonesia
- **Size:** Up to 30 cm (12 in)
- **Diet:** Nectar and fruit, as well as greenstuff, and possibly some seed
- **Sexing:** There are no reliable external sexual differences
- **Compatiblity:** Best kept individually or in pairs
- **Pet appeal:** Colourful and relatively inexpensive

The Red Lory is another species bred quite regularly in collections. As in the Green-naped Lorikeet, young birds can be distinguished by their brown irises and dark markings on their beaks. If obtained shortly after fledging, by about fifteen weeks of age, these birds can make most attractive, albeit messy pets. These lories have proved highly talented mimics, although their natural calls tend to be rather raucous.

Pairs of Red Lories have nested successfully indoors, although simply because two birds spend long periods of time preening each other does not prove that they are of opposite sexes, since they are social by nature. Size can be a useful pointer in some cases only. Cocks generally have broader heads and beaks, and may appear bigger overall. It is important to remember that there is a noticeable variation in size between the four subspecies of the Red Lory. It may be that the birds in question are simply of different races, and not necessarily a breeding pair. You will need to confirm this by a reliable sexing technique, unless the birds have reared chicks.

Although these parrots are quite hardy once properly acclimatized, always provide a nestbox for them to roost in, so that they are not exposed to the worst of the winter weather. Whereas the food of seedeating psittacines will not freeze, nectar solutions will turn into ice

Above: **Red Lory**
Provide these attractive birds with a varied diet based on fruit and nectar, but including seed and greenstuff. Ensure that they have protection from cold weather if they are kept in temperate climates.

quite rapidly. You will need to keep a close watch on the food supply of birds housed in a garden aviary at this time of year.

Make fresh water available to lories and lorikeets, and indoors give them a regular bath or spray. Always remove the water once the birds have finished immersing themselves in a container, since it is likely to be soiled. Provide drinking water in a tubular container to prevent it being splashed around the room.

This group of parrots is susceptible to the fungal disease candidiasis, which often shows as whitish deposits in the mouth. A dietary deficiency of Vitamin A may increase their susceptibility to the infection, and newly imported birds are most commonly affected. Check for any signs of this infection before buying stock.

Other species of lory and lorikeet have similar requirements to the Red Lory and Green-naped Lorikeet. Smaller types, such as Goldie's Lorikeet (*Glossopsitta goldiei*), which is about 19 cm (7.5 in) in length, are possibly better suited to the domestic environment, although less playful than their larger relatives.

SOFTBILLS

The term 'softbill' is applied to a wide variety of birds that do not feed essentially on seed, but on other items, such as fruit, nectar and insects. There are thus various subdivisions within this grouping, such as the nectivorous softbills, which include hummingbirds, and the frugivorous species like many tanagers. As a general rule, the insectivorous softbills are the hardest to acclimatize successfully, since, in most instances, they need to be weaned on to inert foodstuffs that will then form the major proportion of their diet. Although these divisions are useful as a basic guide to the dietary needs of particular birds, they should not be relied upon totally. Indeed, it is doubtful if any bird survives exclusively on fruit, and small insects such as fruit flies are vital in the diet of nectivores.

The management of softbills is much more straightforward today than at any stage in the past. Complete balanced diets and livefood suitable for the diverse needs of all species are available – by mail-order if necessary – from specialist suppliers. There is no longer any need to spend considerable time mixing and preparing complex softbill food from the basic ingredients, and this in turn has led to a greater interest in this group of birds.

Many softbills are colourful, and some are talented songsters. They vary in size from diminutive hummingbirds to hornbills, for example, that may be over 60 cm (2 ft) in length. Certain species are suitable for inclusion in a mixed aviary, whereas others need to be kept on their own in individual pairs. Partly as a result of improvements in the diets available to these birds, breeding results are being achieved with much greater frequency. The following species reflect the individual groups of birds that are usually available and that can be kept easily, sometimes as part of a mixed collection. While the vast majority of softbills will not become pets in the same sense as parrots, the mynahs are a notable exception, and can also prove talented mimics.

Above: **African Yellow White-eye**
This is one of many handsome White-eyes in the genus Zosterops. *Lively birds for a mixed collection.*

Right: **Greater Hill Mynah**
This is perhaps the most well known of all the softbills. It has long been celebrated for its personality.

Greater Hill Mynah
Gracula religiosa

- **Distribution:** India, Southeast Asia and Indonesia
- **Size:** 30 cm (12 in)
- **Diet:** Softbill food, fruit and suitable livefood, such as mealworms
- **Sexing:** Sexes alike, but the wattles of hens may be less conspicuous
- **Compatibility:** Best kept individually or in pairs
- **Pet appeal:** A very talented mimic

Of all softbills, the Greater Hill Mynah is undeniably the most talented mimic, able to intonate words and phrases in a very clear manner. It will also mimic sounds, such as a ringing telephone, with equal precision, which can prove a drawback in the home. Unlike most parrots, these birds are not normally shy in front of strangers, and will run through their repertoire with little need for prompting. They are quite noisy birds by nature, given to a series of whistling calls. Young Greater Hill Mynahs are usually advertised as 'gapers', because of their habit of gaping for food. At this stage, in immature plumage, they tend to be duller in coloration than adults, and lack the distinctive wattles present on the sides and back of the head. These mynahs occur over a wide area, and there is some variation in both size and colour, with the Javan race being accepted as the biggest.

Since mynah birds have very active natures, you must give considerable thought to their accommodation indoors. The cramped box-type cages marketed for these birds are totally unsuitable. Build a small flight indoors, ideally rectangular, so your pet can have adequate exercise. These birds are exceedingly messy, so use melamine-coated board for the solid parts of the structure and build in a sliding tray for cleaning purposes on the floor of the cage. Be prepared to change the floor covering at least daily. Newspaper is ideal for lining the bottom of the cage, since it is fairly absorbent, cheap and easily replaceable.

Mynahs also need to have the opportunity to bathe daily. An earthenware dog bowl is useful for this purpose, enabling the bird to have a thorough soaking without tipping up the container. Provide the bath a short time before you clean the cage out, removing the bowl then. A certain amount of dirt will be washed off, and so the bird should not be encouraged to drink from its bath. If you do not provide a suitable bath, the bird will attempt to soak itself in its waterpot. As an alternative to a bowl of water, you can spray the mynah daily, which helps to keep its plumage in good condition.

In the summer months, it is quite possible to house mynahs satisfactorily in an outdoor aviary. Indeed, in mild areas, they can live outside throughout the year, providing that an adequate shelter is available. They tend to dislike damp, foggy weather more than crisp and clear days, and should be watched closely during such times for any signs of respiratory problems. The fearless, tame natures of these birds can be fully appreciated when they are housed under such conditions. Pairs will almost certainly attempt to nest, although surgical sexing is necessary to recognize a true pair. There are so many races that although minor differences will be apparent between individuals, these should not be taken as sexual distinctions. It may be that cocks have darker eyes than hens, but this is not true in every instance.

These mynahs build an untidy nest, often taking over a parakeet nestbox for the purpose. Accommodate breeding pairs in aviaries on their own and watch them closely; in some instances, the cock's desire to nest may lead him to attack the hen if she does not respond in a positive manner. Even tame birds can become nervous when breeding, and should not be disturbed unnecessarily, especially once the chicks have hatched. The normal clutch consists of two or three bluish eggs, speckled with brown markings. Both sexes share the incubation duties, and the chicks should hatch in two weeks. Provide a regular supply of livefood at this stage to ensure that the young mynahs are reared successfully. Crickets and mealworms are usually taken readily, and these should be dusted with a vitamin and mineral preparation beforehand.

The youngsters fledge when about a month old, being easily distinguished by their duller plumage and the bald, pale yellow areas on the head where the wattles develop later on. They are usually able to feed themselves within days of fledging. Once they have reached this stage, it is safest to remove the young mynahs at the earliest opportunity, since otherwise they may be attacked and killed by their parents. Adult breeding pairs of mynahs can be quite prolific, nesting almost constantly through the year if allowed to do so.

Although these mynah birds share the parrots' powers of mimicry, they are not such long-lived birds as most parrots, for example. Fifteen years is probably their average life-expectancy, but older individuals have been reported. Feather loss is often associated with ageing mynah birds, and it is best to keep elderly birds indoors, certainly over the winter months in temperate climates.

Right: **Greater Hill Mynah**
In common with other members of the starling family, these birds are lively and assertive in character, with a waddling gait and strong flight action. In the wild, Hill Mynahs move through forested areas in small flocks, emitting a cacophony of calls ranging from low laughing sounds to piercing, far-carrying whistles. This wide 'vocal' range undoubtedly accounts for their quite superb talent for imitating tones of the human voice and other familiar sounds.

Chinese Crested Mynah
Acridotheres cristatellus

- **Distribution:** Central and Southern China, Hainan and Taiwan
- **Size:** 25 cm (10 in)
- **Diet:** Good-quality softbill diet and diced fruit, as well as livefood
- **Sexing:** Hens may be distinguished by their smaller crests
- **Compatibility:** House pairs separately
- **Pet appeal:** Hardy and active aviary occupants

While the Hill Mynah is best known by virtue of its powers of mimicry, a variety of other species of mynah are often available. The Chinese Crested Mynah is a typical member of this latter group, which includes the Common Mynah (*A. tristis*). If obtained young, Chinese Crested Mynahs can become quite tame although, like the Hill Mynah, they will not relish such close contact with their owners as do many parrots. Although not especially musical, their natural calls are not unpleasant on the ear. They can learn to talk, but only develop a rather limited repertoire. Again, these birds are active and need to be kept either in a flight or in an outside aviary. Their aggressive tendencies are likely to be displayed, however, if they are kept as part of a mixed collection, especially during the breeding season.

Being naturally omnivorous, these birds are very easy to cater for. Once acclimatized properly, they can be kept outside throughout the year without artificial heat, providing there is an aviary shelter where they can roost. A pair will nest using a

Above. **Chinese Crested Mynah**
Although not as talented a mimic as the Greater Hill Mynah, this species will learn to talk and will provide plenty of activity in an aviary. Hardy once acclimatized and will breed readily in captivity.

parakeet nestbox, which they line with twigs, grass and similar material. The clutch consists of three or four eggs, which should hatch after about two weeks. Be sure to provide plenty of livefood to ensure successful rearing. Fledging occurs about three weeks later, and the young birds are usually quite advanced, being able to feed themselves almost immediately. Transfer them to separate quarters as soon as possible, by which time the adults are likely to be nesting again. The young can be easily recognized by their duller coloration overall.

Green Glossy Starling
Lamprotornis chalybeus

- **Distribution:** Over much of Africa, from Senegal to Sudan and southwards to the Transvaal and Namibia
- **Size:** 24 cm (9.5 in)
- **Diet:** Softbill food or mynah pellets, with a regular supply of diced fruit and insects
- **Sexing:** Hens tend to be smaller, but no clear visual distinctions exist between the sexes
- **Compatibility:** Best accommodated in individual pairs
- **Pet appeal:** Attractive and rank among the easiest softbills to breed in an aviary

This species and the related Purple Glossy Starling (*L. purpureus*) are often available. Although short-tailed, they do not differ significantly from the previous species in terms of care. Breeding details are also similar. Pairs will become aggressive when breeding, and although they may be housed with other large robust softbills for part of the year, it is safest to keep them in separate aviaries at this time.

Ruppell's Long-tailed Glossy Starling
Lamprotornis purpuropterus

- **Distribution:** East Africa, from Ethiopia southwards to Zaire, Uganda and Kenya
- **Size:** 56 cm (22 in)
- **Diet:** Softbill food, diced fruit and insects
- **Sexing:** Hens may be distinguished in some cases by their shorter tail feathers
- **Compatibility:** Best kept in individual pairs. Can prove aggressive
- **Pet appeal:** Striking aviary occupants

The Glossy Starlings are colourful birds, especially when seen in good light, where the iridescence in the plumage can be fully appreciated. They are easy to cater for, and relatively hardy, but need particular care during the acclimatization phase. Glossy Starlings are not really suitable as cage birds, however, because of their active natures, and additionally, with the Long-tailed species, their tails will almost certainly be damaged if the birds are closely confined. The Ruppell's can be distinguished from related species by the presence of violet plumage on the nape, while the remainder of the upperparts are more violet-blue than in the Long-tailed (*L. caudatus*). Ruppell's Starlings are also slightly smaller overall. A third species, Meve's Long-tailed Glossy Starling (*L. mevesii*), is rarer in aviculture and lacks the gold-bronze coloration over the head seen in the Ruppell's.

These starlings will make use of a nestbox for breeding purposes, building a nest of assorted materials, including dry leaves. The clutch of three eggs will hatch in just over two weeks. Once there are chicks,

Above: **Long-tailed Glossy Starling**
Be sure to allow these birds sufficient room in the aviary for their long tails to be appreciated and not damaged. They will appreciate a regular bath or spray with tepid water.

ensure that a varied and constant supply of livefood is offered daily, as invertebrates are vital for the young starlings. Fledging takes place quite rapidly, with the young birds leaving the nest when just over three weeks old. Within a week, they will start feeding independently. Remove them as soon as possible, since the adult birds are likely to be nesting again and may turn aggressive. Glossy Starlings generally spend most of their time moving from perch to perch, rarely descending to the ground. Check that the perches are arranged so that the birds cannot injure their long tails. In an indoor flight, provide bathing facilities or spray the birds regularly.

These birds are also known as Blue-eared Glossy Starlings, and can be confused with the closely related Lesser Blue-eared species (*L. choropterus*), which is virtually identical but smaller overall, rarely exceeding 18 cm (7 in) in size. They are quite vocal birds, with a distinct chatter and some more musical calls, yet they do not talk, in contrast to the mynah birds. Young birds can be recognized quite easily by their blackish plumage, which has only a tinge of green present at this stage.

A number of similar species of African starling are sometimes available. These include the Spreo or Superb Starling (*Spreo superbus*), characterized by its orange breast, and the Amethyst Starling (*Cinnyricinclus leucogaster*). In the latter species, hens can be distinguished by their brownish coloration. Perhaps the most striking member of the group is the Royal Starling (*Cosmopsarus regius*), which tends to be more insectivorous than related starlings.

Right: **Purple Glossy Starling**
One of the several glossy starlings that make graceful aviary subjects.

Pied Barbet
Tricholaema leucomelan

- **Distribution:** Southern Africa to Angola and Zambia
- **Size:** 15 cm (6 in)
- **Diet:** Softbill food, fruit and insects
- **Sexing:** No visual distinctions between the sexes
- **Compatibility:** Will attack smaller species; best housed in individual pairs
- **Pet appeal:** Lively and interesting

The barbets as a group have a wide distribution, being found in tropical regions throughout the world. They are characterized by the bristles around their beaks, which are strong and powerful. Indeed, they resemble woodpeckers in some respects, since they bore nesting cavities into rotten wood. Hollow logs are ideal as nesting boxes, enabling the birds to tunnel into the base. Failing these, build a standard nestbox about 30 cm (12 in) deep and disguise the outside with cork bark. Hammering away at such wood not only serves to protect the woodwork of the flight, it also keeps the birds' beaks in trim and may stimulate breeding activity. A softwood lining within the box will enable the birds to complete their nest. The height of the box seems quite important to some species.

Breeding results are not common, partly because of the difficulty of sexing these birds, but several successes have been reported. Barbets will roost in the nesting site, so this does not necessarily indicate breeding behaviour, although if they use the nestbox during the day, this is a more positive sign. The incubation period is about two weeks, with two or possibly three eggs being laid. The young birds fledge by about three weeks of age, and can be recognized at this stage by the absence of red plumage on the head. They also lack the characteristic serrations, often described as teeth, on the sides of the beak. The youngsters soon feed themselves, and must be removed from the flight in case they are attacked by the cock bird.

It is safest to overwinter barbets indoors in heated quarters, even if they spend the summer months in an outside aviary. Having relatively fine plumage, these birds often appear uncomfortable in cold weather, and can be at risk from frostbite. Fruit should figure prominently in the diets of the more frugivorous species, with a lower level of softbill food being required. Insects of various types are taken readily by all barbets, and appear essential for breeding success. These birds are also avid bathers, and must be given a suitable container of water inside for this purpose. They can live for over a decade in suitable surroundings.

Left: **Pied Barbet**
In the wild, barbets spend much of their time among the trees of their forest home, seldom straying on to the ground for any length of time. It is important to provide the mix of fruits, vegetable matter and insects that makes up their diet. Provide a hollow log for nesting.

White-rumped Shama

Copsychus malabaricus

- **Distribution:** Across Asia, from India to southwest China, and neighbouring islands, including the Greater Sundas and Andamans
- **Size:** Up to 28 cm (11 in)
- **Diet:** Typical softbill diet, including fruit and insects
- **Sexing:** Cock birds are much more colourful, with orange-brown underparts. Hens are smaller and significantly duller, being brownish overall
- **Compatibility:** Can be unpredictable. Best kept with softbills of a similar size, such as fruitsuckers
- **Pet appeal:** Jaunty gait, and cocks have a most melodic song

Long considered one of the most attractive softbills seen in aviaries, shamas prove lively, flicking their tails in a variety of postures. They soon become tame, even feeding from the hand. Livefood is especially important to maintain these members of the thrush family.

Various races of White-rumped Shama are recognized, and the size of these birds does vary somewhat throughout their range. Be sure to acclimatize these birds carefully and give them adequate protection, including heat during the winter months. Related species need identical care. Although shamas are kept in cages throughout their native lands, this is not a satisfactory way to maintain these birds for any length of time. Keep them instead in a reasonably spacious inside flight, where you can appreciate their graceful beauty to the full.

Shamas have been bred successfully on many occasions, although pairs are best kept on their own at this time. The hen will construct an open nest and may be persuaded to use a suitable basket for the purpose. As many as five eggs can be laid, and these start hatching after an incubation period of nearly two weeks, with fledging taking place following a similar period of time. Young cock birds will have shorter tails than those of adults, and their overall coloration is noticeably less distinctive.

Below: **White-rumped Shama**
This male shows the typical orange underparts and long elegant tail. These are lively and melodious birds that thrive in captivity. Ideally, keep them in an indoor flight.

White-crested Jay Thrush

Garrulax leucolophus

- **Distribution:** From northeastern parts of Southeast Asia ranging into southern China
- **Size:** 25cm (10 in)
- **Diet:** Softbill food, plenty of invertebrates, fruit and even seeds
- **Sexing:** Sexes are alike, but cocks may be distinguished by their melodic song
- **Compatibility:** Can be kept with softbills of similar size, but not with smaller birds
- **Pet appeal:** An active, lively songster

The White-crested Jay Thrush is just one of forty-four species of Laughing Jay Thrushes in the genus *Garrulax*. They are popular aviary birds, and easy to cater for, frequently becoming tame. While it is possible

Left: **White-crested Jay Thrush**
An energetic bird that is hardy and full of song. A little aggressive.

Below: **Pekin Robin**
A sprightly, easy-care softbill that will flourish in a planted flight.

to keep jay thrushes together in a group, they do tend to be aggressive, and certainly a breeding pair should be housed on their own.

Jay thrushes have quite a loud call, which is uttered frequently. They are omnivorous in their feeding habits, and may even consume sunflower seed, which they crack open with their powerful bills. Although fairly drab in overall coloration, the contrasts present in the plumage give jay thrushes an attractive appearance.

The White-crested Jay Thrush is found in forests at quite high altitudes throughout its range. It can prove hardy in captivity, providing the birds can roost in a dry shelter. A densely planted aviary should encourage breeding, with a round open nest being built in a suitable locality. Four eggs form a typical clutch and both birds share the incubation duties, with the youngsters hatching after a period of twelve days. The adults can prove nervous at this time; leave them alone as much as possible and provide plenty of invertebrates.

Among other related species often available is the Hoami (*Garrulax canorus*), also known as the Melodious Jay Thrush and the Chinese Nightingale because of its attractive song.

Pekin Robin

Leiothrix lutea

- **Distribution:** From India to Burma and China
- **Size:** 15 cm (6 in)
- **Diet:** Softbill food, fruit and insects. Also seed and nectar
- **Sexing:** The cock's song
- **Compatibility:** Can be included in a mixed collection, but may interfere with the nests of other birds during the breeding season
- **Pet appeal:** A good songster, inexpensive and easy to keep

Because it is so easy to keep, this species provides an ideal introduction to the care of softbills. Since Pekin Robins naturally occur in areas of woodland, be sure to provide adequate cover in their accommodation, especially if you want to encourage a pair to start breeding. There may be minor plumage differences in these birds that may be taken to indicate a sexual difference. The yellowish throat is often paler in hens and the reddish area on the wings may also be absent in some cases, but such distinctions are not entirely reliable. When in breeding condition, however, there will be no doubt once cock birds start their attractive song.

Breeding is quite possible in a planted flight, where the birds weave an open nest, with moss being favoured for this purpose. A clutch of four eggs is typically laid; these should start to hatch after an incubation period of about two weeks and the chicks will fledge when nearly two weeks old. They may then live for over a decade. Livefood is vital during the rearing period. Keep these birds in heated accommodation during the winter. They will thrive in a spacious flight cage and become tame.

White-eye

Zosterops palpebrosa

- **Distribution:** Over the Indian subcontinent, much of Southeast Asia into western parts of China
- **Size:** 11.5 cm (4.5 in)
- **Diet:** Softbill food, nectar, finely chopped fruit and small insects
- **Sexing:** Cannot be sexed by visual means
- **Compatibility:** Agree well in groups, and can also be kept with waxbills and similar small species in a mixed collection
- **Pet appeal:** Alert, lively and social by nature

The Zosterops form a surprisingly large family of approximately eighty-five species with an extremely wide range, from Africa through Asia southwards across the Pacific Ocean to Australia. It can be difficult to distinguish between the various populations, although African species tend to be more yellowish in appearance. Some Zosterops are distinctive, however, such as the Chestnut-flanked White-eye (*Zosterops erythropleura*), characterized by the reddish brown plumage on the sides of the body.

Compared with other nectivores, such as sunbirds, Zosterops are

extremely easy birds to maintain. A proprietary nectar solution suits them well, and should be offered fresh daily, along with other suitable foods. Although it is impossible to sex Zosterops visually, they do best in small colonies, and will not usually squabble, even when breeding. It is at this time that you will hear the male's song. Their nests are surprisingly small, and spiders' webs, along with other more conventional nesting material, should be supplied to encourage breeding. Having built their hanging nest, both birds sit on the eggs. The incubation period is about twelve days, and an adequate supply of small insects, such as fruit flies, should be provided so that the chicks can be reared successfully. Assuming all goes well, the chicks fledge when less than two weeks old, but are still fed by their parents for a similar period of time until they are fully independent.

As may be expected, White-eyes are not hardy in cool temperate climates, and will need to be overwintered inside. In an indoor flight, their inquisitive behaviour and tame nature will be a constant source of fascination. If plants are included in such indoor flights, they can breed successfully under these conditions and raise their young.

Above: **Oriental White-eye**
These social and lively birds thrive on a varied diet based on nectar.

Right: **Fairy Bluebird**
A splendid cock bird showing off its iridescent blue back. Keep warm.

Yellow-vented Bulbul

Pycnonotus aurigaster

- **Distribution:** Southeast Asia, to southern China and offshore islands, including Java
- **Size:** 18 cm (7 in)
- **Diet:** Softbill diet, with fruit and insects
- **Sexing:** Cannot be sexed by visual differences
- **Compatibility:** May be kept with birds of similar size, but pairs are best accommodated separately
- **Pet appeal:** Lively, with a pleasant voice

The bulbuls, like the laughing thrushes, form a large group. They are popular avicultural subjects, in spite of their rather plain coloration. Some species are crested, such as the Red-eared or Red-whiskered Bulbul (*P. jocusus*), but in virtually all instances the sexes are identical in appearance. The Yellow-vented is a typical member of the family. It was first seen alive in Europe as long ago as 1865, when the species was exhibited at London Zoo. Keep these birds in a suitable flight, where a pair may attempt to nest. Cock birds have a rather attractive song,

although they are certainly not such talented songsters as shamas.

The cock's breeding display entails bowing and singing to an intended mate, with wings held slightly away from the body. A nest is often built in suitable vegetation, although some pairs will make use of a canary nest-pan to form the basis of their cup-shaped nest. The hen will incubate the eggs — typically a clutch of four — for about thirteen days. Provide livefood when the young birds are still in the nest. They fledge at the age of two weeks, having been fed by both members of

Above: **Yellow-vented Bulbul**
Cheerful and friendly, the bulbuls are widely distributed across Africa and Asia. This species is representative of the large family and an ideal aviary subject.

the pair. The adults will normally start nesting again after their first round of chicks have fledged, and they can become hostile towards them. Therefore, remove the young birds once they are eating on their own. Bulbuls have fairly fine feathering; for this reason, bring them inside for the winter months.

Fairy Bluebird
Irena puella

- **Distribution:** India and Southeast Asia, including offshore islands, such as Java and Sumatra
- **Size:** 25 cm (10 in)
- **Diet:** Softbill food, with diced fruit and insects
- **Sexing:** Cocks are distinguished by their glossy blue backs and black underparts. Hens are dark blue overall, with red eyes
- **Compatibility:** Can be aggressive. Keep pairs on their own
- **Pet appeal:** Striking coloration

This species is sometimes one of the more difficult softbills to acclimatize successfully, although fruit is more important than insects in its general diet. In common with most softbills, Fairy Bluebirds dislike cold, damp weather. They are prone to foot problems, including frostbite, if they are forced to spend the winter months in unheated accommodation. This is always inadvisable, even with established birds.

The sexes can be easily recognized, and a pair will often attempt to breed, preferring to construct their own nest in a bush rather than using a canary nest-pan for the purpose. The clutch consists of two eggs, which hatch after an incubation period of thirteen days. If you provide sufficient invertebrates to the adult birds for rearing purposes, the chicks should fledge within two weeks. They may not be fully independent until six weeks of age. Young Fairy Bluebirds of both sexes resemble adult hens in appearance, but can be easily distinguished by their darker eyes. Pairs, especially when breeding, should be kept on their own, as cocks in particular may become

fairly aggressive at this time.

Another closely related group of birds in the same small family as the Fairy Bluebirds is the Chloropsis or Leafsuckers. These birds are predominantly green in colour and surprisingly different in their habits, becoming tame very readily, and feeding on nectar, in addition to softbill food, fruit and insects. Male Leafsuckers can prove extremely aggressive towards their intended mates, and may have to be separated as a result. They have an agreeable song, but may also copy the calls of birds housed nearby.

Violet-blue Euphonia

Tanagra violacea

- **Distribution:** Northern South America; Venezuela eastwards to Guiana and Brazil. Also occurs on Trinidad
- **Size:** 10 cm (4 in)
- **Diet:** Softbill food, diced fruit, nectar and a little livefood
- **Sexing:** Cocks are considerably more colourful than the greenish hens
- **Compatibility:** Quite social
- **Pet appeal:** Small and attractive birds

These stocky little birds rank among the smallest members of the tanager group, and are not as easy to cater for as the Palm Tanager. With all softbills, it will pay dividends to travel and select stock personally, but this is certainly the case with euphonias. While cock birds of the various species can be distinguished without

Above: **Violet-blue Euphonia**
A fine cock bird of this lively and colourful South American species.

too much difficulty, this does not apply to the hens, which all tend to look alike.

These birds build an oval nest with a side entrance, and the hen lays four or possibly five eggs within. The incubation period is likely to be about sixteen days; with spiders being a favoured rearing food, as well as fruit. The chicks should fledge when around three weeks old, and the hen may then nest again in rapid succession. Like other euphonias, the Violet-blue has an attractive song, and is also capable of mimicking the calls of other birds. It was first seen in Europe in 1865. Although not common in aviculture, euphonias are ideal occupants for an indoor planted flight, because of their small size and pleasant dispositions.

Palm Tanager
Thraupis palmarum

- **Distribution:** Over a wide area from Central America southwards to Trinidad, the Guianas, Brazil, Bolivia and Paraguay
- **Size:** 18 cm (7 in)
- **Diet:** Softbill food, fruit and invertebrates
- **Sexing:** In some cases, hens are duller in appearance
- **Compatibility:** Can be housed with softbills of similar size
- **Pet appeal:** Unusual coloration

The Palm Tanager is one of the larger species of tanager, and less demanding in its requirements than most of the more colourful *Tangara* species, for example. Four subspecies are recognized throughout its extensive range, and this can complicate the pairing up process. Palm Tanagers will breed successfully in captivity, even making use of a nestbox for the purpose. The clutch typically consists of two eggs, which should hatch after thirteen days. Fruit flies may be taken in large numbers when the chicks have just hatched, along with other small items of livefood. The young tanagers fledge when about three weeks old, and are independent a month later.

Tanagers generally can be difficult to establish, and nectar is certainly required for the smaller species. They are also very fond of bathing, which keeps their plumage immaculate. While many species are not hardy, Palm Tanagers may live satisfactorily in an outside aviary through a mild winter once they are properly acclimatized, although you should bring than in at once if they appear uncomfortable. In common with other tanagers, these birds are not talented songsters. For members of the closely related genus *Ramphocelus*, such as the South American Scarlet Tanager (*R. bresilius*), colour feeding will be necessary to maintain the vivid red plumage over successive moults.

Below: **Palm Tanager**
Less colourful than some tanagers, but reasonably easy to maintain.

Bohemian Waxwing
Bombycilla garrulus

- **Distribution:** Occurs over a huge area; northern Europe, Asia and North America, showing migratory movements
- **Size:** 18 cm (7 in)
- **Diet:** Softbill food, with a good ration of fruit, especially berries in season, such as pyracantha. Also takes greenfood, but less keen on insects
- **Sexing:** No visual distinction possible between the sexes
- **Compatibility:** Not normally aggressive towards birds of similar size
- **Pet appeal:** Sleek, immaculate appearance. Best kept outdoors

These birds are named after the red markings on their inner flight feathers, which resemble wax in appearance. As suggested by their distribution, waxwings are hardy birds that can be kept in an outside aviary throughout the year without heat, although a shelter is recommended. As they are highly social birds, nesting in groups in the wild, a group can be housed together in an aviary quite safely. Waxwings are quite undemanding when breeding; hens will adopt a variety of sites for the purpose, using moss and other materials in order to construct a nest. Once the chicks have hatched, small items of livefood, such as hatchling crickets, will be required. Hens often become extremely tame at this time, and will also catch suitable livefood, such as mosquitoes in their aviary, as dusk falls on a summer evening.

Two further species of waxwing are identified, and although not as common in aviaries, both the Cedar Waxwing (*B. cedrorum*) and the Japanese Waxwing (*B. japonica*) require similar care. The latter species can be distinguished by the red tip to its tail, compared with the yellow coloration present in the Cedar Waxwing.

Below: **Bohemian Waxwing**
These stylish birds will grace any outdoor aviary with their handsome markings and lively nature. They can become tame when feeding young.

PIGEONS AND DOVES

This group of birds is classified in the family Columbidae. Although varying in size from the 18cm (7in) Ground Doves to the Crowned Pigeons, which are nearly 90cm (3ft) in overall size, the pigeons and doves have a fairly uniform appearance. The term 'dove' tends to be reserved for smaller birds, but this does not apply in every instance. Most species eat seed, but a few genera subsist largely on fruit. These are rarely encounted in aviculture, but can be easily maintained and bred on a diet of mynah pellets and diced fruit. Although the fruit-eating pigeons and doves tend to be brightly coloured in many cases, the seed-eating species are less striking. Most doves and pigeons do not require livefood, but some, such as the Tambourine Dove (*Turtur tympanistria*) and the related African Wood Doves, will consume invertebrates. Provide livefoods such as mealworms for these species.

Few aviculturists specialize in keeping pigeons as a group. These birds may appear rather sluggish and are normally kept as part of a mixed aviary. The smaller species will live and breed quite contentedly in such surroundings, but larger birds can create a disturbance, although not harming the other occupants of the aviary. As a general rule, only keep one pair of pigeons or doves in an aviary, especially during the breeding period, as fighting is likely to break out. The following is a selection of species that are often available and that can be housed quite satisfactorily in an aviary with finches.

Above: **Bleeding Heart Dove**
This is one of the many colourful doves that can be kept under aviary conditions. Be sure to provide a varied diet, including greenstuff.

Right: **Pink-necked Fruit Dove**
These handsome fruit doves – this is Ptilinopus porphyrea – live in the dense jungles of the South Pacific islands and Southeast Asia.

Diamond Dove
Geopelia cuneata

- **Distribution:** Over much of Australia, apart from the southwestern and eastern seaboards; not in Tasmania
- **Size:** 20 cm (8 in), including the long tail, which measures about 10 cm (4 in)
- **Diet:** Finch food, notably millets and canary seed, plus chopped greenstuff
- **Sexing:** Cocks in breeding condition have broader eye-rings of red skin and sometimes more spots on the wings than hens
- **Compatibility:** Keep pairs apart; otherwise these doves are ideal for including in a mixed collection of seedeaters
- **Pet appeal:** Dainty appearance and willingness to nest

These doves are popular aviary birds throughout the world. Their small size ensures that they will create no disturbance to other occupants of a communal aviary. Diamond Doves, unlike most pigeons, can also be kept in a large cage indoors, where they may well breed successfully. A canary nest-pan provides an ideal base for their nest, which they make from small twigs, feathers and moss; ensure

Left: **Diamond Dove**
Attractive and free breeding, this is an ideal dove for beginners.

that these materials are available in their quarters. They will spend periods of time walking and feeding on the floor of their aviary, and the cock bird will display by bowing to his intended mate, fanning his tail feathers open at the same time and cooing to her. Two eggs, in common with most pigeons, form the usual clutch, and these are incubated by both birds for a period of about thirteen days.

Unlike some species, the Diamond Dove is usually a model parent, both incubating the eggs and rearing the resulting chicks without difficulty. These develop quickly, and can fledge when only about eleven days old. Keep a watch on them at this stage to ensure that they do not become saturated in a rainstorm. When rearing chicks, give Diamond Doves suitable items such as egg-food. They are capable of producing three or four clutches of eggs in a season, and it will probably be necessary to withdraw the nest-pan during the winter months to prevent excessive laying. These birds are quite hardy, but dislike cold, damp weather. If finches are being transferred to an indoor flight for the winter, move the doves with them.

During recent years, various new mutations have become available; the Silver has been known for a number of years, but now russet-coloured and even pied Diamond Doves are being bred in ever increasing numbers.

Barbary Dove
Streptopelia 'risoria'

- **Distribution:** This is the domesticated form of the African Collared Dove (*S. roseogrisea*), which occurs in northern Africa, with a separate population in the vicinity of the Arabian Peninsula
- **Size:** 25 cm (10 in)
- **Diet:** Seeds, greenstuff
- **Sexing:** Cocks tend to be paler in overall coloration
- **Compatibility:** Best kept in individual pairs
- **Pet appeal:** Extraordinarily tame and gentle

The origins that led to the domestication of the Barbary Dove have been lost. The birds themselves are exceptionally steady and will not panic, unlike many larger pigeons. They are also very free-breeding, nesting even on the floor of a cage, with both birds sitting in turn on the typical clutch of two eggs. Ideally, encourage Barbary Doves to use a platform as a nesting site, and although they will frequently rear both chicks without any additional foodstuffs, a suitable softfood will be beneficial at this time to encourage success.

The young doves are fed initially on crop milk, which has a high level of protein. While Barbary Doves can be used successfully for fostering eggs of other species, it is vital to ensure as far as possible that the

two pairs of birds involved have laid their eggs at approximately the same time. This is because the production of crop milk is tied to the time of egg-laying, and if there is a wide discrepancy there will be no crop milk produced for the hatchling pigeons. This is likely to lead to their rapid demise. It may be possible to foster older chicks successfully, however, since these will be fed on seed rather than crop milk. Barbary Doves are usually good parents, but in some related species there is a tendency for only one member of a clutch to be reared successfully.

Most Barbary Doves are naturally quite tame, and will perch on the hand with little hesitation. It is for this reason that the pure white form, known as the Java Dove, is often popular with conjurors. Young birds in particular can become very trusting, although if kept indoors, do give them adequate space to prevent them becoming morose. Spray the birds regularly to keep their plumage in good condition. This will also serve to damp down the relatively high level of feather dust produced by this and other species of pigeons and doves.

Below: **Barbary Dove**
These extremely amenable doves are also recommended for people new to birdkeeping. Barbary Doves are tame by nature and will breed readily in a cage or aviary. They are often used to foster other species.

Senegal Dove
Streptopelia senegalensis

- **Distribution:** Over the whole of Africa, extending into Asia
- **Size:** 25 cm (10 in)
- **Diet:** Seeds, such as millet and canary seed, greenstuff and invertebrates
- **Sexing:** Hens are duller overall
- **Compatibility:** Keep pairs apart from each other
- **Pet appeal:** Colourful and a ready nester

Various subspecies of the Senegal Dove are recognized over its wide range, each with subtle differences in coloration, so that it can be difficult to select pairs with certainty. These doves are nevertheless easy to keep, and will breed readily if provided with suitable nesting facilities. Like most pigeons, they tend to build rather a loose nest; provide a support in the form of a

plywood tray to prevent eggs being lost from the nest. Two eggs form the usual clutch, with the incubation period being fourteen days. The chicks will fledge rapidly within a further fourteen days. Remove them from the aviary once they are eating independently, in case they are attacked by their parents, who will be keen to nest again.

Cape Dove
Oena capensis

- **Distribution:** Over much of Africa, from Senegal eastwards to the Arabian Peninsula, and southwards to the Cape. Also found on Madagascar.
- **Size:** 23 cm (9 in), including a long tail
- **Diet:** Small seeds, notably millet, greenstuff. May occasionally sample livefood
- **Sexing:** Cocks are easily distinguishable by the large area

of black on the face, extending down to the lower breast
- **Compatibility:** Probably best kept in individual pairs with finches or small softbills, although in a large aviary these doves can be housed successfully in a group
- **Pet appeal:** Graceful, elegant appearance

Common throughout its wide range, the Cape Dove is often available to birdkeepers. Pairs generally will not nest as readily as the Diamond Dove. They need careful acclimatization if imported to temperate regions and must be brought indoors for the winter months, being housed in a suitable flight for this period. It is not unusual for pairs to start breeding during the winter, so nesting facilities should be provided. Two eggs are laid, hatching after a period of fourteen days, with the young fledging after a similar interval. Once a pair start

Above: **Senegal Dove**
It is important to provide some form of support on which these and similar doves can build their fairly insubstantial nests. This will prevent the loss of eggs.

Right: **Cape Dove**
A cock bird, clearly recognizable by the black plumage on the face and breast. These doves are not as hardy as some species and must be carefully acclimatized if they are kept in temperate climates.

breeding, which may not be until their second or third year in new surroundings, they generally continue to nest without problems. Cape Doves have a similar display to Diamond Doves, but cocks do not fan their tails in all cases. Like most other pigeons, they are known under a variety of other common names, including Masked Dove, Namaqua Dove and Long-tailed Dove.

Ruddy Ground Dove
Columbina talpacoti

- **Distribution:** Central America, extending into South America east of the Andes as far as Paraguay and Argentina
- **Size:** 18 cm (7 in)
- **Diet:** Small seeds such as millet, with greenstuff
- **Sexing:** Hens are duller, being greyish brown overall
- **Compatibility:** Although it is possible to keep small groups of these birds successfully in large and well-planted aviaries, pairs are best housed individually
- **Pet appeal:** Ideal for a mixed collection

Several species of Ground Dove are occasionally available, all from Central and South America. They are also sometimes known as Pygmy Doves, in view of their relatively small size. These doves tend to nest quite close to the ground, often in a shrub, where they will build a fairly tight nest. Preferably, however, provide a support in the form of a wooden platform or a canary nest-pan. The Ruddy Ground Dove, also known as the Talpacoti Dove, was first bred at London Zoo as long ago as 1868, and repeated successes have occurred since then. The two eggs will hatch after a period of about fourteen days, and the chicks will fledge after a similar period. Pairs usually raise several broods over the course of a season. The Ground Doves generally are quite undemanding in terms of their care, although better breeding results occur in a planted aviary, where there is cover available to them. They are unlikely to be completely hardy, however, and it will be safest to bring them indoors for the duration of the winter months in temperate regions.

Other related species need similar care. The Gold-billed Ground Dove (*C. cruziana*) from the western seaboard of South America, characterized by the yellow base to its beak, is quite often seen.

Right: **Gold-billed Ground Dove**
As with other Ground Doves, keep this species in a planted aviary.

FANCY PIGEONS

A vast number of fancy pigeon breeds is recognized. Many of them can be kept in dovecotes in small numbers, although most fanciers prefer to have a special loft for their birds, on the same basis as for housing racing stock.

The so-called flying breeds of pigeon are probably most suitable for housing in a dovecote. There is a group of birds known as the high-flyers, because of their spectacular flying ability, which takes them high up into the sky. Breeds in this category include three that originated in the United Kingdom. The West of England Tumbler, popularly known as the West, is noted for the acrobatic nature of its flight. Another related breed with Tumbler ancestry, the Birmingham Roller, also occurs in a wide range of colours, although this feature is judged less significant than the birds' flying skills. A group of pigeons flying together is known as a kit, and the Rollers will actually spin through the air as they perform their flight pattern. (See Further Reading on page 198 for specialist books.)

The other British high-flying breed is the Flying Tippler, which has great endurance. These pigeons can remain on the wing for long periods, often for eighteen hours or even longer, during which time they neither feed nor drink. Their management is rather specialized, as may be expected, and the prevailing weather conditions are important. Never fly these birds during periods of fog or rain, as this will seriously hamper their abilities and is likely to lead to birds being lost. Flying competitions are carried out under prescribed rules for these pigeons.

Continental breeds of high-flying pigeons are also known. The Cumulet, whose name is said to reflect the ability of these birds to ascend to cumulus clouds, is a French breed. The Danzig High Flyer, somewhat similar to a Fantail in appearance, will fly on its own rather than as part of a kit.

The Fantail is probably the most universally kept breed of fancy pigeon, and is also one of the oldest, being known as long ago as the seventeenth century. Pure white birds are popular, but Fantails can be bred in a very wide range of colours, since they are popular exhibition subjects rather than high-flyers. Indeed, a most bizarre range of exhibition pigeons has been developed. In some cases, such as the Owl Pigeons, the beaks are so reduced in size that the birds are not even able to feed their own chicks; these pigeons are described as being short-faced.

Although the management and breeding of exhibition birds can be quite demanding, the care of pigeons kept in a dovecote is quite straightforward. They will be quite hardy, but at first enclose them in their new accommodation. If you have obtained them locally, this will also prevent them from returning to their former abode. It is probably best to get young birds, as they will be more likely to settle in new surroundings. Ensure that the pigeons are safe from potential predators; fix wire around the bottom of the dovecote pole, for example, so that cats cannot climb up.

Ideally, the birds should have food and water in the dovecote, although this may not always be practical. All fancy breeds require a standard mixture of pigeon corn, with each bird eating perhaps 5 gm (2 oz) of food daily. Three-quarters of the mix should consist of barley, wheat and kibbled maize, plus a quarter of peas

Above and right: **Fancy Pigeons**
The White Fantails shown above are exhibition birds par excellence, bred specifically for their elegant appearance. The pigeon shown at right is perhaps more typical of those kept at liberty. A wide variety of pigeons and doves can be kept in a suitable dovecote.

and beans. Other seeds, including plain canary seed, hemp and tares can also be supplied. When adding peas and beans, bear in mind the size of the individual bird's gape, since some beans are too large for small breeds. The proportions will also vary according to the bird concerned; racing stock, for example, is typically fed a diet with a higher proportion of peas and beans. It is easy to buy an appropriate mixture. A diet intended for young birds will also be suitable for the smaller pigeons.

Pigeons will drink a surprisingly large volume of water, and this must be freely available, along with an appropriate pigeon grit. Place the food in an earthenware vessel that cannot be tipped over. Provide the water in a covered container; otherwise it will become fouled.

The breeding period rarely presents any difficulties. The usual clutch of two eggs is incubated in turn by both birds, and the chicks should hatch after a period of approximately eighteen days. Unfortunately, it is difficult to sex the young pigeons, known as squeakers, until they themselves are in breeding condition. Under normal

circumstances, the population of a dovecote will increase quite rapidly during the breeding season. Sell off any surplus stock to avoid overcrowding in the accommodation.

Pigeons flying free in an urban area can cause complaints. Also bear in mind that, even with the best possible supervision, some birds will be lost and this can be upsetting. It may be helpful to ring the offspring so that in the future there is an increased possibility that straying pigeons may be returned to you. Special breed rings of the appropriate size are available. Apply these closed rings before the feet become too large. Take the three

long toes and slide the band over them, then, with the short back toe pressed vertically against the leg, slip the band up until this toe is freed. The ring will then be able to move freely up and down the leg, from above the toes to the next joint.

Always keep a close watch on free-flying birds. They are more likely to pick up diseases carried by wild birds than their aviary counterparts. Runny eyes are a symptom of the disease known as infectious coryza; this infection can be spread easily, especially in the confined conditions of a dovecote. Catch affected birds and transfer them to separate accommodation for treatment.

BANTAMS AND OTHER FOWL

Bantams are small fowl, which in some instances have larger counterparts, such as the Rhode Island Red. They are valued as foster-parents, being capable of hatching the eggs of waterfowl, pheasants and similar birds. Yet they have much in their favour as birds to be kept in their own right. They are colourful in many cases, and hardly, being easier to keep in the confines of a garden than their larger relatives. Hens will lay quite readily and, although their eggs are not as large as those of standard poultry, they are still highly edible.

There is also a considerable interest in exhibition bantams, with about fifty distinct breeds being recognized, and many distinctive varieties within these categories. Such birds are often a regular feature of agricultural shows. Stock is usually available at relatively low cost but, if possible, always choose young birds rather than mature stock, which may be nearing the end of its useful reproductive life. For this reason, it is often best to avoid auctions, where older birds may be included, and buy direct from a breeder instead. Here, we look at the three main categories of bantam – Light, Heavy and Fancy – and then consider the management of broody bantams and their use as foster-parents. Certain birds are more suitable for this purpose than others.

Above: **Golden Sebright Bantam**
A hen and cock bird of this outstanding exhibition breed. Showing standards for bantams are as exacting as for every other subject.

Right: **White Crested Dutch**
The extraordinary crest of this bantam creates a stunning display that wins many admiring glances at an exhibition of Fancy Breeds.

Light Breeds

The Light Breeds of bantam weigh up to about 850 gm (30 oz). They are generally active and lively, doing best in a screened run from which they cannot escape. These bantams tend to be more flighty and, at liberty, are best kept with one wing clipped, otherwise they may fly on to a neighbour's property. The various Mediterranean breeds, such as the Minorcas, feature in this group, as well as the popular Old English Game bantams. The latter have been bred in a wide range of colours, and have the typical upright stance of other Light Breeds. Many bantams in this group do not become broody yet prove good layers and, although interesting in their own right, they will not be suitable for fostering purposes.

Heavy Breeds

As a rule, the so-called Heavy Breeds of bantam tend to prove the best broodies. These include the Australorps, which are black in colour, and the Marans, which lay brown eggs. The Araucana produces bluish eggs, which are perfectly edible in spite of their unusual coloration. The Silkie Bantam, universally accepted as being the most suitable breed as a broody hen, is not strictly a bantam, but a fowl, in view of its large size.

Fancy Breeds

The third category features Fancy Breeds that are primarily kept for their decorative appearance. These include the Barbu d'Uccles and the Barbu d'Anvers, which are variants of the Belgian, but with feathered legs. (This can be significant in a practical as well as a decorative way, since, as a general rule, those bantams with feathers extending over their legs show a greater tendency to go broody.) Other Fancy Breeds include the Polish, with its profuse head feathering, and the strikingly attractive Sebright bantams. These are essentially valued as exhibition birds. It can take a considerable period of time to prepare bantams for a show, where they will be judged to the appropriate standards for the breed concerned. Nevertheless, their decorative appeal will enhance any garden. Cockerels can be vocal at an early hour, however, as with larger domestic fowl, so they may need to be confined to avoid complaints.

Bantams are normally kept in small groups consisting of one cockerel and several hens. If kept without artificial light, the birds will come into lay in early spring, although this can be earlier if a light bulb is used in their quarters through the winter. While sudden changes in the pattern of lighting will depress egg-laying, a gradual increase or constant pattern of lighting ensuring fourteen hours daily will encourage the bantams to lay during the winter. Manipulation of the lighting regimen in this way is essential for exhibition breeders so that bantam chicks are ready for shows later in the season.

Managing broody bantams

A broody bantam is simply a hen in breeding condition. It is possible to induce this behaviour by placing a

Above: **Frizzle Bantam**
The contrast of black and white creates a striking spectacle.

Above: **Silkie Bantam**
This handsome breed makes an excellent broody hen for fostering. It is large for a bantam, however, and can be classified as a fowl.

dummy egg in the desired nesting site. She will spend long periods sitting on the nest, refusing to leave unless physically removed, and returning at the earliest opportunity.

Separate quarters are necessary for broody hens, where they will not be disturbed. It may be preferable to move the bird right at the end of the day, so that hopefully she will continue roosting on the new nesting site after dark. The steadiest bantams are likely to prove the most reliable sitters. Wheat or corn are the only foods that should be offered, in

addition to water and grit. The hen will come off the eggs for short periods, and it will then be possible to check their fertility.

The fertile egg passes through several distinct stages as the chick develops. After an incubation period of approximately a week, it should be possible to detect a pattern of

developing blood vessels and a lighter area, known as the air space. The technique used is sometimes described as candling, since formerly the egg was held in front of a candle to illuminate the egg's contents. Today, a torch or electric light bulb is used for the purpose. Take care not to keep the eggs out of the nest longer than necessary, nor to overheat them in front of the light source. Never handle eggs excessively, especially during the early part of the incubation period, when the developing embryo is most vulnerable to jarring movements.

By twelve days into the incubation period, the fertile eggs will appear almost opaque. Those which are infertile or in which the developing germ has died will be clear. (It is for this reason that the description of 'clear eggs' arose for those that were not fertilized.) The air space should increase in size throughout the incubation period until hatching. If an incubator is being used, then a check on the fertility of the eggs and the development of the embryos is certainly to be recommended. Discard infertile eggs or those containing dead embryos as they take up space and may present a danger to fertile eggs. They could explode in the incubator, scattering their contents around the interior.

Right: **English Game Cock**
These very popular show birds can be recognized by their upright stance.

Bantams as foster-parents

There are both advantages and drawbacks to the use of broody bantams as foster-parents. Not all hens will sit properly and a few may desert their clutches. Also, particularly with larger fowl, chicks can be inadvertently injured while they are small. Maintaining a flock of bantams entails considerably more work than having an incubator on hand for a clutch of eggs; the birds must be treated routinely for parasites, for example. Yet, conversely, the more natural system of using broodies can yield dividends, especially when the chicks hatch. The bantam will encourage the birds to eat and they will not become imprinted towards humans as do hand-raised chicks.

The difficult period with a broody is when she and the young chicks are transferred to the breeding coop, with an attached run. Avoid placing this in an area of long grass, as the chicks can get soaked and cold in heavy rain. Check the young birds several times during the day at first to ensure that they have remained close to the broody and have not become chilled. Water pots should be very shallow, so there is no risk

of the chicks drowning, and food should be supplied in similar containers. Watch the youngsters closely; ducklings, notably various teal and carolinas, may be reluctant to eat at first. Livefood may encourage them, particularly if mixed in with the rearing food. Alternatively, sprinkle a little egg-food on the backs of the ducklings; they will remove this as they preen each other in the normal way.

Keep the broody within the coop, where she cannot steal the chicks' food, but allow her out for regular periods of exercise. If you are using a broody to raise ducklings, increase the depth of the water container as the ducklings grow, so that they can start to bathe. They will then venture into the run for longer periods. It is vital that the coop and run remain in a sheltered locality, however, so that the chicks will not be exposed to prolonged sunshine, which may precipitate heatstroke and rapid death. Screen and shade at least part of their enclosure as an additional precaution. The broody can be left with her chicks for five weeks or so, by which time they will be nearly fully feathered and able to lead independent lives.

Left: **Silver Sebright Bantam**
This is one of the most attractive of the Fancy Breeds. Each white feather is outlined in black, producing an elegant plumage display. This cock bird has the fine red comb - a 'pea' comb rather than the serrated type - and wattles typical of male fowls.

Right: **Curly Lyonnaise**
An appealing French breed of bantam with ruffled feathers in black.

Below: **A bantam fostering ducklings.**
Using a bantam to hatch out and raise such birds has natural advantages over using an incubator.

PHEASANTS AND QUAIL

T hese birds spend much of their time on the ground, and although some can be kept satisfactorily at liberty, the majority are housed in aviary surroundings. Take particular care with the floor covering; it must drain well, so a thick layer of sand should be ideal. Gravel can be used in some instances, but the birds may swallow a sufficient quantity to cause digestive problems, notably impaction of the crop. Grass provides a natural base for an aviary, and will be eaten by most birds in this group. Since they will often spend considerable periods of time walking close to the perimeter of the aviary, it is often recommended to construct paths of sand around the edge and plant up the central area. Plant this not only with grass but also with suitable vegetation that will provide cover for these rather nervous birds. This in turn should discourage them from flying vertically and injuring themselves on the roof of the aviary. As an added precaution against injuries of this type, you may want to include a false roof in the aviary (see page 46).

Preferably, erect solid barriers between aviaries in a block. This is especially important with pheasants, as cock birds will attempt to attack each other through the mesh of their enclosures.

Do not be surprised if you see these birds with sand in their plumage; dust-bathing is common with some species, and helps to keep the feathering in good condition.

When first introducing such birds to new aviaries, remember that they are likely to be very nervous until they have settled in these quarters. Keep disturbances down to a minimum. Prepare to protect newly planted shrubs, using plastic covers around their sides to prevent the birds attacking them before they have an opportunity to become established.

Above: **Crested Partridge**
A colourful species from the forests of Southeast Asia. The bright crest of feathers shows this to be a cock bird. Be sure to provide warmth and shelter during temperate winters.

Right: **Golden Pheasant**
A cock bird, showing the splendid colouring that has earned it justifiable acclaim around the world. Various colour mutations available include a paler form.

Californian Quail

Callipepla californica

- **Distribution:** The western side of North America, from California to Oregon, extending also into Mexico
- **Size:** 25 cm (10 in)
- **Diet:** Chick crumbs, millet; will also take some greenfood and invertebrates
- **Sexing:** Hens are easily distinguished by their smaller crests and the lack of white plumage on their heads
- **Compatibility:** Pairs should be kept apart from each other
- **Pet appeal:** Unusual appearance and ease of maintenance

The Californian is one of the less demanding species of quail, and its care presents no great difficulty, although these birds do best in a relatively large aviary. They will perch in the flight, and thus, because of their size, they can disturb smaller birds. Yet quails will not attack their companions, even when breeding, although cocks will be aggressive towards each other and must be kept apart.

Californian Quails will attempt to nest quite readily, with breeding success being significantly more likely in a planted aviary. Here, typically beneath a bush, the hen will prepare a simple hollow and lay as many as twenty eggs, which she broods alone for a period of twenty-three days. The young quails will start to run around shortly after hatching. Offer them suitable rearing foods, including a softbill food, egg-food and greenstuff chopped into small pieces. In terms of seed, offer them blue maw; this comes from poppies and, being extremely fine, can be eaten by young quail with little difficulty. As the chicks get older, introduce them to adult foods, notably crumbs containing about twenty percent protein.

If the eggs are abandoned by the hen, or if you want to maximize on egg production, use an incubator. Set the temperature of the incubator at about 38–39°C (100–102°F) and transfer the hatchling birds to a brooder once they have emerged from the eggs. On occasions, bantams have also hatched these quails successfully. Be prepared for some rearing losses, since the Californian Quail is not always an easy species in this regard, with chick mortality sometimes being high. These quail dislike damp weather, but are otherwise hardy under general circumstances. Always provide a suitable entrance to the shelter of the aviary, enabling the birds to roost inside.

Below: **Californian Quail**
A cock bird. These quails will thrive in a well-planted aviary.

Bobwhite Quail
Colinus virginianus

- **Distribution:** Southwards from Arizona extending to Sonora in Mexico
- **Size:** 23 cm (9 in)
- **Diet:** Typical mixture of chick crumbs and millets, with some greenfood
- **Sexing:** Hens are paler overall, with buff rather than white throats
- **Compatibility:** Keep pairs apart from each other
- **Pet appeal:** Attractive, unusual coloration and ease of taming

Twenty-one subspecies of Bobwhite Quail are recognized, many of which have evolved local names, such as the Texas Bobwhite (*C. v. texanus*). They will happily take a variety of seeds, being associated with agricultural areas throughout their natural range, where they will also feed on insects that cause damage to crops growing in the fields.

Left: **Bobwhite Quail**
Familiar and widely bred in captivity, these quails will prosper in a planted aviary. This is a cock bird.

Bobwhite Quail are well established in aviaries worldwide, with pairs usually being keen to breed. A hen will go to great lengths to disguise her nesting site, building a more elaborate structure than the Gambel's Quail, often with a dome to hide the nest from above. The clutch size is quite variable, normally in the range of twelve to twenty eggs. These are white in colour, and should hatch just over three weeks after laying. When the chicks emerge from the eggs, be sure to give them adequate space, as they may otherwise start to pluck their feathers in such stressful conditions.

Bobwhite Quail also dislike periods of cold, damp weather, so ensure they can find sanctuary in the interior of the aviary shelter by making a small hinged door to fit an appropriate gap. The potential lifespan of these birds can be as long as a decade under suitable environmental conditions.

The Bobwhite is a colourful and attractive species and justifiably popular, although again, these birds will perch in an aviary, which can be disturbing to the other occupants on occasion. Can become quite tame.

Gambel's Quail
Callipepla gambelii

- **Distribution:** Northwestern California to southern Nevada and Utah, extending to western Texas and New Mexico
- **Size:** 25 cm (10 in)
- **Diet:** Chick crumbs and mixed millet, with some greenstuff and livefood
- **Sexing:** Hens can be distinguished by their smaller crests, as well as by their grey rather than black heads
- **Compatibility:** Pairs need to be kept apart from each other
- **Pet appeal:** Considered by some as being more striking than the Californian Quail

This species is very similar to the Californian Quail, but tends to settle better in the confines of an aviary, being more terrestrial in its habits. A pair will thrive even in indoor surroundings, but require cover in their enclosure, especially for breeding purposes. Both clutch size and incubation period are as for the Californian Quail.

Insects are less vital during the rearing period than in the case of other quails. Young birds can usually be sexed by two months of age. These quail are even less keen on damp surroundings than their relatives, however, since they originate in arid terrain. (They are also known as the Desert Quail for this reason.) Quail chicks can drown if they become saturated in a rainstorm. Ensure that the hen can nest under cover, rather than in the open exposed to bad weather.

Right: **Gambel's Quail**
The natural range of this species borders that of the Californian Quail but does not overlap it, concentrating principally on the drier habitats of the western USA. This is a cock bird, as is clear from the distinctive black head and the prominent crest.

Rain Quail

Coturnix coromandelica

- **Distribution:** India, Sri Lanka and Burma, including the Shan States
- **Size:** 15 cm (6 in)
- **Diet:** Chick crumbs, millet seeds, chopped greenfood, some invertebrates
- **Sexing:** Hens can be easily distinguished since they lack black markings on the head and breast
- **Compatibility:** Pairs need to be kept apart from each other
- **Pet appeal:** Small and easy to cater for

Cock birds of this species are characterized by a prominent area of black plumage in the centre of their breasts, giving rise to their alternative description of Black-breasted Quail. While not bred on the same scale as the Japanese Quail, this species will frequently nest, even in a large cage. Yet like many quails, the hen may lay in a haphazard fashion, unless provided with adequate cover. In addition, a cock may persecute a single female to the extent that she is not permitted to sit for any length of time. For this reason, it is preferable to house these quails in trios for breeding purposes, with two hens being kept with an individual cock bird.

Breeding details are similar to those for the Japanese Quail, with young birds growing rapidly. Take particular care during the breeding period, however, to ensure that the quail are not panicked, causing them to fly up with considerable force, possibly injuring themselves badly, if not fatally. Severe lacerations to the scalp caused by flying hard into aviary mesh can heal, but the affected area may not refeather and the bird will be permanently disfigured. Since they come from a tropical area, these birds are again at risk from the effects of frostbite.

Below: **Rain Quail**
Quite appropriately, this cock bird has been photographed in the wild in the pouring rain. Evidently, these Asian quails can endure damp conditions more readily than their North American counterparts, but it is always advisable to provide shelter in their aviary.

Japanese Quail

Coturnix coturnix

- **Distribution:** Eurasia into northern Africa
- **Size:** 18 cm (7 in)
- **Diet:** Chick crumbs, with mixed millets plus greenfood
- **Sexing:** Hens have less black markings on the underparts
- **Compability:** Keep pairs apart from other quails
- **Pet appeal:** Free feeding and an ideal introduction to quail breeding

The Japanese Quail is now bred in large numbers for commercial purposes, whereas formerly their wild counterparts were caught for food. As domestication has proceeded, so hybridization has occurred, and stock today tends to be less nervous than its wild relatives. The various strains that have been evolved are known under separate names. Both Manchurians and Pharaohs can be sexed by slight differences in breast coloration, with the plumage of hens being more greyish, and speckling is clearly apparent here. The English White variety cannot be sexed in this way, however, nor can the British Range, which is dark in overall coloration. In terms of appearance, the Tuxedo is effectively a combination of these two latter types. These birds can be sexed when only a fortnight old, and hens in some instances will be laying within weeks of hatching. At this stage, female quail become progressively larger than their mates, and with adult stock that show no difference in coloration, it can be possible to distinguish pairs by this means. When weighed, hens are significantly heavier overall.

A clutch may consist of a dozen eggs, which should hatch after a period of eighteen days. The young birds soon start to feed themselves, taking small seeds, such as blue maw, sprinkled on egg-food at first. These quail are essentially terrestrial by nature, and will rarely disturb perching birds if provided with adequate cover on the floor of their enclosure. They will prove quite hardy, but should be encouraged to roost under cover. Also, it is inadvisable to allow them access to an outside area where there is thick snow on the ground, because of the risk of frostbite.

Right: **Japanese Quail**
Now bred on a commercial basis, these quails make excellent aviary subjects. Easy to feed and breed.

Chinese Painted Quail
Excalifactoria chinensis

- **Distribution:** Over much of Southeast Asia, from India to southeastern China, as well as Sri Lanka, Formosa and Hainan
- **Size:** 12.5 cm (5 in)
- **Diet:** Chick crumbs, mixed millets, greenstuff and some insects
- **Sexing:** Hens are easily recognized by their brownish overall coloration, lacking the bluish plumage of the male
- **Compatibility:** Cocks need to be kept apart from each other
- **Pet appeal:** Quite colourful, freely available and easy to keep

The Chinese Painted Quail has long been valued as an aviary occupant to clear up the seeds spilt by finches in a mixed collection. Yet these small quails are more than just effective scavengers. They provide colour and charm to a part of the aviary that otherwise may not be used, and their breeding behaviour is fascinating, especially the development of their chicks. A great advantage of these quails is that they will live exclusively on the ground and will not interfere with other birds, although if there are low perches in the flight, they may use these on occasions. Chinese Painted Quail show much less of a tendency to fly up than related species, even when disturbed, preferring instead to seek out cover.

Always keep these birds in trios, with two hens being housed in the company of a cock bird. Otherwise, a single hen is liable to be persecuted, and will certainly be plucked – typically around the neck – by her intended mate. In cage surroundings, screen off a corner with cardboard to encourage successful breeding. If the cock bird appears to be harassing a hen that has laid, then remove him.

The clutch size for this species can be relatively small, with possibly only six eggs being laid at a time. Unfortunately, as domestication of the Chinese Painted Quail has proceeded, so the incidence of hens that refuse to incubate their own eggs has also risen. This is almost certainly linked to the fact that incubators have been used extensively in the breeding of these birds. Wild-caught birds, although rarely available in avicultural circles, have a much better reputation for incubating their own eggs.

If the hen does refuse to sit, transfer the eggs to an incubator set at a temperature of 39°C (102°F) and a relative humidity of 50 percent. In either instance, the chicks should hatch within eighteen days, and possibly even earlier. At this point, they are truly tiny, often being compared with bumble-bees. In an aviary flight with 1.25 cm (½ in) mesh of any kind, they will be able to escape through the wire. For this reason, before the breeding season, fit a mesh of smaller dimensions around the base on the inner surface of the wire panel to a height of at least 23 cm (9 in). Hold the upper edge firmly in place by thin battening running around the flight and fixed to the uprights.

The young quail are especially

Above: **Chinese Painted Quail**
A pair of these charming birds, the hen being generally brown in colour. These quails will stay mainly on the ground and rarely fly up.

vulnerable to the weather. They can become saturated, and so never provide open pots of water on the ground for these birds. Use tubular containers fixed to the mesh instead. With these there is no risk of the hatchlings drowning themselves. The chicks are brooded by the hen for several days after hatching and will develop rapidly. While the cock bird may not show any resentment towards the offspring, it might be necessary to remove him if he attempts to persecute the hen while she is caring for her brood. Once the young quail start to moult into adult plumage, be prepared to remove them to separate quarters, as fighting between cock birds will be almost inevitable.

Handle quail extremely carefully; their plumage is easily lost, and rough handling will leave you with a handful of feathers when the bird is ultimately released. A certain degree

of feather loss under these circumstances is inevitable, however. Various mutations of the Chinese Painted Quail are now established. These include a fawn type, which is paler than the normal, as well as a silver and a pure white variety, the latter tending to be the most scarce.

Common Button Quail
Turnix suscitator

- **Distribution:** India to China and Taiwan
- **Size:** 15 cm (6 in)
- **Diet:** Chick crumbs, millets and similar small seeds, greenfood and small invertebrates
- **Sexing:** Cocks can be distinguished by their cream throats; those of hens are black
- **Compatibility:** Hens will disagree with each other, and thus pairs should be kept apart, although these birds can be kept as part of a mixed collection
- **Pet appeal:** Unusual habits; can become quite tame

Button Quail are not related to the other species of quail in any way.

They form a separate group, and are considered to be more closely related to both pigeons and sand grouses, in spite of their superficial similarity to true quail. These birds are also sometimes known as Bustard Quail and Hemipodes.

Unusually, it is the hen that is the more colourful and larger bird in the fifteen recognized species of Button Quail. They are not difficult birds to maintain in aviary surroundings, especially when housed in a planted flight. Indeed, their needs are very similar to those of quail, except when breeding.

Although both sexes prepare a nest, it is the cock bird that incubates alone. A dome-shaped nest is typically constructed, being hidden close to the ground The hen will lay up to five eggs at a time, and normally moves from male to male, producing several clutches in rapid succession. In a large flight, therefore, try to include several cock birds in the company of a single hen. The eggs should hatch after a period of thirteen days and the hatchlings will soon learn to feed themselves, taking softfood and

some small seeds, such as blue maw, in the early stages. Both cock and hen may share parental duties, brooding the chicks and feeding them at first. Again, a fine layer of mesh, or even boarding, at least 30 cm (12 in) high will be necessary, in order to prevent the young birds escaping from the flight shortly after hatching.

Button Quail mature rapidly, and can be laying by the age of twelve weeks. Keep a close watch on the birds to ensure that a hen does not seriously threaten an intended mate, as they can be aggressive. When in breeding conditon, the unusually loud purring calls of the hens will be heard with increasing frequency. These serve to attract mates and deter potential rivals. Button Quail lack hind toes, and are therefore especially at risk from the potentially crippling effects of frostbite.

Right: **Common Button Quail**
This photograph highlights the excellent camouflage of these quail-like birds. Maintain them the same way as true quails, in a planted aviary. Unusual breeding habits.

Golden Pheasant
Chrysolophus pictus

- **Distribution:** Central and northwestern parts of China
- **Size:** Cocks can be 110 cm (43 in) overall; hens are smaller
- **Diet:** Commercial poultry diet, augmented with seeds and greenstuff
- **Sexing:** Hens lack the bright coloration of cocks, being essentially brownish
- **Compatibility:** Cocks need to be kept apart from each other
- **Pet appeal:** Very striking, easy to maintain and breed

Whereas quail are often kept as part of a mixed collection, pheasants are maintained as aviary birds in their own right. They are not suitable for being kept indoors, however, unless their enclosure is unusually spacious. The cock Golden Pheasant is one of the most striking members of the family, and these birds can be cared for without difficulty. Problems are most likely to arise during the breeding season, however, as cocks are naturally polygamous, requiring several hens. Having mated, the hen then retires to lay and rear her chicks. For this reason, it can be preferable to introduce the cock to a hen in separate accommodation and then transfer him to another mate soon afterwards. Planted flights offer the best likelihood of successful breeding results. Here a hen can lay and hatch the chicks unmolested.

A clutch may consist of up to twelve eggs, and these should hatch after an incubation period of just

Top: **Golden Pheasant**
A male bird at semi-liberty proudly displays its magnificent plumage.

Above:
Ghigi's Yellow Golden Pheasant
A cock bird of this paler form, the most commonly seen colour mutation of the Golden Pheasant.

over three weeks. Provide a suitable rearing food once they have hatched, in addition to the normal diet, which should include some small seeds such as millets. Some Golden Pheasants will also take insects. The young pheasants will take two years to achieve the full adult plumage.

Perhaps not surprisingly, in view of the numbers of Golden Pheasants that are bred annually in collections around the world, various colour mutations have occurred. These include a paler form, described as the Yellow Golden Pheasant, which appears to have originated in Germany, and was then developed by an Italian professor. This is the most commonly available colour form at present, although, conversely, a darker variant called the Dark-throated is also known, as well as a salmon form. Hybridization with many other pheasants has also taken place, but this is not recommended, in view of the need to keep breeding strains pure. Indeed, various pheasants often seen in aviaries are considered endangered in the wild, and thus captive-bred stock can be vital to ensure their long-term survival. Release schemes in certain areas have already been undertaken using birds bred in aviary surroundings.

Lady Amherst's Pheasant

Chrysolophus amherstiae

- **Distribution:** Southeastern Tibet, southwestern China and parts of Burma and the Shan States
- **Size:** Cocks can be 173 cm (68 in) overall, including a tail of 110 cm (43 in); hens smaller
- **Diet:** Commercial poultry diet, plus seeds and greenstuff
- **Sexing:** Hens are easily distinguished, being significantly duller than their mates
- **Compatibility:** Cocks should be housed away from each other
- **Pet appeal:** Colourful, and with undemanding habits

This pheasant bears the name of the wife of the English ambassador to China, who introduced the species to Europe at the beginning of the nineteenth century. Like the Golden, Lady Amherst's Pheasants have been persecuted for the ruffs of plumage present on the necks of cock birds; these have been used for hat decorations and to make artificial flies for fishermen.

Unfortunately, when Lady Amherst's Pheasants were first imported during the nineteenth century, there was a surplus of cocks and, as a result, a considerable degree of hybridization occurred with Golden Pheasants. The effects of this are still apparent in stock today. Look for signs of red plumage on the sides of the body of cock birds, notably in the thigh region, and evidence of spots on the tail feathers. An excessively large crest can also indicate a hybrid ancestry, as are scarlet tips to the tail coverts. Hens with yellow rather than greyish legs, and brown coloration on the head and throat are also likely to be impure.

Like other pheasants, the Lady Amherst's needs a spacious enclosure, especially if the magnificent tail plumes of the cock bird are not to be damaged. Keep these birds away from muddy areas for this reason. In a well-secluded and fenced garden, it may be possible to keep these pheasants successfully in a state of semi-liberty, providing that their wings are clipped. Keep food within the aviary, however, so that the birds will return to feed and hopefully roost within the shelter. It is dangerous to leave them free at night, especially when they are unable to fly, since this will leave them readily exposed to foxes. Like the Golden, these pheasants are quite hardy and will nest just as readily, although the resulting chicks can prove harder to rear successfully. It will take two years for young birds to obtain their adult plumage, but before this time, they can be distinguished by the greyish ruff around the back of the neck and the appearance of red in the upper tail-coverts. After their first year, although not in full colour, cocks may mate successfully; hens are also able to breed at a similar stage in their development.

Left: Lady Amherst's Pheasant
A perching cock bird shows off its long, highly coloured tail plumes.

Silver Pheasant

Lophura nycthemera

- **Distribution:** China, ranging into adjoining parts of Southeast Asia, including Burma, Vietnam and Thailand
- **Size:** Cocks are about 122 cm (48 in) long overall, with tails of 71 cm (28 in)
- **Diet:** Commercial poultry diet, with seeds and greenstuff
- **Sexing:** Hens are predominantly brown and smaller than cock birds
- **Compatibility:** Cocks need to be kept apart from each other
- **Pet appeal:** Colourful and hardy

Thirteen subspecies of Silver Pheasant are recognized throughout its large range, but in captive stock the subtle distinctions between them have been lost in many cases through indiscriminate pairings over countless generations. These pheasants naturally inhabit mountainous areas of forest, where, outside the breeding season, they often forage for food in groups. Silver Pheasants have long been kept in Europe, and may have bred for the first time in London as long ago as 1700. A large, well-planted aviary is essential for these birds, with one cock being housed in the company of several hens. Try to avoid keeping pheasants in closely adjoining aviaries, in order to minimize the risk of cocks fighting through the mesh. Erect some form of screening to give the birds seclusion if this form of housing is adopted. Silver Pheasant cocks can become

Above: **Silver Pheasant**
A cock bird kept at semi-liberty, displaying his elegant tail plumage.

Below: **Silver Pheasant**
The hen bird, shown here, clearly lacks the splendour of the cock.

extremely aggressive during the breeding period, using the sharp spurs on the backs of their legs to devastating effect.

Clutches can be relatively small, often numbering between four and six eggs per hen. Hens normally incubate on their own, although a cock bird will return at intervals to a mate, and may even take over the task of incubation if the hen refuses to do so, or dies. Similarly, once the chicks hatch – after a period of about twenty-five days – the cock may then brood the offspring, remaining with them overnight rather than seeking to roost elsewhere.

In an aviary, arrange the perches

so that the tail plumes are not damaged. With their wings clipped, the birds can be allowed out into a garden, but, unfortunately, the aggressive nature of the cock bird in breeding condition is not only directed to other pheasants, and people may also be attacked on occasions. Clearly, it is not advisable to let them mix directly with young children, but the sight of a family group of these pheasants at semi-liberty in a suitable area is truly magnificent. Always encourage hens to breed within the confines of an aviary, however, where they will be less at risk from protential predators, such as foxes.

Nepal Kalij

Lophura leucomelana

- **Distribution:** Nepal
- **Size:** Cocks about 71 cm (28 in); hens about 56 cm (22 in)
- **Diet:** Commercial poultry or pheasant pellets, seeds, greenfood and invertebrates
- **Sexing:** Hens have smaller crests, which are dark brown rather than glossy black in colour
- **Compatibility:** Keep pairs in separate accommodation
- **Pet appeal:** Hardy and attractive crested appearance

Although lacking the bright colours associated with some pheasants in this genus, the Nepal Kalij and related species are easy to keep and prove interesting aviary occupants. They have tended to be neglected in the past, but stock is usually obtainable without too much difficulty Various distinctive subspecies are recognized, including the White-crested Kalij (*L. l. hamiltoni*), and these forms have been bred rather indiscriminately in captivity, although it appears that they may also hybridize in the wild.

The Kalij Pheasants should be kept in large, well-planted enclosures, with one cock bird in the company of at least two hens. After mating, the hens will retreat under bushes, where they will proceed to incubate their eggs. As many as a dozen eggs may be laid, and the chicks should hatch after a period of twenty-five days. They usually prove reliable parents, and do not eat their eggs like certain *Lophura* pheasants. When the chicks hatch, offer them suitable rearing food, as well as insects and chopped greenfood, such as chickweed. They will gain adult coloration within the first year. The main drawback of keeping these birds in a planted flight, however, is their tendency to hide in the vegetation; this secretive behaviour applies especially to chicks.

Below: **Nepal Kalij**
An unusual pheasant best housed as separate pairs in a large enclosure.

Swinhoe's Pheasant

Lophura swinhoei

- **Distribution:** Found only on the island of Formosa (Taiwan)
- **Size:** Cocks are about 84 cm (33 in) overall, with hens being about 53 cm (21 in)
- **Diet:** Commercial poultry diet, seeds, greenstuff
- **Sexing:** Hens are easily distinguished by their black crests and duller overall appearance
- **Compatibility:** As with other species, cocks must be kept separate from each other
- **Pet appeal:** Attractive and easy to maintain

Left: **Swinhoe's Pheasant**
The outstanding colours of the cock bird's plumage and its ease of maintenance commend this species to beginners keen on pheasants.

Discovered during 1862, the first pair of these pheasants seen alive in Europe were bought by Baron Rothschild for a vast sum of money, but soon repaid the investment by breeding readily. Obtained in 1866, the birds produced a dozen chicks that year, with a further sixty-eight being reared over the next two years. They are thus an ideal species for newcomers to pheasants. Breeding them is a very worthwhile undertaking, moreover, since they are considered to be an endangered species in their restricted natural range in the highland regions of Formosa (the island now known as Taiwan).

Swinhoe's Pheasants do not need especially spacious surroundings, and are quite hardy. When in breeding condition, the cock displays his crest feathers and inflates the bare scarlet skin on the head. The

clutch size normally varies between six and twelve, and the chicks should hatch about twenty-five days after laying. Hens tend to nest earlier than other pheasants, but some young stock might be reluctant to breed until they develop adult plumage after their second year.

A rare cinnamon form of Swinhoe's Pheasant has been recorded, but proved difficult to establish. It was seen first in France towards the end of the nineteenth century, and subsequently reappeared in the aviaries of Professor Ghigi of Italy, but, in spite of a number of cinnamon young being reared, the mutation was again lost. Pheasants of this colour may nevertheless re-emerge in the future, especially in view of the fact that Swinhoe's are represented in captivity by a limited number of closely related birds.

Reeves' Pheasant
Syrmaticus reevesi

- **Distribution:** The more mountainous regions of northern and central China
- **Size:** Cocks, with their long tails, can be nearly 203 cm (80 in) in length; hens are smaller, about 76 cm (30 in)
- **Diet:** Commercial pheasant or poultry food, seeds, greenstuff and invertebrates
- **Sexing:** Cocks are easily recognized by their long tails and brighter overall colouring
- **Compatibility:** Do not house cocks together
- **Pet appeal:** Attractive coloration

Reeves' Pheasant is named after the man who first introduced this species to Europe in 1831. The spectacular feathers of cock birds have been widely featured in Chinese art for centuries. Not surprisingly, these pheasants have become very popular in the West, and are bred in quite large numbers every year. The first captive breeding took place during 1867, at the London Zoo.

Cock birds can become excessively aggressive during the breeding season. House each cock with several hens, so that one is not persecuted excessively. Adequate cover in the aviary is also to be recommended, partly for this reason. Clutches vary from seven to fifteen eggs in number, and should hatch after a period of twenty-five days. The chicks develop rapidly. If they start squabbling among themselves, separate the chicks.

Reeves' are hardy pheasants, and can be kept out of doors throughout the winter. They may also be kept in

Above: **Reeves' Pheasant**
The resplendent tail plumes of the cock bird look their best when this pheasant is kept in a state of semi-liberty. It originates from the mountains of China, and not surprisingly, Reeves' Pheasant can tolerate the winters of temperate climates around the world. House cock birds separately.

a state of semi-liberty, but not, of course, in the company of other species that are likely to be persecuted. Do not forget to trim the birds' wings and repeat this as necessary in order to prevent the pheasants escaping from your property. There is always a danger that the cock's magnificent tail plumes will get damaged in aviary accommodation. In more spacious surroundings, the Reeves' beauty will be seen to best effect.

Satyr Tragopan
Tragopan satyra

- **Distribution:** Central and eastern parts of the Himalayas
- **Size:** Cocks average about 71cm (28 in); hens about 61 cm (24 in)
- **Diet:** Pheasant or poultry ration, with seeds, greenfood and invertebrates
- **Sexing:** Hens are smaller and duller overall, with paler skin around the eyes
- **Compatibility:** Cocks will prove aggressive towards each other
- **Pet appeal:** Colourful

The Tragopans as a group do not rank among the most common pheasants kept in aviaries. Nevertheless, the cock Satyr Tragopan is an extremely beautiful bird, and pairs of this particular species are most frequently available. These pheasants need spacious surroundings because they tend to fly more than members of other genera, and they will also spend considerable periods of time perching. They nest off the ground, making use of a suitable platform for the purpose in an aviary, and will collect twigs and other debris with which to line the nesting site. Tragopans are best kept in breeding trios, so that the cock will be less inclined to persecute a hen

incessantly. The clutches are quite small, with up to six eggs being laid at one time. If the eggs are transferred to an incubator, the hen may well lay a second round quite soon afterwards. Alternatively, hatch the chicks under a suitable broody bantam (see page 157). The incubation period is twenty-eight days. Provide suitable rearing foods, including insects and chopped greenfood, to the young birds at first. Another unusual feature of the Tragopans is their fondness for berries and fruit, which should be offered on a regular basis.

The young birds may nest in their first year, before they gain adult plumage. They can become quite tame if kept at liberty in a garden, but it will be essential to clip their flight feathers to prevent them straying. Although hardy – they inhabit mountainous areas in the wild – try to encourage Tragopans to roost under cover so that they are not at risk from frostbite. As an additional precaution, some breeders attach heating strips to the perches where the birds roost. These do not become hot, but simply provide a gentle warmth for the toes. Unfortunately, a similar system cannot be used for all birds, since parrots, for example, are likely to destroy the strips containing the heating element.

Above: **Satyr Tragopan**
A cock bird sporting its iridescent colours to perfection. Allow these pheasants to nest off the ground.

Below: **Brown- eared Pheasant**
This close-up shows the tufts that arise from beneath the eyes and give this bird its common name.

Brown-eared Pheasant
Crossoptilon mantchuricum

- **Distribution:** Western China, in mountainous areas
- **Size:** About 100 cm (39 in)
- **Diet:** Commercial poultry or pheasant food, seeds, greenfood
- **Sexing:** Hens are generally smaller, and lack the spurs present on the legs of cock birds, but this is by no means an infallible guide in all cases
- **Compatibility:** Pairs should be kept on their own
- **Pet appeal:** Unusual appearance and docile nature

The Brown-eared Pheasant was first introduced to western aviculture in 1864, when one cock and two hens were received by the Jardin d'Acclimatation in Paris. They then passed into the care of Mlle. de Bellonet and started breeding successfully, to the extent that from this original stock literally hundreds of chicks were reared. Classed as an endangered species in the wild, it is from these original three birds that today's captive stock has been evolved, with just a further two cock birds being acquired from China by London Zoo during 1866.

Brown-eared Pheasants have proved a justifiably popular species for aviaries, becoming quite tame

and less likely to panic than other pheasants. Their main drawback, however, is their destructive habits. In the wild, they normally forage for food on the ground, digging for roots, insects and other edible items, and thus they can rapidly destroy a grass floor in an aviary. They also need a large area; if they are closely confined, they may resort to plucking each other's feathers. Aggression, even during the breeding season, is not common however.

Brown-eared Pheasants are unlikely to breed until their second year, although they develop adult plumage earlier. A typical clutch consists of between five and eight eggs, with an incubation period of approximately twenty-seven days. Unfortunately, a relatively large proportion of clutches consist of infertile eggs. This is because the stock may be closely related, but the problem has been overcome to a great extent during recent years by artificial insemination of hens. Indeed, in the first trial approximately three-quarters of the eggs were fertilized successfully by this means.

The other Eared Pheasants need similar care; the Blue-eared is most common, while the White-eared, which lacks the characteristic tufts beneath the eyes, is now being bred in increasing numbers, as befits its endangered status in the wild.

Copper Pheasant
Syrmaticus soemmerringii

- **Distribution:** Japan
- **Size:** Cocks are about 122 cm (48 in) in overall length, including the tail feathers, which are approximately 76 cm (30 in) long. Hens are smaller, not exceeding 61 cm (24 in) long
- **Diet:** Commercial poultry or pheasant diet, seeds, greenstuff and insects
- **Sexing:** Hens are predominantly brownish
- **Compatibility:** Need to be kept individually for much of the year
- **Pet appeal:** Impressive appearance

Several subspecies of the Copper Pheasant are recognized, occurring in various parts of Japan. As avicultural subjects, these pheasants are not as easy to keep as previous species, largely because of their aggressive behaviour. Cocks are not only extremely pugnacious towards each other but they will also attack and may even kill their mates. For much of the year, therefore, it is safest to house pairs individually, in adjoining flights, and only introduce the birds when both show signs of wanting to breed. In Japan, where these pheasants are popular game birds and are bred commercially for

Above: **Copper Pheasant**
This is a cock bird of the Ijima subspecies, one of several subspecies that occur in Japan. In the wild, these impressive pheasants live at the forest edge in rugged mountainous areas and are acclaimed as sporting birds. They prove more difficult to keep in captivity than many pheasants, because of their aggressive nature.

release, artificial insemination has been used to overcome compatibility problems. Even hens need to be kept apart, however, as the dominant individual will bully her weaker counterparts. It is not unknown for a few individual pairs to live together in harmony, especially in a planted flight, but trouble is liable to break out unexpectedly, so very close supervision is essential.

Copper Pheasants are not generally as prolific as the related Reeves' Pheasant. A clutch will consist of up to a dozen eggs, which should hatch after an incubation period of twenty-five days. The chicks are not always easy to rear, requiring suitable small food and insects during their early days. Adult plumage develops in the first year, and the young birds will then have to be separated before they start showing clear signs of aggression towards each other.

Crested Partridge
Rollulus roulroul

- **Distribution:** Southeast Asia; Thailand to the Malay Peninsula
- **Size:** 28 cm (11 in)
- **Diet:** Commercial poultry diet, seeds, fruit, greenfood and invertebrates
- **Sexing:** Hens lack the chestnut crests of cocks
- **Compatibility:** Pairs are best kept apart to prevent fighting
- **Pet appeal:** Unusual and distinctive coloration

Whereas the majority of other species featured in this section are quite hardy, the Crested Partridge, or Roul-roul, cannot be expected to overwinter successfully in an outdoor aviary in temperate areas. They are essentially birds of the forest, where their greenish plumage merges into the background. Although these partridges have been bred successfully, they do not always prove reliable parents, and the eggs may well have to be transferred to an incubator. This behaviour may be caused in certain cases by an inadequate provision of suitable cover for the birds. A domed nest of twigs is usually constructed, with the hen hiding inside for the eighteen days of the incubation

period. The cock bird will remain in the vicinity throughout this time, and subsequently will help with the care of the newly hatched chicks. A range of rearing foods should be supplied at this stage. The young birds have brownish plumage and develop rapidly; they are perching by the time they are two weeks old.

In an indoor flight, provide adequate screening for these birds and, as always, treat them for internal parasites before releasing them in their quarters. This is especially important with newly imported stock, since they may be carrying a fairly heavy burden of worms and have not been treated previously. Birds reared in captivity are likely to have received some medication but, nevertheless, always dose them as a precautionary measure. It is easier to treat birds for such parasites in the first instance, rather than having to deal with the consequences of a severe infestation at a later stage. (See pages 30-31 for parasite treatment.)

Below: **Crested Partridge**
A cock bird, distinguishable from the hen by the crest. Ensure that this tropical bird has adequate warmth and shelter during the winter months in temperate climates. They may not prove reliable parents.

Himalayan Monal
Lophophorus impleyanus

- **Distribution:** The Himalayan Mountains, from eastern Afghanistan through to Tibet
- **Size:** Cocks average 71cm (28 in); hens are slightly smaller
- **Diet:** Commercial poultry or pheasant diet, seeds, greenstuff
- **Sexing:** Hens are predominantly brown in colour
- **Compatibility:** Pairs need to be kept separately
- **Pet appeal:** Attractive and easy

This is the only species of Monal established in aviaries at present. Cock Himalayan Monals are most striking birds, with a natural iridescence that emphasizes the beautiful coloration of their plumage. These birds are much stockier in appearance than other pheasants, and can be kept without difficulty. They dislike damp conditions, however, and so ensure that their aviary is well drained. Monals naturally inhabit areas of forest in mountainous terrain, and need planted flights for breeding purposes. They are quite able to withstand spells of cold weather.

At the onset of the breeding period, cocks can become aggressive towards their mates; with

some pairs, it may be necessary to keep them in separate enclosures for much of the year. The hen usually selects a site under a conifer or a similar shrub to excavate a simple hollow for her eggs. An artificial egg is said to attract her to a suitable locality, where a typical clutch of six eggs will be laid over the course of several days. These can be removed for artificial incubation, in order to encourage the hen to lay again. There is a record of one hen producing no less than fifty eggs in the course of a season, but excessive egg production should not be encouraged. The incubation period is about twenty-seven days, and the young monals will take egg-food and similar items, as well as insects, soon after hatching. In spite of their hardy nature, monals – unlike other peasants – will invariably choose to roost in an aviary shelter, seeking out the highest perch. Young birds gain their full colour during their second year; before this time, it may be possible to distinguish cocks by a trace of black plumage in the throat region.

Right: **Himalayan Monal**
A fine pair of these amenable birds, the cock identifiable by its crest and handsome iridescent plumage. These are hardy, easy-care birds.

Chukor Partridge
Alectoris graeca

- **Distribution:** Himalayan region, India to Nepal
- **Size:** 35.5 cm (14 in)
- **Diet:** Poultry food, seeds, greenstuff, berries and invertebrates
- **Sexing:** Hens can often be distinguished by their smaller size and the absence of spurs
- **Compatibility:** Pairs need to be housed individually
- **Pet appeal:** Easy to maintain and nest quite readily

While this partridge is Asiatic in its distribution, a closely related form known as the Rock Partridge occurs in Europe. They are not difficult to maintain, but these birds can be very aggressive towards each other in a confined space. Cocks are even likely to attack hens if a number are housed together. As always with such birds, ensure that there is adequate cover in the aviary so that a solitary hen will not be attacked.. An area of rocks in the aviary will help to recreate the natural environment of these partridges, while access to an area of sand will enable them to dust-bathe. Up to a dozen eggs may be laid in a clutch, often concealed behind rocks, and they should hatch after twenty-four days. Supply typical rearing foods at this stage and provide shelter in the aviary. These birds roost at night, and a suitable perching area must be arranged for them. Although some individuals become tame, others will remain nervous and can disturb perching birds, such as jay thrushes, sharing their aviary.

Left: **Chukor Partridge**
This Asiatic partridge will benefit from a landscaped, planted aviary.

Javanese Green Peafowl
Pavo muticus

- **Distribution:** Burma, Thailand and the Malay Peninsula, extending to Java
- **Size:** Cocks can be up to 3 m (10 ft) overall, with hens being about 100 cm (39 in) in length
- **Diet:** Commercial poultry or pheasant rations, seeds, greenstuff and invertebrates
- **Sexing:** Hens resemble the cock bird, but are duller and smaller
- **Compatibility:** Cocks should be kept apart
- **Pet appeal:** More beautiful than the Indian Blue Peafowl

The various subspecies of the Green Peafowl are not as common in capitivity as the Indian Blue Peafowl, and they have been hunted more extensively in the wild. They are similar in most respects, however, except that their calls are not as disturbing. The Green Peafowl is less hardy, being at risk from frostbite. Mature cocks can be aggressive towards people, and for this reason it may not be possible to keep them at liberty. Beware of their sharp spurs when catching and handling these birds.

Like all gallinaceous birds, peafowl are susceptible to enteric parasites, notably the protozoa called *Histomonas meleagridis* that causes the disease popularly known as blackhead. This is passed from bird to bird by an intestinal worm, *Heterakis gallinae*, which lives in the caeca (pouches in the lower intestine wall). Regular deworming is recommended, since blackhead is often fatal in peafowl. (See also pages 30-31 for advice on parasites.)

Grey-breasted Guinea-fowl
Numida meleagris

- **Distribution:** Western Africa, north of the equatorial forest
- **Size:** 46 cm (18 in)
- **Diet:** Commercial poultry or pheasant ration, seeds, greenstuff and insects
- **Sexing:** Hens are generally slightly smaller
- **Compatibility:** Live in groups
- **Pet appeal:** Tames easily

Guinea-fowl belong to the separate family Numididae, but are similar in their requirements to pheasants, partridges and quail. In some areas of the world, they are farmed for meat. Guinea-fowl can be kept in an aviary or allowed to roam around in a garden, where they will prove useful watchdogs, calling loudly at the approach of strangers. Unfortunately, they tend to roost in trees, and it can be difficult to persuade them to adopt a shelter for this purpose. Although relatively hardy, they will not thrive in damp surroundings and can be susceptible to frostbite.

Hens prepare a simple scrape in the soil before laying up to twenty eggs, and these should hatch in twenty-four days, although not all hens will sit readily. The young birds,

Above: **Javanese Green Peafowl**
An impressive bird that rivals the Indian Blue Peafowl for good looks.

Below: **Grey-breasted Guinea Fowl**
A hen sitting on her clutch of eggs laid in a scrape in the ground.

sometimes described as 'keets', are relatively slow to develop. Occasionally, guinea-fowl may become aggressive, especially if kept in the company of poultry.

Over twenty subspecies of the Grey-breasted Guinea-fowl are recognized. These include the well-established silver form which, as its name suggests, is paler than the normal. Of the other species, the Vulturine Guinea-fowl (*Acryllium vulturinum*) has been imported, but invariably commands a high price. It is a particularly attractive form, but needs dry conditions to thrive.

Indian Blue Peafowl
Pavo cristatus

- **Distribution:** India and Sri Lanka
- **Size:** Cocks can be nearly 254 cm (100 in) in length, including their tail feathers; hens may reach 100 cm (39 in)
- **Diet:** Commercial poultry or pheasant diet, seeds, greenstuff and invertebrates
- **Sexing:** Cocks are instantly recognizable by their magnificent tail plumes
- **Compatibility:** Cocks should be kept apart from each other
- **Pet appeal:** Stunning appearance and keenness to breed

The Indian Peafowl is probably the best-known member of the family Phasianidae. It has been kept in captivity for three thousand years, being held in high esteem by both the Greeks and Romans. The large size of these birds means that they really need to be kept at liberty in a suitable garden, with high fences. Peafowl tend to perch in trees and are capable of jumping 1.8 m (6 ft), even with their wings clipped. In their favour, however, is the fact that once established in a territory a group consisting of a cock with several hens will rarely fly far away. It may be preferable to cover an area of the garden with netting, allowing the birds to roam free beneath; in spite

Left: **White Peafowl**
The peacock of the white mutation, a striking alternative to the familiar colours of the original form.

Above: **Indian Blue Peafowl**
The tail plumes of the peacock, a widely celebrated display.

of their size, they are at risk from foxes. Peafowl are very easy to maintain, and quite hardy. In an urban area, however, their far-carrying, ghostly calls uttered after dark could give rise to complaints from neighbours.

Hens nest on their own, laying a clutch of six eggs or so in a secluded spot. These should hatch after a period of twenty-eight days, and the resulting chicks, although soon able to perch, will develop only slowly. A hen will brood her offspring at night, covering them with her wings, for as long as two months. It will take three years for young cock birds to acquire their magnificent, beautifully marked tail plumes.

Several mutations of the Indian Peafowl have occurred, but to most people they are not as attractive as the original form. White Peafowl, for example, are pure white, but the ocellae, or eyes, apparent on the train of peacocks can still be distinguished. The Pied mutation, with white and normal areas present on the same bird, is extremely variable in extent, as in other birds. Another, more appealing mutation is the so-called Black-winged, which was recognized as long ago as 1823. It is also known as the Black-shouldered, as this is the part of the body where the change is most distinctive in cock birds of this type. Hens are significantly paler than those of the normal Blue Peafowl.

WATERFOWL

W hile some waterfowl need to be kept on a large pond if they are to thrive, others will do well in the confines of a typical suburban garden. Waterfowl generally are easy to keep, and many species will also nest quite readily. The smaller birds can be kept satisfactorily in an aviary if they are fully flighted i.e. if their flight feathers are intact. When buying stock, check whether or not the birds have been pinioned. This is easy to carry out in young waterfowl, and ideally should be done within days of hatching, and not later than about ten days old. Subsequently, the removal of the so-called bastard wing will need to be carried out by a veterinarian, who will administer an anaesthetic to the bird.

Waterfowl are surprisingly long-lived birds; reliable records reveal that geese can live for half a century, and many ducks will live well into their teens. Part of the appeal of waterfowl, in addition to their coloration, is their tameness. For this reason, always try to obtain young stock, which will settle more rapidly in a new environment. Encourage the birds to come to you at feeding time, rewarding them accordingly. Do not move suddenly, but allow the birds to feed around you without being disturbed. Gradually, they will come to accept your presence without fear, simply moving out of the way as you walk slowly towards them.

In the same way that bantams and other breeds of poultry have been evolved from wild stock, a similar situation has occurred in the case of waterfowl. The many commercial and fancy breeds of duck are believed to be derived essentially from the Mallard. Various forms of geese have also been developed, with the Chinese being especially favoured for its egg-laying abilities. This particular breed is a domesticated descendant of the Swan Goose.

A representative selection of both fancy ducks and geese can be found at most agricultural shows. Stock can also be obtained at such venues, although generally, it is preferable to contact a commercial breeder directly; look up the addresses in the advertisement columns of specialist magazines.

You may find it difficult to decide upon a particular breed or species, since there are now so many waterfowl well established in aviculture. Yet, in some cases, it is possible to keep a mixed collection. The following representative sample highlights the major groups. (In the text, the term, 'eclipse' refers to the dull plumage of certain male ducks outside the breeding season.)

Above: *A Mandarin Duck at home on a small pond. Many waterfowl are quite content with a limited amount of water in their enclosures, although diving ducks need deeper water.*

Right: *A Mallard Duck with its ducklings. This is perhaps the most widely known species of duck, being adaptable to a wide range of conditions and situations.*

Fulvous Whistling Duck

Dendrocygna bicolor

- **Distribution:** Occurs over a vast area, including the Americas, East Africa and parts of Asia
- **Size:** 51 cm (20 in)
- **Diet:** Suitable duck food, greenstuff and invertebrates
- **Sexing:** No visual external differences
- **Compatibility:** Live happily in groups and are unlikely to molest other ducks
- **Pet appeal:** Lively, colourful and inoffensive

The terms 'tree duck' and 'whistling duck' are synonymous. The latter description is derived from the calls of these birds, which resemble a shrill whistle, most commonly heard when a rival is being challenged. A pond for this group of ducks needs to be at least 61 cm (24 in) deep, enabling them to dive without difficulty. In common with the other seven species of *Dendrocygna*, the Fulvous Whistling Duck is not entirely hardy, and should be given adequate protection during periods of bad weather.

They normally lay in late spring,

with the young developing a full covering of plumage by the time they are seven weeks old. It is usual for birds not to breed until their second year. Some Tree Ducks prefer to use nesting boxes and may on occasions roost off the ground. Close examination of the vent, in order to reveal the rudimentary penis

Above: **Fulvous Whistling Duck**
A peaceful and colourful species that will breed without fuss.

associated with drakes, can be helpful in sexing these waterfowl, but this is not reliable in all cases. Using this method, some drakes will be classed as ducks.

White-faced Tree Duck

Dendrocygna viduata

- **Distribution:** occurs both in tropical South America – extending to Argentina, Paraguay and Uruguay – and also in southern Africa, as far as Angola and the Transvaal. Also represented on Madagascar and the Comoro Islands
- **Size:** 51 cm (20 in)
- **Diet:** Commercial poultry diet, grain, greenstuff
- **Sexing:** There are no external plumage distinctions between the sexes
- **Compatibility:** Live happily in groups, although there is a strong pair bond
- **Pet appeal:** Quite colourful and tame easily

The Tree Ducks can be instantly recognized by their very upright stance, emphasized by their long necks and legs. They do require a fairly large expanse of water, however, where they can swim and dive, as they are not entirely terrestrial by nature. Their enclosure will need to be planted to encourage breeding, with tall grass being especially favoured for this purpose. Up to sixteen eggs may be laid in a simple nest, hatching after a period of about twenty-eight days. The young ducklings can be difficult to rear successfully, since they need to be kept relatively warm and encouraged to take food. If you hatch the chicks artificially, do not allow them immediate access to water other than in a dish, since their feathers will not be waterproofed and they are likely to sink and drown. Normally, the ducklings would obtain the oil from their mothers' feathers. Once they start preening themselves adequately they smear the waterproofing oil from the preen gland onto their own feathers.

Left: **White-faced Tree Duck**
Provide a spacious pool for these ducks and a planted enclosure with tall grass where they can nest. The relatively upright stance is characteristic of the Tree Ducks.

Black Swan
Cygnus atratus

- **Distribution:** Western and eastern Australia, extending to Tasmania and New Zealand
- **Size:** 100 cm (39 in)
- **Diet:** Duck diet, corn, with chopped greenstuff and fruit
- **Sexing:** Hens (known as pens) are smaller, with shorter necks
- **Compatibility:** Aggressive, pairs need to be kept on their own
- **Pet appeal:** Rather for the specialist

While swans generally are among the most majestic of the waterfowl, they also tend to rank among the most demanding, and this certainly applies in the case of the Black Swan. There is a strong pair bond in this species; males (cobs) will fight each other ferociously, and so pairs need to be housed individually. They will also attack and kill other waterfowl, and in breeding condition may prove aggressive towards people. Unlike other swans, however, this species does not require a large area of water, being content with a pond of modest dimensions and a surrounding grassy area, where the birds will graze in a similar manner to geese. They are relatively noisy, and their calls can cause disturbance to neighbours after dark.

When breeding, a fairly bulky nesting platform is constructed, typically in a reed bed. A pair will share the incubation of the five or six eggs, with the cygnets hatching after a period of about thirty-six days. Both adults care for their offspring, and may even be seen carrying them on their own backs in

Above: **Black Swan**
A pair with at least one cygnet in evidence. These swans form a strong pair bond and become aggressive to other waterfowl and even people when breeding. Suitable for specialists in this type of bird.

the water. Two clutches of eggs may be hatched successfully in a season. It may be possible to accommodate pens together without fighting, but young cobs will soon need to be removed. Black Swans should be pinioned, otherwise they may stray.

Lesser Snow Goose
Anser caerulescens

- **Distribution:** Northern Canada and Greenland, heading to southern parts of the United States over the winter period
- **Size:** 71 cm (28 in)
- **Diet:** Grass, commercial diet, seeds
- **Sexing:** Sexes are identical in appearance, but the gander is often larger
- **Compatibility:** Tolerant nature
- **Pet appeal:** Docile and readily tamed

The Snow Goose is popularly regarded as being white, but in fact there is also a blue form, in which much of the body is bluish grey in coloration. The Greater Snow Goose (*A. c. atlanticus*) is larger than the Lesser, and does not occur in a colour form. Young birds in both instances are greyer than their adult counterparts. Snow Geese generally do not prove difficult to keep or breed, with as many as eight eggs being laid in a clutch and incubated for about twenty-eight days. Like the majority of geese, these birds prove reliable parents, although it is useful to have an incubator or broody bantam available in an emergency. This is most likely to arise at the end of the incubation period, once some of the chicks have hatched. The adult birds will then tend to wander away from the nest with these goslings, and other eggs still to hatch may become chilled. This may happen with relatively large clutches. Young geese are not difficult to rear, and soon start browsing on grass and other foodstuffs offered to them.

Below: **Lesser Snow Goose**
This is the more familiar white form; there is also a blue form.

Whooper Swan
Cygnus cygnus

- **Distribution:** Migratory, breeding in northern areas – notably Scandinavia and Iceland, extending east to Japan – and wintering further south, in Europe, North Africa and Asia
- **Size:** 152 cm (60 in)
- **Diet:** Duck diet, with grain, and greenstuff
- **Sexing:** No visual distinction between the sexes
- **Compatibility:** Aggressive, especially when breeding
- **Pet appeal:** Striking appearance

These swans tend to be less pugnacious than the familiar Mute Swan, but need an extensive area of water, with adequate adjoining grassland for grazing purposes. They are noisy, being named after their whooping calls, which are most commonly heard when the birds are flying. They may construct a breeding platform on the water, and here as many as seven large eggs may be laid. The pen sits alone, while her mate remains close by. The cygnets should hatch after forty days, and are normally capable of flying by the time they are two months old. Sprinkle food on the water for them, since this is where they will spend much of their early life. Like other swans, these birds are slow to mature, only breeding during their third year.

Right: **Whooper Swan**
The pen (female bird) incubates the eggs as the cob (male) stands by in a suitably proprietorial manner. Although less aggressive than the Mute Swan, these swans will still defend their breeding site from all comers with appropriate defiance. Provide a large pond and paddock.

White-fronted Goose

Anser albifrons

- **Distribution:** Migratory, breeding in the Arctic area of Asia and Europe, moving southwards as far as the Mediterranean during the winter months
- **Size:** 68.5 cm (27 in)
- **Diet:** Duck diet, grain, greenstuff
- **Sexing:** No external differences between the sexes
- **Compatibility:** Quite social, even with other geese of similar size
- **Pet appeal:** Attractive and tames readily

Geese are far less dependent on the provision of an area of water than other related birds. They will range widely when grazing on land, and do best in a large enclosure where they can be maintained in a state of semi-liberty. It is important to keep the grass in a paddock in suitable conditon for geese; they will not take long grass, and a well-mown lawn is essential in the first instance. The birds will then keep cropping the grass, and should prevent it from becoming overgrown. If a particular area appears to be suffering from their attentions, move them to an adjoining strip so that the original plot can recover. Indeed, if you have a large area, it is probably best to divide it up into separate sections for this purpose.

A drawback of geese is their fairly loud cackling calls, but they also serve to announce the arrival of strangers by this means. The White-fronted Goose is also sometimes known as the Laughing Goose, because of its jovial sounding calls. They become tame and will breed readily, having an incubation period of about twenty-eight days.

Left: **White-fronted Goose**
A sociable and easily tamed species that will thrive at semi-liberty.

Bar-headed Goose
Anser indicus

- **Distribution:** Central Asia, moving across the Himalyas to India when migrating
- **Size:** 71 cm (28 in)
- **Diet:** Grass and, especially during the winter, commercial diet and seeds
- **Sexing:** No visible distinction between the sexes
- **Compatibility:** Reasonably social, even with other waterfowl
- **Pet appeal:** Hardy and relatively colourful

The Bar-headed Goose was first represented in the collection at London Zoo during 1845, and today is probably more often seen in zoological rather than in private collections. Yet its requirements are as straightforward as those of related species, with suitable grazing being of primary importance. They can become very tame and interestingly, once settled in their quarters, these geese rarely stray, even if they are not pinioned. Nevertheless, it is best to keep them in this fashion.

A raised nest, often featuring moss and lined with feathers, is prepared and normally a clutch of about four eggs laid within, although larger numbers are not unknown. It can be as long as thirty days before the goslings emerge, and they may seek out a pond or similar area of water early in life. The young birds should start breeding three years later.

Pink-footed Goose
Anser brachyrhynchus

- **Distribution:** Greenland, Spitzbergen and Iceland, migrating to northern Europe for the winter
- **Size:** Up to 76 cm (30 in)
- **Diet:** Mainly vegetable matter, but will also take commercial diets and seeds
- **Sexing:** Sexes similar, but females are often smaller
- **Compatibility:** Live happily in groups
- **Pet appeal:** Hardy and undemanding

A European species, sometimes classified as part of the Bean Goose (*A. fabalis*) group, the Pink-footed Goose is easy to maintain. For breeding purposes, home-bred stock is essential. In most waterfowl, and geese in particular, wild-caught birds are exceedingly slow to start breeding in captivity. Yet once this hurdle has been overcome, their offspring in turn tend to nest readily. Pink-footed Geese typically start nesting in mid-spring, with as many as eight eggs being incubated by the goose alone. The gander never strays far away from his sitting mate, however, and subsequently helps to chaperone the offspring.

Although not becoming as tame as the Greylag (*A. anser*) and other related grey geese, the Pink-footed is nevertheless an interesting species, well worth including in a waterfowl collection. They are relatively quiet compared with other geese, and can be sexed by their calls. Those of ganders are higher pitched than the calls of the goose.

Above: **Bar-headed Goose**
When provided with suitable grass on which to graze and a commercial duck diet, this hardy breed should prove loyal and rewarding.

Below: **Pink-footed Goose**
This is a worthwhile addition to any waterfowl collection, being fairly quiet and undemanding in captivity. Ideally, choose home-bred stock.

Red-breasted Goose
Branta ruficollis

- **Distribution:** Soviet Union; Siberia, migrating to the Caspian Sea for the winter
- **Size:** 56 cm (22 in)
- **Diet:** Grass, commercial diet, seeds
- **Sexing:** No visual distinction between the sexes, but geese may be smaller than ganders
- **Compatibility:** Reasonably tolerant of other species
- **Pet appeal:** Colourful and easily tamed

This species has never been common in aviculture, and invariably commands a high price. It is probably not the most prolific of the geese, although once they start breeding, pairs can produce nine goslings from a clutch of eggs. They are also long-lived, so that although these geese may not breed until their third year, a pair can produce a considerable number of offspring in their lifetime, especially as they prove very diligent parents. Red-breasted Geese often prefer a relatively exposed spot for nesting, and should be encouraged to breed in an area where they can be protected from predators.

Interestingly, Red-breasted Geese may once have ranged over a much wider area - a pair is portrayed on an Egyptian tomb at Medum dating back to 3000 B.C.

Right: **Red-breasted Goose**
A colourful and long-lived species that, once settled, will breed consistently year after year.

Barnacle Goose
Branta leucopsis

- **Distribution:** Greenland and other northern areas, including Spitzbergen, moving south to winter in northern Europe
- **Size:** Up to 68.5 cm (27 in)
- **Diet:** Grass, other greenstuff, plus commercial diet, including seeds
- **Sexing:** Geese are generally smaller than ganders
- **Compatibility:** Tends not to be aggressive, even towards other waterfowl
- **Pet appeal:** Hardy and attractive

The Barnacle Goose is easy to look after, provided that it is kept with access to a suitable area of grass. Like other geese, these birds tend to pair up indiscriminately when kept in the company of related species. In spite of their peaceful natures, therefore, it is preferable to keep them in a group on their own to prevent hybridization. They form a strong pair bond, and although the goose sits alone, the gander remains close by and will hiss angrily to deter any intruders into their breeding territory. The clutch of up to six eggs may be incubated for twenty-six days, and the young geese soon head for water. They will be mature by their third year.

Left: **Barnacle Goose**
A hardy and peaceful goose best kept apart from related species to prevent random hybridization.

Egyptian Goose
Alopochen aegyptiacus

- **Distribution:** Africa, to the south of the Sahara, frequenting lakes
- **Size:** 71 cm (28 in)
- **Diet:** Grass and greenfood, plus commercial food, corn, insects
- **Sexing:** No visual distinctions between the sexes, but the calls of ganders are quite gruff; those of geese are high pitched
- **Compatibility:** Pairs should be kept apart, as they are aggressive
- **Pet appeal:** Straightforward requirements and tame by nature

These geese have been kept for ornamental purposes since the time of Ancient Egypt, and, in temperate climates, have proved very hardy. Unfortunately, however, they also tend to be highly aggressive, and will not hesitate to kill small waterfowl as well as fight among themselves. A pair will graze contentedly on an area of grass, and do not require a great deal of additional care. As always, however, be sure to provide additional food during the winter, especially when there is snow on the ground. These geese usually prefer to roost in trees, and although they will nest on the ground, they also breed in trees, where a suitable platform is available. Like other waterfowl, they moult their flight feathers almost simultaneously, being unable to fly at this stage. If threatened then, they take to water.

Egyptian Geese are not difficult to breed; a clutch of as many as ten eggs can be anticipated, and these should hatch after an incubation period of thirty days. While the goslings will remain with their parents in a family group for a period of time, they will need to be separated before the onset of winter. It is not surprising that over the vast natural range of this species, various slight colour variants have arisen; in captivity, an almost pure white form has been evolved.

Right: **Egyptian Goose**
A robust long-domesticated species that will thrive in captivity.

Hawaiian Goose
Branta sandvicensis

- **Distribution:** The island of Hawaii
- **Size:** 61 cm (24 in)
- **Diet:** Grass and other greenstuff, plus commercial food and seeds
- **Sexing:** Geese smaller than ganders and darker overall
- **Compatibility:** Pairs are best kept apart from other waterfowl, as they tend to be aggressive
- **Pet appeal:** Unusual

The Hawaiian Goose, or Ne-ne, was almost certainly saved from extinction by a programme of captive breeding co-ordinated by the Wildfowl Trust in Britain. So successful was the project that not only has stock been released back to the wild, but also these geese are readily obtainable for private collections, enabling considerable stocks to be built up in captivity throughout the world. Formerly occurring on other islands in the Hawaiian group, the Ne-ne has evolved unusual feet to cope with the volcanic environment of its native habitat. The webbing between the toes has become reduced in size, while the digits themselves are relatively long and powerful, enabling the birds to exert a strong grip in a loose terrain. Unfortunately, this has also rendered them susceptible to frostbite. Ideally, spread straw (not hay, because of the danger posed by fungal spores) around their quarters during the winter months to ensure that the birds are not exposed to frozen surfaces and to protect the feet of birds roosting on the ground at night. The birds may also use some of this straw to build their nests. The goose sits alone for the duration of the incubation period, which can extend over thirty days. When breeding, these geese are liable to become very pugnacious.

Left: **Hawaiian Goose**
A fascinating species saved from the brink of extinction. Provide suitable protection from frostbite.

Cape Barren Goose
Cereopsis novae-hollandiae

- **Distribution:** Southern Australia and offshore islands, including Tasmania
- **Size:** 100 cm (39 in)
- **Diet:** Grass and other greenstuff, commercial diet and seeds
- **Sexing:** Goose smaller than gander, with a deeper call
- **Compatibility:** Pairs need to be housed strictly on their own
- **Pet appeal:** Unusual appearance

The Cape Barren or Cereopsis Goose has a very limited distribution in the wild, but captive-bred stock is well established. They feed primarily on grass, and do not often venture on to water, so they can be kept essentially in a paddock without a pond. It is said that when grazing they secrete a noxious smelling chemical that will deter other animals, including sheep, from feeding on the grass. Cereopsis Geese have distinct territories and can prove highly pugnacious; keep pairs in individual enclosures to avoid any conflict developing.

Be prepared for the fact that they may choose to breed during the winter months in the northern hemisphere. Their nest is not elaborate, merely a hollow scrape in the ground lined with their feathers and other materials, including grass. If the weather is bad, it may be preferable to transfer the eggs to an incubator. Sitting birds may be hostile even towards people and will resent any disturbance. The incubation period is about thirty-five days and the young goslings, unlike their parents, will venture readily into water. Try to encourage the birds to nest and roost under cover; a fairly large shelter in their enclosure is therefore to be recommended. As the goslings grow, so the adult birds are liable to become aggressive towards them.

Below: **Cape Barren Goose**
An unusual and large species from the southern hemisphere.

Ashy-headed Goose
Chloephaga poliocephala

- **Distribution:** Argentina and southern Chile, extending to the Falkland Islands
- **Size:** 56 cm (22 in)
- **Diet:** Grass and greenstuff, commercial diet and grain
- **Sexing:** Geese are generally smaller, and again, can be distinguished by their harsh cackling sounds; the ganders' calls consist of softer whistling notes
- **Compatibility:** Keep pairs on their own, as they can be aggressive
- **Pet appeal:** Smaller than other geese and quite hardy

This species is one of a number of geese originating in South America. Others include the Lesser Magellan (*C. picta*) and the Ruddy-headed (*C. rubidiceps*). They are not particularly difficult to care for, being content to browse freely over a suitable area of grass. They will start laying in the spring, and produce relatively small clutches, numbering perhaps just five eggs. The incubation period is approximately thirty days, and the goslings will soon become tame. This particular species was first bred in 1852, at the London Zoo.

Right: **Ashy-headed Goose**
A compact and amenable species suitable for a small grassy paddock.

Ruddy Shelduck
Tadorna ferruginea

- **Distribution:** Migratory, breeding in southern parts of Europe and Asia, moving further south for the duration of the winter
- **Size:** 63.5 cm (25 in)
- **Diet:** Commercial duck diet, seeds, greenstuff and insects
- **Sexing:** Ducks smaller than drakes, with more white present on the head
- **Compatibility:** Best kept apart, especially at breeding time
- **Pet appeal:** Tame and attractive

The ruddy coloration of these shelducks can vary quite considerably in intensity between individuals, and this feature may be reflected in the wild. The species is very easy to keep, but tends to be rather quarrelsome, especially during the breeding period. The repetitive calls uttered by these ducks can also prove disadvantageous in an urban area. They will call with increasing frequency at the onset of the breeding season, before laying. Hens will seek out a nestbox or even a suitable hollow in the ground, and lay a clutch of around eight eggs, which should hatch about thirty days later. The ducklings are normally reared without problems, and will be fully feathered by about two months of age. They will breed during their second year. The Common Shelduck (*T. tadorna*) is similar in its habits, but is less aggressive.

Right: **Ruddy Shelduck**
A colourful species that will tame easily but may disturb neighbours!

Baikal Teal
Anas formosa

- **Distribution:** Migratory, breeding in eastern Siberia and moving to Japan and China for the winter
- **Size:** 40.5 cm (16 in)
- **Diet:** Commercial duck diet, including grain, plus greenstuff
- **Sexing:** Ducks are significantly duller than drakes and brownish overall
- **Compatibility:** Reasonably peaceful
- **Pet appeal:** Drakes are extremely attractive

The striking appearance and hardy nature of the Baikal Teal make it one of the most desirable of this group of waterfowl. Unfortunately, compared with other teals, it has proved reluctant to breed in the past. As domesticated strains are being built up, however, so this problem is being overcome to a great extent. Nevertheless, Baikal Teal still rank among the more expensive species. They appear to need adequate cover for breeding purposes. A typical clutch consists of eight eggs, which will hatch after an interval of about twenty-three days. The ducklings will feed on land or on the water and are almost fully feathered eight weeks after hatching.

Right: **Baikal Teal**
A boldly marked drake of this handsome and placid species.

Chilean Teal
Anas flavirostris

- **Distribution:** Northern South America, and from southern Brazil, northern Argentina and central Chile to Tierra del Fuego. Also present on the Falkland Islands
- **Size:** 40.5 cm (16 in)
- **Diet:** Commercial duck diet, with seeds and greenstuff
- **Sexing:** Ducks are smaller and duller overall than drakes
- **Compatibility:** Fairly trustworthy
- **Pet appeal:** Straightforward and peaceful

Since they are quiet and tame easily, Chilean Teal are an ideal species for the newcomer to duck-keeping. Pairs also nest readily, using nestboxes provided for the purpose, and may even adopt the disused nests of other species. Although occurring over a wide area of South America, it is the southern subspecies that have been seen most commonly. These teal will lay clutches of six eggs, with the ducklings emerging about twenty-six days later. Two or more clutches may be laid in a season. In the following year, the young ducklings will be capable of breeding. Chilean Teal are relatively hardy, but protect them during periods of bad weather.

Below: **Chilean Teal**
An excellent peaceful species for beginners to try; this is a drake.

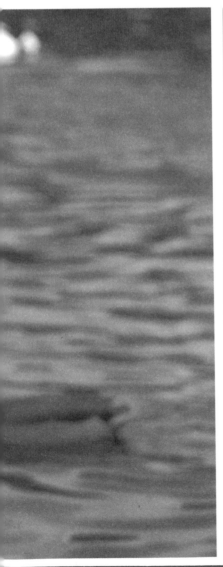

Blue-winged Teal
Anas discors

- **Distribution:** Canada and the United States, migrating southwards to Mexico, northern South America and the Caribbean
- **Size:** 35.5 cm (14 in)
- **Diet:** Typical duck diet, seeds and greenstuff
- **Sexing:** Drakes in breeding plumage are more colourful than ducks, with black prominent on their heads
- **Compatibility:** Can be kept safely with other small ducks
- **Pet appeal:** Social and quiet nature

These teal present no great problems with regard to their care, and they are well established in captivity. They do not require a large enclosure and prefer a fairly shallow pond. The Blue-winged Teal is not entirely hardy, however, and must have adequate protection during the winter months. Typically, they disguise the nest in aquatic vegetation, and the birds may construct a tunnel leading to their eggs, rather than leaving them open to potential predators. About twelve creamy coloured eggs are laid, and these should hatch after a period of twenty-three days. These teal will readily escape through a small gap in their enclosure, so check the perimeter regularly for this reason.

Below: **Blue-winged Teal**
A drake of this sociable, rather shy species. In severe climates, always ensure that it has suitable shelter in cold weather conditions.

Chestnut-breasted Teal
Anas castanea

- **Distribution:** Western, southern and eastern Australia, including Tasmania
- **Size:** 56 cm (22 in)
- **Diet:** Commercial duck diet, with greenstuff
- **Sexing:** Ducks are predominantly brown, lacking the bright coloration of the drakes
- **Compatibility:** Will not prove aggressive
- **Pet appeal:** Colourful and hardy

Although first seen alive in Europe as long ago as 1870, it was not until 1909 that this species was first bred in captivity. Some pairs prove much more successful breeders than others. Unlike certain Australian birds, the Chestnut-breasted Teal has adapted to breed successfully in the spring of the northern hemisphere. They prefer to use nestboxes, where as many as a dozen eggs may be deposited. The duckling should hatch within about thirty days, and, unless pinioned, will be capable of flying within two months. It is important to establish a pair bond between such birds if they are to be kept in a mixed collection. This will virtually eliminate the risk of hybrid pairings occurring with closely related species, which may otherwise arise. Indeed, solitary members of this genus housed in a mixed collection of waterfowl are likely to pair up with other ducks, so try to ensure that all birds are paired beforehand to avoid unnecessary hybridization taking place.

Below: **Chestnut-breasted Teal**
The highly coloured drake of this southern hemisphere species.

Versicolor Teal
Anas versicolor

- **Distribution:** Over a wide area from Bolivia, southern Brazil and Paraguay to Tierra del Fuego and the Falkland Islands
- **Size:** 35.5 cm (14 in)
- **Diet:** Commercial duck diet with seeds and greenstuff
- **Sexing:** Ducks tend to be smaller and duller overall than drakes
- **Compatibility:** Social by nature
- **Pet appeal:** Small and quiet

These ducks are typically found on stretches of water where there is plenty of vegetation on which they can browse. Even on a garden pond they can display an avid appetite for duckweed and other available plants. They are not noisy, even when breeding. At this time of year, the ducks will usually adopt a nestbox for the purpose. Not all females prove keen to breed, however, and, in any event, appear slow to mature, often not breeding until their second year. Up to ten eggs may be laid, with the ducklings being cared for by both adult birds. Versicolor Teal can become quite tame, and cock birds remain in colour throughout the year; they do not have eclipse plumage, as seen in certain other species.

Left: **Versicolor Teal**
A quiet, amenable and compact species that will become tame.

Common Pintail

Anas acuta

- **Distribution:** North America, Europe and northern Asia. Migratory, moving to the tropics in winter
- **Size:** 58.5 cm (23 in)
- **Diet:** Typical duck diet, plus greenstuff
- **Sexing:** Ducks are predominantly brown
- **Compatibility:** Drakes may be aggressive towards each other

when breeding, but are generally docile towards other waterfowl
- **Pet appeal:** Hardy, and the drakes are colourful

The Pintails as a group can be recognized by the narrow tail feathers. This particular species closely resembles the Mallard in its habits, and is equally able to withstand adverse winter weather. Clearly, however, they will require extra care during the winter, especially if their pond is frozen over.

These Pintails do appear to need a relatively large area of water, and adequate cover seems essential for breeding purposes. They may adopt a nestbox, and here the duck will lay possibly seven or more eggs, which should hatch after a period of twenty-four days. Wild-caught stock is slow to breed in captive surroundings, but captive-bred birds may nest during their first year.

A distinct race, known as the Kerguelen Pintail (*A. a. eatoni*), from the small islands of the St. Paul,

Above: **Common Pintail**
A pair of these elegant birds, clearly recognizable by their narrow tail feathers. Hardy and peaceable.

Kerguelen and Amsterdam group in the Indian Ocean, is now also established in captivity. In this race, however, both sexes resemble ducks of the Common Pintail. Other species of Pintail, even those from tropical areas, such as the colourful Bahama Pintail (*A. bahamensis*), are relatively hardy in temperate climates.

Mallard

Anas platyrhynchos

- **Distribution:** Over a wide area of North America, Europe and Asia
- **Size:** 61 cm (24 in)
- **Diet:** Typical duck diet, plus greenstuff
- **Sexing:** Ducks are essentially brown, lacking the colours of the drake in breeding condition. Ducks also have orange markings on the beak, which serves to distinguish the sexes when the birds are out of breeding condition
- **Compatibility:** Drakes can prove troublesome
- **Pet appeal:** Attractive, even if common

Mallard Ducks are a common sight on lakes and ponds, even in city centres, and their genuine beauty can sometimes be ignored as a result. Not surprisingly, they are easy to look after, and are bold birds by nature. The breeding season can be difficult, however, since drakes will become aggressive to ducks housed in their company, and if there is a serious imbalance, a number of drakes will descend on a duck and

are capable of drowning her. They are quite undemanding in the choice of a mate, and are reputed to have hybridized successfully with no less than fifty species of waterfowl. Unfortunately, there is no strong pair bond, with the result that after mating a duck leaves the group to nest, and a preponderance of cock birds will remain on the water, persecuting any hen in their vicinity.

The eggs, typically between seven and eleven, may be laid in a nest under cover some way away from water. The ducklings will hatch after about twenty-six days. Some ducks may even choose a nesting site in a tree, but they are not able to fly properly until they are at least two months old. In view of their promiscuity, it is perhaps not surprising that mallards are usually kept in groups on their own. Domestication has been undertaken primarily in China, where these birds are reared both for eggs and meat.

Right: **Mallard**
A justifiably popular species worldwide for its colour and ease of maintenance. Squabbles may arise at breeding time, however.

Common Shoveler

Anas clypeata

- **Distribution:** Over much of 'North America, especially the eastern side, and across northern Europe into Asia
- **Size:** 51 cm (20 in)
- **Diet:** Typical duck diet, plus greenstuff; also invertebrates, notably worms
- **Sexing:** Ducks are predominantly brown; blue wing patches are present only in drakes, enabling them to be distinguished when in eclipse plumage
- **Compatibility:** Drakes become aggressive during the breeding season
- **Pet appeal:** Distinctive and colourful appearance

Although a typical dabbling duck in most respects, feeding on land or water like the Gargenay, the Shovelers as a group are much more dependent on the provision of invertebrates in their diet than related

ducks. They will search in flower beds diligently for worms, slugs, snails and insects, when kept at liberty. Shovelers tame readily, and nest on land, usually in a spot hidden by tall grasses. A clutch may vary from eight to twelve eggs, and these should hatch within about twenty-five days. Livefood is very important for the successful rearing of the ducklings, and they can prove rather sensitive to the cold. Provide these ducks with a suitable shelter during the winter when there is a threat of frost. Their enlarged beaks can get chilled quite easily, which will severely restrict the birds' ability to feed themselves. Indeed, in the wild, Common Shovelers migrate southwards to warmer climates to escape the winter weather.

Right: **Common Shoveler**
An interesting species that in the wild frequents ponds and flooded marshes, using its long spatulate bill to feed in shallow water. Provide shelter in severe weather.

Red-crested Pochard

Netta rufina

- **Distribution:** Parts of Europe, extending to Spain, and Asia. Migrates south outside the breeding season
- **Size:** 56 cm (22 in)
- **Diet:** Typical duck diet, with a regular supply of greenstuff
- **Sexing:** Drakes, even out of colour, can be distinguished by their red bills and irises
- **Compatibility:** Drakes can become aggressive at the onset of the breeding season
- **Pet appeal:** Attractive and hardy

Left: **Red-crested Pochard**
Provide these diving ducks with an adequate expanse of water and a spacious enclosure to make them feel at home. They are easy to breed and usually make reliable parents. This is a drake.

These diving ducks spend much of their time on water and appear rather ungainly on land, where they will also browse for greenstuff. Their enclosure needs to be relatively large, if grass is not to be rapidly destroyed. Ducks will frequently adopt nestboxes for breeding purposes and build quite a bulky nest. They are reliable parents, and have been used as foster-parents for the eggs of other species. The ducklings, hatching after a period of about twenty-five days, are not difficult to rear, and most normally begin to feed without any hesitation. Livefood will often encourage reluctant ducklings of any species to eat. As the ducklings develop, it is soon possible to distinguish between the sexes by the brighter coloured bills of young drakes. Red-crested Pochards can breed during their first year, and drakes may well attack ducks of other species at this time.

Gargenay
Anas querquedula

- **Distribution:** Southern England right across Europe to Asia
- **Size:** 51 cm (20 in)
- **Diet:** Commercial duck diet, plus some plant matter
- **Sexing:** Ducks are brownish
- **Compatibility:** Tend to associate in small family groups
- **Pet appeal:** Tames readily

The Gargenay, in common with other related species, has eclipse plumage. In this species, the male moults into breeding feathering surprisingly late, so that drakes are only in colour for about three months of each year. Their mates will lay up to thirteen eggs, but the resulting ducklings that hatch about twenty-three days later are not easy to rear, and indeed, these ducks tend to be nervous breeders. It is not unknown for them to lay eggs around their enclosure in a haphazard fashion, and Gargenays should not be disturbed when sitting, in case they desert their nest. These ducks can become quite tame, however, and have an unusual but not disturbing call, which has led to their alternative common name Cricket Teal. They are relatively hardy, but may need to be kept in a suitable outbuilding or shelter when their pond is frozen.

Left: **Gargenay**
A drake in breeding plumage, with the distinctive white eye-stripe.

Rosybill
Netta peposaca

- **Distribution:** Southern South America; Paraguay, Uruguay, Argentina and Chile.
- **Size:** 56 cm (22 in)
- **Diet:** Mixed duck food, with a regular supply of greenfood
- **Sexing:** Ducks have dark beaks; those of drakes turn rosy red by the time they are fully feathered
- **Compatibility:** Quite peaceful, and can be kept with other ducks
- **Pet appeal:** Subtle coloration and docile nature

The Rosybill is a diving duck, and thus the depth of water is significant for this species. Provide a pond about 76 cm (30 in) deep. These ducks have a large appetite for vegetation and will destroy any plants within reach. The nest is usually constructed close to water, often hidden in rushes or similar vegetation, and a clutch may consist of a dozen eggs. The young ducklings that hatch about twenty-six days later will need chopped greenfood, such as chickweed, readily accessible to them. They are unlikely to breed successfully until their second year, although signs of mating behaviour may be observed before this time. Rosybills are able to withstand the winter weather of temperate climates, but will need extra food supplies. Cultivate suitable greenfood, such as cress, to provide a fresh supply during snow cover.

Right: **Rosybill**
A drake, with the typical red bill. Provide deep water for this species.

Tufted Duck
Aythya fuligula

- **Distribution:** Northern and central Europe, into Asia. Moves south for the duration of the winter
- **Size:** 40.5 cm (16 in)
- **Diet:** Typical duck food, plus greenfood
- **Sexing:** The bills of drakes are a paler grey than those of ducks
- **Compatibility:** Social by nature
- **Pet appeal:** Lively, with an agreeable disposition

These small diving ducks are very common throughout their range. They are very adaptable, becoming tame and soon settling in new surroundings. Nevertheless, always opt for domestically bred stock whenever possible, as such birds will be more likely to breed successfully. Surprisingly, these small ducks do not always prove prolific, and tend to nest relatively late in the season, in late spring. In the wild, pairs may breed in close proximity to each other, and thus keeping a group of these social ducks together can encourage reproductive activity. Females sit alone during the incubation period of about twenty-six days, with up to eleven eggs being laid in some cases. The young ducklings require a relatively high proportion of invertebrates (worms, slugs, snails, insects, etc) in their diet during the early stages, if they are to be reared successfully. They should develop quite rapidly, being fully feathered when five weeks old.

Brazilian Teal
Amazonetta brasiliensis

- **Distribution:** Over the entire eastern side of South America
- **Size:** 51 cm (20 in)
- **Diet:** Typical duck diet, plus greenstuff
- **Sexing:** Ducks have grey rather than red bills
- **Compatibility:** Quite social, although drakes may become aggressive
- **Pet appeal:** Easy to keep, not requiring a large area of water

These teal do not rank among the most colourful of waterfowl, but remain in breeding plumage throughout the year, undergoing no eclipse moult. The Brazilian Teal is more arboreal than members of the *Anas* genus, in this respect resembling the Wood Ducks. These

birds will frequently perch in trees, although they display more of a tendency to nest on the ground. Ducks sit alone, with their mates nearby, incubating a clutch of perhaps eight eggs, which should hatch after a period of approximately twenty-five days.

Unfortunately, Brazilian Teal are susceptible to frostbite; they do not protect their feet, but roost alternately on one foot at a time, warming the other in their body plumage. Therefore, confine them in a suitably warm area with a thick floor covering of shredded paper or straw, particularly when there is snow or ice on the ground.

Two distinct subspecies are recognized, with the Greater form (*A. b. ipecutiri*) being significantly larger than the Lesser (*A. b. brasiliensis*), and darker in overall coloration. The former race is confined to Argentina.

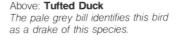
Above: **Tufted Duck**
The pale grey bill identifies this bird as a drake of this species.

Below: **Greater Brazilian Teal**
A drake of the larger of the two subspecies. Prone to frostbite.

European Widgeon
Anas penelope

- **Distribution:** Across Europe, extending into Asia
- **Size:** 46 cm (18 in)
- **Diet:** Typical duck diet, with grass and other greenstuff, as well as invertebrates
- **Sexing:** Drakes are a deeper chestnut-brown, even in eclipse plumage
- **Compatibility:** Generally not aggressive
- **Pet appeal:** Colourful and hardy

Left: **European Widgeon**
These birds will graze like geese and also take food on water.

Keep these widgeon in an area where they can have access to grass, which they will graze like geese. They may also take garden plants, such as aubretia, if given the opportunity. A pair will nest quite readily, with the eggs being laid on the ground, hidden in grass or under a bush. The incubation period is about twenty-five days, and the eggs, up to ten in number, will be laid at daily intervals. The ducklings are easy to rear successfully, and are feathered by six weeks of age. It is possible to sex young ducklings since the wing coverts of drakes will be paler in coloration. Domestically reared birds breed quite readily, but wild stock may prove disappointing.

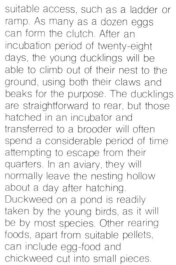

Mandarin Duck
Aix galericulata

- **Distribution:** Eastern parts of Asia, extending to Japan and Taiwan
- **Size:** 46 cm (18 in)
- **Diet:** Commercial duck diet, including grain
- **Sexing:** Even in eclipse plumage, drakes can be distinguished from ducks by their yellow rather than greenish feet, and red rather than grey beaks
- **Compatibility:** Not aggressive
- **Pet appeal:** Drakes of this species are probably the most beautiful of all ducks

In view of the striking appearance of these birds, it is perhaps not surprising that they rank among the most popular of waterfowl. They are quite at home either in a small aviary with a pond or at semi-liberty. The former arrangement may be preferable, because these birds are tree dwelling by nature, even nesting in tree holes·a considerable distance off the ground. The pair bond is very strong, and the bright coloration of the drake is seen to best effect during the display period.

In an aviary, the birds may be persuaded to use a nestbox or even a hollow drainpipe firmly positioned off the ground. This should have

Left: **Mandarin Duck**
The drake is supremely handsome among waterfowl and rightly popular. A hardy and agreeable species.

suitable access, such as a ladder or ramp. As many as a dozen eggs can form the clutch. After an incubation period of twenty-eight days, the young ducklings will be able to climb out of their nest to the ground, using both their claws and beaks for the purpose. The ducklings are straightforward to rear, but those hatched in an incubator and transferred to a brooder will often spend a considerable period of time attempting to escape from their quarters. In an aviary, they will normally leave the nesting hollow about a day after hatching. Duckweed on a pond is readily taken by the young birds, as it will be by most species. Other rearing foods, apart from suitable pellets, can include egg-food and chickweed cut into small pieces.

Stock available today is almost exclusively captive-bred. Pinioning will be essential, since Mandarins will wander; indeed, some feral populations have become established in certain areas. Mandarins are hardy ducks, in spite of their exotic appearance.

Carolina Duck
Aix sponsa

- **Distribution:** Two distinct populations exist in North America: on the western seaboard from British Columbia to California; and on the eastern side, from the Great Lakes southwards
- **Size:** 46 cm (18 in)
- **Diet:** Typical duck diet, including greenstuff
- **Sexing:** The more colourful beak of the drake serves to distinguish the sexes, even when in eclipse plumage
- **Compatibility:** Not aggressive
- **Pet appeal:** Highly colourful and undemanding

Very similar to the Mandarin Duck in its habits, the Carolina, or North American Wood Duck, lives in areas of coniferous forest in the wild. They nest in trees, up to 10 m (33 ft) above the ground, with the ducklings tumbling down shortly after hatching. Domestic stock is inclined to reproduce more freely than Mandarin Ducks, and they invariably make reliable parents. Two clutches can be laid in quite rapid succession, with pairs remaining in close contact, although the hen alone is responsible for incubating the eggs. The ducklings can be sexed by the time that they are fully feathered, when they are about two months of age.

In a mixed collection of waterfowl, hybridization involving this species is not unknown; pairings with at least twenty other species of duck have resulted in offspring being produced. Since Carolinas tend to remain separate from other waterfowl sharing their accommodation, it is usually preferable to house them in a group on their own.

Left: **Carolina Duck**
An attractive drake of this amenable species. They will breed readily, and usually make steady parents.

Chiloe Widgeon
Anas sibilatrix

- **Distribution:** Southern half of South America
- **Size:** 48 cm (19 in)
- **Diet:** Typical duck diet, with greenstuff and vegetation
- **Sexing:** Ducks have greyish wing coverts; those of drakes are pure white
- **Compatibility:** Relatively tolerant of other waterfowl
- **Pet appeal:** One of the most colourful members of the group

In terms of care, these widgeon differ little from the European Widgeon, and have been bred in captivity for over a century. Some drakes may show aggressive tendencies during the breeding season, harassing unpaired ducks in their midst. Ducks lay up to eight eggs in a clutch, with an incubation period of twenty-five days. The young ducklings will feed readily, even those hatched in an incubator. Indeed, they can encourage other more difficult species to start feeding and it may be worth having a pair in the collection for this reason. Nestboxes are preferred by these ducks for laying, and over the course of a season they may lay two or three times in succession. Chiloe Widgeon are hardy birds, but be sure to provide a shelter for them in bad weather when the temperature is below freezing.

Right: **Chiloe Widgeon**
A fine drake of this reliable, free-breeding species that brings colour to any waterfowl enclosure.

Left: **Philippine Duck**
A newcomer to domestication that is easy and rewarding to keep.

Below: **Hooded Merganser**
A female of this relatively uncommon species. Provide a deep pond.

Philippine Duck
Anas luzonica

- **Distribution:** Philippine Islands
- **Size:** 53 cm (21 in)
- **Diet:** Duck diet, with greenstuff
- **Sexing:** Drakes may be distinguished by the black streak at the base of their bills
- **Compatibility:** Relatively docile
- **Pet appeal:** One of the more unusual species, tames readily

The Philippine Duck, a relative of the Mallard, has only become popular in waterfowl collections during recent decades. It is not a particularly striking bird, but it is quite hardy and makes no great demands with regard to care. Do not keep them with Mallards, however, since the latter are likely to assault the ducks ferociously during the breeding period. Philippine Ducks construct quite large nests, often hidden in grass. Up to ten eggs may be laid, and these should hatch in about twenty-six days. The ducklings require plenty of finely chopped greenstuff during their early days. Subsequently, the adult pair may nest again quite rapidly. The birds remain in colour throughout the year; they do not go into eclipse plumage.

Muscovy Duck
Carina moschata

- **Distribution:** From Mexico southwards, extending to Uruguay and Peru
- **Size:** Drakes approximately 81 cm (32 in); ducks smaller, about 61 cm (24 in)
- **Diet:** Usual duck diet, including grain and greenstuff
- **Sexing:** Drakes are significantly larger, and with a prominent red swelling on the upper beak close to the nostrils
- **Compatibility:** Drakes are pugnacious and need to be kept apart
- **Pet appeal:** Tames easily

The wild Muscovy Duck is relatively scarce in waterfowl collections, whereas its pied domesticated counterpart is often seen. Indeed, these birds stand out by virtue of their size and, with their grazing habits, may at first sight appear more akin to geese than ducks. In their natural habitat, Muscovy Ducks live in dense areas of woodland close to water, and are arboreal by nature. Their claws are sharp, and help the birds to maintain a grip on the branches.

A drake should be kept with several ducks, and the resulting eggs have a relatively long incubation period of around thirty-six days. Ducks will lay either on the ground or in trees, using a suitable nestbox for the purpose in captivity. Although certainly not birds for a mixed collection of waterfowl, Muscovy Ducks have hybridized with various other species, ranging from dabbling ducks and shelducks to geese. They can be used to incubate the eggs of other species, and, with their naturally long sitting period, will not leave the eggs before they are likely to hatch successfully.

These ducks are named because of a gland in the neck region that produces a musk secretion that rapidly contaminates the flesh after death, unless it is removed.

Left and below: **Muscovy Duck**
The head of a wild drake (left) shows the characteristic swelling on the upper beak. The familiar pied domesticated form is shown below.

Hooded Merganser
Mergus cucullatus

- **Distribution:** In North America, from southern parts of Canada, southwards and eastwards across the United States
- **Size:** 46 cm (18 in)
- **Diet:** Pellets, grain, even mealworms; naturally take fish
- **Sexing:** Drakes, even in eclipse plumage, have yellow irises; those of ducks are dark brown
- **Compatibility:** Can be aggressive when breeding
- **Pet appeal:** Unusual and tame

The Hooded Merganser is the best-known member of this group, but stock is nevertheless quite scarce and commands a relatively high price. These waterfowl have rather specialized requirements, feeding in the wild on fish, which they dive for and pursue under water. A deep area of water is therefore essential for these birds. If the ducks are not allowed free access to water for any reason, they must be able to immerse themselves in a suitable container in order to maintain the condition of their feathering. Captive-bred stock now available is not too difficult to manage, and, in turn, may be induced to breed in a suitable nestbox or hollow tree. A clutch of as many as nine eggs may be laid, with the young hatching about thirty days later. Mealworms are often popular with recently hatched Hooded Mergansers, as well as softfoods of various types. If they have been hatched in an incubator, introduce them to a shallow dish of water when they are about two weeks old. Under normal breeding circumstances, the duck alone cares for her offspring.

Ring-necked Duck
Aythya collaris

- **Distribution:** Central and northwestern parts of North America, moving southwards as far as the Caribbean for the winter
- **Size:** 40.5 cm (16 in)
- **Diet:** Typical duck diet, with greenstuff
- **Sexing;** Ducks have white areas of plumage on their heads
- **Compatibility:** Drakes may be aggressive when breeding
- **Pet appeal:** Elegant appearance

Ring-necked Ducks live in areas with aquatic vegetation in which they can conceal themselves. This is especially important at breeding time. Their nest is typically constructed in a bed of reeds, near the water. About nine eggs form the usual clutch, and incubation takes about twenty-six days. This species was first seen alive in Europe as recently as 1935, and an initial breeding success did not follow for almost a further three decades, although captive-bred stock is now reasonably well established. These ducks are relatively hardy, but will not thrive if the water in the pond is frozen for any length of time. Be sure to transfer them to suitable indoor accommodation in good time during such difficult conditons.

Right: **Ring-necked Duck**
A drake of this graceful species. Provide a densely planted pond.

Common Scoter
Melanitta nigra

- **Distribution:** Much of northern Europe, extending into Asia. Migrates south for the winter. Also represented in North America
- **Size:** 48 cm (19 in)
- **Diet:** Feed essentially on fish and other aquatic livefoods; a substitute diet of high protein pellets, such as those produced for trout, along with grain and strips of fish should be adequate to maintain these ducks
- **Sexing:** Drakes have an orange spot on their beaks
- **Compatibility:** Pairs are probably best kept apart
- **Pet appeal:** Attractive, but likely to be problematical to keep

Above: **Common Scoter**
A female of this marine species that may prove difficult to keep.

The Scoters are a group of marine ducks and need similar care to that outlined for the Common Eider (see page 197). These ducks require a large expanse of water if they are to thrive; when kept in dry surroundings, Scoters invariably develop foot ailments. Relatively little is known about their habits, although they tend to lay about nine eggs, which hatch approximately twenty-eight days later. The ducks abandon their progeny quite early on, after about five weeks in some cases. They cannot be regarded as being free-breeding in captivity, and stock is not commonly available.

Ferruginous Duck
Aythya nyroca

- **Distribution:** Eastern Europe into Asia, plus a small population around the Straits of Gibraltar, extending to North Africa
- **Size:** 43 cm (17 in)
- **Diet:** Typical duck diet, including grain
- **Sexing:** Drakes have white irises; those of ducks are brown
- **Compatibility:** Will not prove aggressive, although drakes may be pugnacious towards each other in the breeding season
- **Pet appeal:** Tame and social nature

These ducks, also known as the Common White-eye, are members of

Above: **Ferruginous Duck**
The white irises identify this bird as a drake. This species is easy to keep in a well-planted enclosure.

the diving group, yet prefer quite shallow stretches of water. They are among the easiest of the diving ducks to keep and breed, especially if the surrounds of the pond are well planted. The birds will nest here, possibly perilously close to the water. Between seven and ten eggs form the usual clutch, with the ducklings starting to hatch about twenty-six days later. The young birds will take plenty of duckweed at first, or other greenfood chopped into pieces. They will be almost fully fledged by the age of seven weeks and mature by twelve months old.

White-breasted Water Rail

Laterallus leucopyrrhus

- **Distribution;** Southeastern South America, from Brazil to Paraguay and Uruguay
- **Size:** 18 cm (7 in)
- **Diet:** Seeds, softbill food, livefood
- **Sexing:** Hens may have more silvery white underparts than cocks
- **Compatibility:** Not aggressive
- **Pet appeal:** Small, can be housed safely in a mixed collection

A variety of rails and waders are occasionally available, with this species probably being most commonly kept. Although these birds can be kept outside in a planted flight during the summer months, they are not hardy and need to be brought inside for the duration of the winter. Their long toes are vulnerable to frostbite, which also applies to related species. White-breasted Rails, sometimes known as Red and White Crakes, do not need a large area of water, preferring the shallows in any event. Their enclosure must be well planted, however, especially close to the water. They are shy birds by nature and cover of this

Right: **White-breasted Water Rail**
A lively but shy species that will appreciate sufficient cover in its enclosure in which to hide away and provide privacy at breeding time.

kind is essential for them, especially if a pair show signs of breeding behaviour. These rails nest above ground, seeking out a suitable shrub in which they will weave a cup-shaped nest.

A clutch of four or five eggs can be anticipated, and the hen will sit alone throughout the incubation period of twenty-five days. The cock remains in close attendance, walking in the typical jerky manner of the species. The small rails leave the nest shortly after hatching, and, in the company of their parents, will seek out livefood, which is crucial for the early stages of rearing. They are exceedingly nervous at this point,

seeking cover if at all alarmed. Considerable patience may be necessary to spot the family. These birds can be surprisingly difficult to catch in any event, being exceptionally nimble. In common with related species, White-breasted Rails are interesting if somewhat specialist avicultural subjects.

Common Eider

Somateria mollissima

- **Distribution:** Coastal areas of northern North America, parts of Asia across the Bering Straits, as well as Greenland, Iceland and northern Europe
- **Size:** 63.5 cm (25 in)
- **Diet:** Commercial duck diet with a relatively high protein content
- **Sexing:** Drakes are darker than ducks, even in eclipse plumage
- **Compatibility:** Quite social
- **Pet appeal:** Communal nature

This species was once heavily persecuted in the wild for the soft breast plumage that the female uses to line her nest, so-called eiderdown. Today, however, this trade has declined and Eider Ducks are again increasing their distribution. They are birds for the specialist, as are most marine ducks, since they seem to be more at risk from the fungal disease aspergillosis than their freshwater counterparts. Deep clean water, extending over a large area, is to be recommended. (They will live quite happily on fresh water.) A significant proportion of their diet should be in the form of animal protein; in the wild, these ducks feed on mussels and other similar creatures, including fish. Since Eider Ducks can succumb with heat stroke in the summer, keep them in a cool locality. Between four and six eggs are usually laid, with the offspring emerging after twenty-six days.

Left: **Common Eider**
A female of this sociable marine species. Only for specialists.

FURTHER READING

Alderton, D. *Looking After Cage Birds* Ward Lock, 1982

Alderton, D. *Beginner's Guide to Lovebirds* Paradise Press, 1984

Alderton, D. *Beginner's Guide to Zebra Finches* Paradise Press, 1984

Arnall, L and Keymer, I. F. *Bird Diseases* Bailliere Tindall, 1975

Batty, J. *Bantams* Saiga Publishing, 1981

Bracegirdle, J. *The Border Canary* Saiga Publishing, 1981

Cross, J. S. *The Gloster Fancy Canary* Saiga Publishing, 1978

Delacour, J. *Pheasants of the World* Nimrod Book Services, 1977

Dodwell, G.T. *Encyclopedia of Canaries* TFH Publications, 1976

Dodwell, G.T. *The Lizard Canary and Other Rare Breeds* Triplegate, 1982

Forshaw, J. M. *Parrots of the World* David and Charles, 1978

Goodwin, D. *Estrildid Finches of the World* British Museum (Natural History), 1982

Goodwin, D. *Pigeons and Doves of the World* British Museum (Natural History), 1983

Howman, K. C. R. *Pheasants – Their Breeding and Management* K & R Books, 1979

Houson, E. *The Yorkshire Canary* Saiga Publishing, 1980

Immelmann, K. *Australian Finches* Angus and Robertson, 1982

Jennings, G. *Beginner's Guide to Parrots* Paradise Press, 1985

Johnson, A. A. and Payn, W. H. *Ornamental Waterfowl* Spur Publications, 1979

Kolbe, H. *Ornamental Waterfowl* Gresham Books, 1979

Low, R. *Parrots – Their Care and Breeding* Blandford Press, 1986

Martin, R.M. *Cage & Aviary Birds* Collins, 1980

Mobbs, A. *Gouldian Finches* Nimrod Book Services, 1985

Robbins, G. E. S. *Quail – Their Breeding and Management* World Pheasant Association, 1984

Rutgers, A and Norris, K.A. (Editors) *Encyclopaedia of Aviculture* (Volumes I to III) Blandford Press, 1977

Trollope, J. *The Care and Breeding of Seed-eating Birds* Blandford Press, 1983

Smith, G.A. *Encyclopaedia of Cockatiels* TFH Publications, 1978

Vince, C. *Keeping Softbilled Birds* Stanley Paul, 1980

Walker, G. B. R. *Coloured Canaries* Blandford Press, 1976

Watmough, W. and Rogers, C.H. *The Cult of the Budgerigar* Nimrod Book Services, 1984

Wheeler, H.G. *Exhibition and Flying Pigeons* Spur Publications, 1978

Below: Diamond Sparrow (*Emblema guttata*)

GENERAL INDEX

Page numbers in **bold** type indicate major references including accompanying photographs or diagrams. Page numbers in *italics* indicate captions to other illustrations. Less important text entries are shown in normal type.

Above: Reeves' Pheasant
(*Syrmaticus reevesi*)

INDEX OF SPECIES

Page numbers in **bold** type indicate major references including accompanying photographs or diagrams. Page numbers in *italics* indicate captions to other illustrations. Less important text entries are shown in normal type.

Right: Mealy Amazon
(*Amazona farinosa*)